A GERMAN IDENTITY

IDENTITY

1770 to the Present Day

Harold James

PHŒNIX

A PHOENIX PAPERBACK

This paperback edition published in 1994
by Phoenix, a division of Orion Books Ltd,
Orion House, 5 Upper St Martin's Lane,
London WC2H 9EA

A CIP catalogue record for this book is available
from the British Library.

ISBN: 1 85799 179 6

Printed and bound in Great Britain by Butler & Tanner Ltd, Frome and London

ACKNOWLEDGEMENTS

The manuscript of this book has been read either in part or in whole by friends and colleagues to whom I am very grateful for illuminating and helpful suggestions: Timothy Blanning, Felix Gilbert, Diane Kunz, Arno Mayer, Charles McClelland, Peter Paret and Fritz Stern. Jane Dailey Nirenberg assisted me greatly in preparing the manuscript for publication. Juliet Gardiner at Weidenfeld and Nicolson provided useful and sympathetic advice, and Linden Lawson has been an exemplary editor.

Contents

Abbreviations

APO	Ausserparlamentarische Opposition (Extra-Parliamentary Opposition)
CDU	Christlich-Demokratische Union (Christian Democrats, Bonn and GDR)
CPSU	Communist Party of the Soviet Union
CSU	Christlich-Soziale Union (Bavarian Christian Democrats, Bonn)
DDP	Deutsche Demokratische Partei (Democratic Party, Weimar Republic)
DDR	Deutsche Demokratische Republik (German Democratic Republic, GDR)
DGB	Deutscher Gewerkschafts-Bund (German Federation of Trade Unions)
DNVP	Deutsch-Nationale Volkspartei (Nationalist Party, Weimar Republic)
DVP	Deutsche Volkspartei (People's Party, Weimar Republic)
ECSC	European Coal and Steel Community
EDC	European Defence Community
EEC	European Economic Community
ERP	European Recovery Programme
FDP	Freie Demokratische Partei (Liberals, Bonn)
FRG	Federal Republic of Germany
GDR	German Democratic Republic
KPD	Kommunistische Partei Deutschlands (German Communist Party, Weimar Republic)
LDPD	Liberal-Demokratische Partei Deutschlands (Liberals, GDR)
NDPD	National-Demokratische Partei Deutschlands (Nationalists, GDR)
NKVD	People's Commissariat of State Security (Soviet)
NÖS	Neues Ökonomisches System (New Economic System, GDR)
NPD	Nationaldemokratische Partei Deutschlands (Nationalists, Bonn)
NSDAP	Nationalsozialistische Deutsche Arbeiter Partei (Nazi party, Weimar and Nazi dictatorship)
SA	Sturmabteilung (Storm-troopers)
SED	Sozialistische Einheitspartei Deutschlands (socialist-communist party, GDR)
SPD	Sozialdemokratische Partei Deutschlands (socialist party, Kaiserreich, Weimar, Bonn)
VdgB	Vereinigung der gegenseitigen Bauernhilfe (peasant party, GDR)

Introduction

Already before the dramatic political upheavals of 1989, most Germans worried about problems of national identity. During the course of the nineteenth century, German thinkers developed a messianic nationalism, claimed to represent a 'universal nation', and promised to the whole world salvation through the German people. Then, once the rise and the eventual collapse of National Socialism had discredited the radical claims of the German nationalist tradition, there appeared to be little left over. The new post-war peculiarity of German nationalism after 1945 was often thought to be simply its non-existence. After 1989, the question that haunted observers of Germany was: would there be a new and destructive nationalism in the wake of German unification?

Conventional ways of assessing the level of nationalist sentiment offered little help. At the end of the 1980s, public opinion surveys concluded that Germans then had less national pride than other European peoples. According to the investigations of the Allensbach Institut für Demoskopie, 55 per cent of Britons were 'very proud' to be British; the equivalent figures for France and Italy were 33 and 41 per cent. Only 21 per cent of West Germans declared themselves 'very proud' of being German. More strikingly still, Germany had the highest number of respondents claiming to be 'not at all proud' of their nation. To the extent that they were proud, they said it was because of such national attributes as 'Goethe, Schiller and other great poets', or because of the German landscape. It was remarkable how national identity in these surveys was not associated with political memories or institutions. These results did not change dramatically after the unification of 1990.

Most accounts view this problematic nationalism as merely a characteristic of nations which have lost wars and are divided politically. Disillusionment is no more than a natural result of military defeat. While this interpretation is not absurd, it fails to answer an obvious objection. After 1945, German nationalism apparently withered away,

1

whereas after other lost wars – say after 1806 or after 1918 – powerful, destructive, and ultimately radical nationalisms sprang up. Perhaps a more adequate explanation of the German peculiarity in the present would take into account the features of Germany's longer-term historical development.

This book explores two themes of that story: first, the dangers of an excessive focus on economics in national life; secondly, the effects on German development· of her place in the international system. The argument of the first part of the book is that Germany's historical peculiarity in the nineteenth century lay in the close association between nation-building and economic evolution. Some Germans engaged in the self-conscious construction of their nation as a planned social unit. This was a vision that emerged out of an act of collective reflection, between the mid-eighteenth and the mid-nineteenth centuries, on what societies should be made to become. The new unit would be linked by economic ties and would in turn foster a dynamic growth that could be translated into military power. The second part of the book is concerned with the deleterious consequences, in the subsequent period, of the association between economics and nationalism. It traces the story of economic instability and eventual collapse and the reformulation of nationalism as an extremist doctrine in the first half of the twentieth century.

The philosopher Max Scheler made a similar, highly prescient, point about the links in Germany between political behaviour and economic activity, in an essay published in 1917. He warned in that essay that the Germans were not really historically peculiar, but rather were blazing the trail of materialism – the national obsession with economics – for everyone else. Germany just showed the rest of the world the way of the future. Scheler's prophecy about the function and identity of nations has been vindicated in the course of the twentieth century. Particularly since 1945, and outside Europe, many new nations have tried to link nation-building with economic advance. One way of reading German history is as a lesson of *how* this should be done, and at the same time *why* it should not be done.

This account, then, tries to point a moral rather than to adorn a tale: it looks for lessons from the past about the identification of politics and economics. It also examines the past as a guide to how German politics have reacted to the circumstances of the international order. The analysis selects, in an inevitably and admittedly personal way, certain ideas and figures important to German reflection about Germanness. Though it draws on cultural, social, economic, diplomatic, and political descriptions, it cannot claim to be a complete and comprehensive history of Germany. It is intended as an interpretative essay, not a political

2

narrative. Its aim is to show links between reflection and imagination concerning nationhood, on the one hand, and, on the other, the institutions of public life and the politics of the international order. Underlying this analysis is the question of connections between economic development and the instability of political identities, institutions and allegiances – the instability that was so characteristic of recent German history.

My argument is concerned with the emergence in the mid-nineteenth century of a doctrine of nationality that justified the existence of the nation primarily by reference to the inexorable logic of economic development. Such a view took the place previously occupied by theories emphasizing cultural identities. Instead of being a cultural community, or a political unit based on a shared culture, the nation became the framework for an economic process that would in turn create political and cultural consciousness.

Increased wealth could eliminate the evils of the *ancien régime*, and promote social solidarity. It might bind together a true national community. In time, however, and certainly by the end of the century, the economy as a source of national legitimacy appeared spiritually and psychologically unsatisfying. The old idealism about national development vanished. Commentators pointed out that industrialism and economic change had produced large disparities in income and wealth rather than social harmony. They castigated their contemporaries with the biblical image of the Dance around the Golden Calf. A new critique stressed the cultural nature of Germanness, and called for a reassertion of 'ideal values'. Though this demand for a new identity influenced the youth movement at the turn of the century, it remained an undercurrent as long as Germany's economy continued to be strong, and while Germany could build a claim to being a Great Power – even a world power – on the basis of her economic strength.

Both these pillars of the German doctrine of nationality were, however, demolished by the First World War. Claims to be a Great Power collapsed. In the aftermath of the war, the economy was weakened, and the 1920s turned out to be a decade of instability and stagnation. As a result, the claims of the nation to be an economic unit that could mould a new and better society through increasing national wealth looked more and more hollow. The cultural and political versions of nationalism gained in appeal – and became charged with a radical version of the late nineteenth-century attack on the shallow 'materialism' of a social order predicated solely on economic success. Nazism took up these older cries. Only the military defeat of 1945 put an end to this radical nationalist tradition – a tradition that had underpinned the ideology of the National Socialist dictatorship.

The story of this cycle of German national doctrines from cultural to political to economic and then back all the way, becoming ever more radical in the course of this progression, is, I believe, not just of historical interest. There is an immediate and present interest behind the telling of the tale. The occasion for this book is my belief that since 1945 the same cycle of development of nationalist doctrine in Germany has emerged once more, though in a muted form. I hope that we can learn something from the first terrifying cycle of the breakdown of economic theories of nationhood – that we should put our faith in something other than economics or economic success. Clio should warn us not to trust Mercury (the economic god) too much. Economies are unlikely to be forever flushed with the rosy bloom of optimism and expansion: when they sicken, it may be helpful to have a dense network of loyalties, traditions, and old institutions which can retain a legitimacy more profound and more satisfying.

In the 1950s and 1960s a majority of politicians in both East and West Germany believed the political legacy of the war to be so appalling that the only way of reconstructing national life lay in the successes of a buoyant and dynamic economy. The triumphs of a *Wirtschaftswunder* would allow Germans to forget the pain of the past (the West German theory); or might produce a totally transformed social order that would erase for ever the problems of the past which had arisen from the logic of the fatal social constellation of a bourgeois-capitalist order (the East German theory).

At the same time, and in both states, such theories provoked among a small and intellectual minority the accusation that the postwar order had devoted itself too enthusiastically to money-grubbing materialism. More fundamental values (though no one dared to say German values) had suffered. Money could not do away with the past, buy out morality, or eliminate historical guilt. This critique grew louder in the 1960s; it played an important part in the student movement in the West. During the 1970s scepticism about the transformative capacity of economic growth became even more appealing, and captivated more people, as that growth faltered. Belief in economic performance and in theories of management (Keynesianism in the West, central planning in the East) looked less respectable. In response, on all parts of the political spectrum, the quest for a substitute of the economic goal – for national identity – became more of a political issue. Left and right in the Federal Republic, the government and dissidents in the Democratic Republic, once more examined what it meant to be German. This required a re-examination of the past – which has proved painful and even traumatic.

The past of the German nation contains the evils and the horrors of National Socialism. Some politicians on the right in the Federal Republic recommend 'walking tall' despite the legacy of the past. Especially after German unification, a wider group believes that it is unrealistic to expect German policy towards the rest of the world to be perpetually constrained by a past now over forty years old. Others – notably the Federal President Richard von Weizsäcker – call for an open confrontation and reckoning with the past as the only possibility to identify ways in which the 'new', post-1945 nation has transcended the social and political limitations of the 'old' Germany.

When we ask what has changed, what is new about Germany, one answer lies in international politics. Part of the image of the new Germany depends on a vision of the international order. Here again, in regard to world politics and the Germans, Clio can give us a lesson.

The identity of Germany came apart much more obviously and much more explosively in the interwar years than in the 1970s and 1980s. The nationalism of that past was infinitely more radical and destructive than almost any modern statement about German nationhood – though British, French and Italian journalists suffer from periodical fits of hysteria about German revanchism. Part of the reason is clearly that the economic crisis of the later 1920s, at the time of the world depression, was far more devastating than the oil price shocks of the 1970s. German society has also changed, and may be less receptive to extreme statements. But there is also a connection between doctrines of nationhood and the state of international politics.

Both the ill-fated Weimar Republic and the two post-1945 German states came out of military defeat and had to begin their lives at the centre of an international system constructed around the need to restrain the potential resurgence of aggression in defeated Germany. These constraining systems moulded the character of the German states, and consequently changes in world diplomacy had an immediate impact on the political conduct of Germans.

In the case of Weimar, the world view of the Paris peace settlement of 1919 disintegrated relatively rapidly. The crumbling began as early as 1920, when the US Senate refused to ratify the peace treaties; and the whole edifice fell apart during the world depression. The failure of the League of Nations to deal with the Japanese invasion of Manchuria (1931), and the Lausanne conference which cancelled German reparations (1932), spelt the end of the peace treaties, but also – it will be argued – the end of the Weimar Republic. It may not have been the severity of the 1919 peace treaties that caused the political breakdown – a view still often expressed in order to explain the 1920s – but rather the disintegration of the peace settlement twelve years after the end of the war. Once the shackles were lifted from the German body politic, nationalist exertions became possible. The Republic lasted, to put it most simply, as long as reparations.

The post-1945 order was much more secure. But by the 1980s, a crisis in the Soviet system began to undermine the Yalta–Potsdam settlement. Between 1989 and 1991 the dissolution of Soviet power first destroyed the GDR and then, to the surprise of the world and of Germans themselves, made possible German unification in October 1990. The new instability of international relations in combination with an economic crisis in the wake of German unification posed a completely new challenge to the political structures and identities that had developed over the course of the old Federal Republic's forty year existence.

How can Germany rebuild its security? As long as concepts of identity are produced by intellectual speculation rather than being anchored in institutional realities, they are likely to be volatile, and disruptive. Finding institutional sources of identity – for instance in the legitimacy of the Federal Republic's parliamentary process – takes time, but increases political stability. This in turn is essential for dealing with the changes that will inevitably occur in world politics. But it is also important to realize how much of this precariously evolving German identity was associated with the foreign political, military and strategical attachments developed after the war: in short the policy of integration in the Western alliance. Links of this kind give the necessary concreteness which is lacking in metaphysical musings about the true nature of Germanness.

The book's first chapter examines the problem of how national identity has developed since the eighteenth century. It explains how Germans, lacking any institutional basis for identity and faced by a hostile international system at the beginning of the nineteenth century, engaged in what might be termed the promiscuous construction of a national image, a national identity, and a national mission. They went to classical antiquity as a guide; and they seized models and examples supplied by foreign countries. This chapter tries to show where modern Germany began, and specifically how unstable nationality may be in the absence of a strong set of institutional identifications. Chapter II traces the transition from cultural to political nationalism in the first half of the nineteenth century: this movement brought with it the notion of national uniqueness, and, increasingly, also national superiority. One of the grounds for superiority was the dramatic growth of the economy after

6

the mid-century, a growth which many Germans hoped would bring social stability as well as a position of advantage relative to other peoples in the area of central Europe. The association of economics and state-building for academics, civil servants, and politicians is the focus of Chapter III. Chapter IV examines the criticism of the mutual association and identification of state, nation, and economy: on the one hand from cultural opponents of 'materialism', on the other from those who came by the end of the nineteenth century to argue that the old-style nation-state had become too small a unit for rational economic progress. Chapter V associates a crisis about nationality in the Weimar Republic with poor economic performance. The theme of Chapter VI is the culmination of previous cultural and political traditions of nationalism in the National Socialist dictatorship, and their eventual discrediting as a consequence of Nazi barbarism and then of Germany's military defeat. Chapters VII, VIII and IX deal with the postwar order, and raise the question of how the German problem of the 1990s can be understood in the light of the German past.

1

Prelude: The Building Blocks of German National Identity

What makes a nation a nation? Shared traditions (a common culture), or shared history, or a common language? Nationalism depends on the application of imagination to formulate, and indeed even sometimes invent, all of these common features. It works through a powerful, but nevertheless usually highly fictional, account of shared historical, linguistic, and cultural identities.[1] Nationalists, however, frequently disagree as to what constitutes these shared identities. There are always, in any society, not one but several storytellers in the invention of nationality, who usually cannot agree even about the general structure of the narrative. This chapter is concerned with the construction in the eighteenth and nineteenth centuries of German identity out of a promiscuous mixture of traditions and models.

The elaboration of a doctrine of national mission long preceded the establishment of a German state in 1871 and the rise of Germany to the ranks of the Great Powers of Europe. In establishing their vision of a nation in the century before 1871, Germans could not look to the present to establish what German identity meant. Their territory was politically fragmented, and most of the units were highly ineffective in international politics. Often when the present looks threatening or hostile, we look back to the comfort of heroic stories from the past. In common with other 'new nations' of the nineteenth century – Italians, Hungarians, Czechs, South Slavs – Germans could find no justification for national existence in any existing set of institutions. The German Confederation as established in 1815 did not appear to be a body capable of satisfying demands for a specifically German institutional identity: it was yoked by the Habsburg Emperors to the international cause of political and social reaction.

8

Finding identity in the past, however, brought problems for Germans, in spite of the existence of a German language and what might be claimed as a cultural tradition. Politically, the past had little to offer. There certainly had been until 1806 the venerably old Holy Roman Empire 'of the German Nation' (Heiliges Römisches Reich deutscher Nation), but this imperial past, after the French Revolution, had no obvious applicability to practical problems of the present. The old Empire, already described in the seventeenth century as an 'unnatural monster' (by the legal philosopher Samuel Pufendorf), could excite the medieval imagination of political romantics – as did the Roman Empire, or the Crown of St Stephen, or the Crown of St Wenceslas. But it could not do much more than that.

Western Europe was far more fortunate in having a constitutional and administrative framework in which identity might develop. English nationality found its expression in laws and political bodies. Laws separated the Anglican church from Rome in the sixteenth century. An institution – the monarch in parliament – defined this separation. France's legal system and institutions were much more contested than Britain's. There were clearly distinct alternative visions of France. According to conservative thinkers, France had been created by its monarchs, and by the centralizing bureaucracies they had built up. Obedience to the monarch cemented Frenchmen together. For revolutionaries, France was an idea – Liberty – and an historical act – the French Revolution. But for them, and for moderate liberals, France was also the institutions and the constitutional arrangement born out of the Revolution, and above all the reworking of law.

Part of the elaboration of theories of nationhood in the modern period lay in defining a set of attributes as the 'national character' of a people. Such properties could provide the answer to questions of the type 'What is it to be German?' or 'How does nationality manifest itself in personal and in political behaviour?' Describing character invariably involves idealization and a substantial amount of myth-making. The problem appears most acutely in situations where there is no institutional context for nation-building.

If national identity lies in political and institutional arrangements, there is no need to be preoccupied with the search for an elusive national character.[2] The institutions themselves provide centres of attention and activity. People gradually regard them as a fine way of settling the numerous disputes that naturally arise from everyday life. They generate a sense of legitimacy in themselves and in the community of which they are part, and which they come to represent. In the end they create patterns of behaviour which can be eventually identified as national properties.

It then becomes possible to speak of typical actions, or even of national character. Out of the English Act of Supremacy and from the activity of Tudor and Stuart parliaments came an idiosyncratic notion of the English gentleman. A gentleman was less a precise description of a certain standing in the pyramid of English society than a depiction of conduct and deportment.[3] Gentlemen possessed a sense of fairness and dignity which might make parliamentary processes work without undue corruption or overt antagonism. Political passion and corruption both belonged not to England or English life, but to foreign countries.

In France another myth about behaviour flourished – it might be called the 'Voltaire effect'. French institutions, being in rapid change, produced other stereotypes – the socially engaged intellectual or journalist or politician who made politics into an act of thinking and willing. Great intellectual statesmen – Lamartine, Thiers, Jaurès, Clemenceau, de Gaulle – cast their shadows on French politics.

It should not be necessary to point out that English and French realities differed greatly from these images and self-images. There was a civil war in seventeenth-century England. Eighteenth-century English politicians were corrupt, and popular politics passionate and frequently violent. With great frequency, French intellectuals in politics turned into self-seeking hypocrites. A substantial literature grew up which pointed out the fragility of claims to high standards of political behaviour. Balzac and Maupassant could mock pretences at political high-mindedness.

But the claims nevertheless mattered as an ideal of national character against which a more mundane or more sordid reality could be tested. Germans – as well as other new nations of the nineteenth century – found it much more difficult to work out what the pattern for national life should be. They saw in politics only weakness and fragmentation. They could not find a stereotype in religion, because of the confessional division between a largely Protestant north-east, and a largely Catholic west and south-east. How could such diverse regions be brought together? At the beginning of the nineteenth century, Germaine Necker (Madame de Staël) wrote a highly sympathetic study of the German mental world in which again and again she pointed out the debilitating consequences of the lack of effectively operating political bodies. 'Political institutions alone', she concluded, 'are capable of forming the character of a nation.'[4]

At the end of the eighteenth and the beginning of the nineteenth century, German political disunity contrasted with the existence to the west of two states organized along national lines, with national institutions. Britain and France proved to be economically and above all militarily effective: successes which meant a political control of the affairs of the European continent. In the French case, a view of the state as the political expression of the nation produced a new and powerful citizens' army. And to the east, Germany had the military power of the Tsarist empire.

It is not surprising that – at the same time as Madame de Staël was writing about Germans' national modesty – Germans from their observations of French and British triumphs acknowledged the historical superiority and the eventual inevitability of the nation-state. Some of them deduced that they should imitate this form of political organization if they were not to be defeated and subjected to the rule of other nations. The nation-state became not simply a blueprint for desirable development, but a necessary formula for political survival.

In the absence of institutions which might determine appropriate behaviour, Germans had to manufacture their own concept of nationality. Again like other new nations, they needed self-consciously to formulate an imagined national past and an idealized future. How to do this? Partly they relied on the rejection of some types as 'alien': defining Germans in opposition to other peoples, Frenchmen, or Russians. But the German quest for identity also required the absorption of foreign models into German life.

One answer that underlay many formulations about the nation in the nineteenth century was in essence a very simple one: imitation. Look at other peoples and treat their national images and ideals as a set of variegated and diverse building blocks from which German identity could be constructed, synthesized, or manufactured. Imaginative projections of other national types helped Germans to decide who they were. Although Germany had a very vigorous and powerful cultural tradition of her own and scarcely needed to import any kind of foreign culture, she needed a way of understanding that strong cultural traditional as an alternative to French or British power politics. She needed in fact a model for national thought.

In Western Europe loosely defined (Britain, France, Switzerland, Spain, Portugal, Denmark and Sweden), old states had established a territorial framework for political activity long before the beginning of the nineteenth century. Elsewhere, where in the era of the French Revolution nationalism developed outside the context of a territorial state, the theorists of the new movement had a double or split vision. They looked with one eye back at the ancient multiplicity of nations and peoples (*Völker*). The other eye was cast forward, to the possibilities of borrowing behaviour and institutions from already existing states.

Marx and Engels made this point with reference to economic development when they spoke in the *Communist Manifesto* of the power of markets and prices to compel 'all nations, on pain of extinction, to adopt the bourgeois mode of production'. In the preface to *Das Kapital*, Marx explained that the more advanced country simply showed the less advanced one what it would become in the future. Or, as a modern writer puts it, 'in effect, by the second decade of the nineteenth century, if not earlier, a "model" of "the" independent national state was available for pirating'. Britain, as an example of an old nation-state, or France and America as models of revolutionary new ones, laid down a blueprint for the historical development of other peoples.[5]

Friedrich Meinecke's *Cosmopolitanism and the National State* (1907) provides the most systematic explanation of how the thought of German identity emerged not in opposition to a universal ('cosmopolitan') set of values, but in the context of generally held, Europe-wide ideals:

Cosmopolitanism did not merely sink to the ground, pale and exhausted; and the new national idea did not then spring up in its place, unimpeded and victorious. Cosmopolitanism and nationalism stood side by side in a close, living relationship for a long time. And even if the idea of the genuine national state could not come to full bloom within such a relationship, the meeting of these two intellectual forces was by no means unfruitful for the national idea.[6]

The philosopher Georg Wilhelm Friedrich Hegel did most to identify the existence of universal 'world historical nations', which at a particular moment embodied all that was progressive in world history:

The nation to which is ascribed a moment of the Idea in the form of a natural principle is entrusted with giving complete effect to it in the advance of the self-developing self-consciousness of the world mind. This nation is dominant in world history during this one epoch, and it is only once that it can make its hour strike.[7]

At the beginning of the nineteenth century, the Germans had distilled and synthesized the world spirit. Hegel's account of this synthesis was notoriously murky; but it profoundly affected the vision of nineteenth-century Germans.

Not everyone faced the problem as honestly as Bogumil Goltz, a strange ethnographer who lived all his life in Thorn (Torun) on the Vistula. In the middle of the century he explained exactly how Germany had pieced itself together out of a whole range of different national images. He took quite literally the Hegelian idea of Germany as the universal nation:

As man is the supreme creature, so one might call the German the most perfect human, because in fact he unites all the characteristic

12

properties, talents and virtues of all countries . . . The German
nation has no national character in the way that other nations have,
because it has become generalized as a world people through the
application of reason . . . We are as conscientious, hard-working
and skilful as the Chinese; we have or had their piety towards old
people . . . We have English thoroughness and accuracy . . . We
have French skill and elegance in all technical arts . . . We
understand music and all beautiful arts better than the Italians . . .
We are tillers and herdsmen with a love of nature and a patriarchal
sentiment as are the old Poles and the Hungarians.[8]

Goltz was clearly an over-enthusiastic eclectic, and he carried his
argument to absurd lengths. But less erratic, and more profound,
authors saw in Germany the same eclectic quality. Madame de Staël
wrote in the aftermath of Napoleon's defeat of Prussia, an era usually
reckoned to be one of national revival and patriotic assertion. She
appreciated little of this. She did not refer to Fichte's rousing patriotic
addresses delivered in contemporary Berlin. Her Germans were rather
modest and lacking in self-confidence. 'In literature, as in politics, the
Germans show too much consideration for foreigners, and not enough
national prejudices. Self-abnegation and esteem for others are qualities
in individuals, but the patriotism of nations must be egotistical.'[9]

Looking back over a century which had brought national unity and the
creation of a powerful state which had a great deal to boast about, the
nationalist historian Heinrich von Treitschke rather surprisingly echoed
the thoughts of the French observer of Prussia in the Napoleonic era.
National consciousness had not yet been achieved – at least not in his
eyes. In lectures given in Berlin in 1893, Treitschke referred to 'this pride
of our nation, that it is powerful enough to be cosmopolitan in the noble
sense, that it is capable of absorbing the immortal element of other
peoples'. Because of their island mentality, Englishmen had 'limited
horizons' that prevented the adoption of new cultural patterns. Germans
did better. 'The Germans are the opposite, and the vast majority are
born world citizens who must always work at toning down the perpetual
regard for foreign ideas so that they can sometimes think of themselves
by themselves. The German people should be described as having a
"selfless" characteristic – a word whose meaning has been seriously
distorted over time.'[10]

This vision of what constituted national identity saw a number of
modes of behaviour from which selections could be made at will by a
group of self-defining national-intellectual consciousness-raisers.
Treitschke argued that there were many different types of national

virtue: 'the rays of divine light only appear in individual nations endlessly refracted. Each has a different picture and different thoughts about the diversity. Each nation has the right to believe that in it are manifest particular parts of divine reason.' God's Englishmen, French-men, Poles, and so forth were secure in their particular privileges. Because Germans were aware of the multiplicity of claims to an especial standing in the universe, they were more sceptical, more hesitant, and more neurotic. Germans, Treitschke said, 'are always in danger of losing their nationality, because they have too little of such pride'.[11]

Other nations' heroes became those of Germany. In Caspar Scheuren's lithograph of 1840, *The German*, the brooding, central figure sits with a Bible and a volume of 'German history', but also admires a picture of George Washington and a statuette of Napoleon. Protestant Germans looked to the heroic seventeenth-century Swedish king Gustavus Adolphus.

The risk that Germany would be too eclectic or that she would absorb too many inappropriate models put the consciousness-raisers on their guard. It was predictably Goltz who provided the longest list of improbable models:

> We are as obedient and imitative as Chinese and Russians, from whom we have the idea of Emperor and Emperor worship . . . We love wandering as much as Tartars and Kirghiz . . . In our love of knowledge and in all other things we have a Jewish-Talmudic inventiveness and skill at categorizing, Jewish toughness, indestructability, a Jewish sense of envy and private quarrels . . .[12]

The definition of nationality by reference to others went alongside a view about German geography. Because Germany lay in the centre of things – in physical terms, but also economically, politically and culturally – circumstances forced it into a passive and accepting role (Goltz said 'the woman among nations').[13] This view of the German character as constrained by the political layout of Europe was common enough to become a frequent joke. One German politician wrote in 1948 about Konrad Adenauer: 'I don't know what so many people have against Adenauer. I have known him the longest and the best. He is less reliable than a Frenchman, more deceptive than an Englishman, more brutal than an American and more inscrutable than a Russian – in short the ideal statesman for our beaten and mistreated nation!'[14]

Even at the zenith of aggressive German nationalism, the fascination with national comparisons and with borrowing remained obsessive. When the Olympic games were held in National Socialist Berlin in 1936, the SA newspaper *Der Angriff* exhorted Germans to show the world their best side: 'We must be more charming than the Parisians, more light-living than the Viennese, more vital than the Russians, more cosmopolitan than Londoners, more practical than New Yorkers.'[15]

In fact an extreme willingness to make comparisons went hand in hand with ever more aggressive German nationalism. National imitation proved to be more destructive than constructive. There was in practice little that was civilizing about Treitschke's (and others') use of the ideal of a 'universal people'. If anything, it operated as a decivilizer. Why?

One of the most obvious answers is that there were too many models to choose from and that this made for a fundamental instability in the national self-image. There are parallels in the modernization of Japan after the Meiji restoration, when the Japanese borrowed indiscriminately from British, French, American and German models, and when national ideologues castigated their compatriots for their lack of 'stick-to-itiveness' (*mikka bōzu*).[16] Germans too had built up identity out of a series of over-schematic visions of what other peoples' national identity represented to them. The universal people looked universally for models: to the modern world of France, England, America, Russia, Italy, Poland, Switzerland, and the Netherlands; as well as to the vanished worlds of Greece and Rome.

France: Liaison dangereuse

In the eighteenth century, there was little difficulty in selecting an exemplary country. Though France's political dominance in German affairs in the aftermath of the Peace of Westphalia (1648), and the brutal sack of the Palatinate in 1674 and again in 1688, engendered a natural Francophobia, this was more than compensated by admiration for French society and manners. In the eighteenth century, French became the language of polite conversation. Frederick the Great often expressed his aversion to the barbaric German tongue.

One of the pioneers of the German revival was Christian Thomasius. He believed that German should replace Latin in educated talk – but his model for this suggestion was the triumph of the vernacular in France. What might be termed the French cultural dictatorship over Europe fascinated him. His *Discourse on What Forms Should Be Imitated from the French in Daily Life and Behaviour* (1687) began with the observation that 'today everything must be French with us. French clothes, French food, French household goods, French language, French morals, French sins, and even French diseases are everywhere the rage.'[17] He pointed out that such imitation was perfectly natural and – far from constituting an outrage to German patriotic sentiment – showed the way for reason and progress. 'Frenchmen are after all today the most skilful people and know how to order all things in the appropriate way.'[18] They could conduct an 'expert and well-mannered love affair'.[19] They preferred the lute or the violin to the drum and the bagpipes. They held Cicero, Cujas, Grotius and Descartes in higher esteem than the clerical and medieval obscurantists, the scholastics and Aristotle.

How could Germany resist so powerful an attraction? In large and even middling-sized states, the princes felt attracted by new concepts of power – which were associated linguistically with France, and also politically, since France tried to bolster the rights of princes *vis-à-vis* the Holy Roman Emperor. During the Westphalian peace negotiations in the middle of the seventeenth century, German princes began to set out a view of their '*droit de souveraineté*'. They later thought it important to apply the most sophisticated and newest methods to statecraft – or as they put it to know their '*intérêt*' and on the basis of this formulate a '*dessein*'.[20] They spoke French, and across the German countryside they built imitations of Versailles.

The French influence went far beyond power-hungry princes, and also beyond the writers of the Enlightenment. Thomasius, a native of Saxony, claimed that the French language had become so commonplace that in many places shoemakers, tailors, and even children and common servants (*Gesinde*) could speak it adequately. The linguistic impact lasted long after the French appeal as a model of national identity had faded. North Germans in particular delighted in taking over French vocabulary in the nineteenth century.[21] They walked along the *Boulevard* on the *Trottoir*, with a *Parapluie* outstretched if it should be raining. Their female domestic servant was a *Mamsell* (Mademoiselle). Travelling on the train meant a new inundation of French words: before walking onto the *Perron*, they bought a *Billet*, and took a seat in a *Wagon* under the supervision of the *Conducteur*.

Some observers believed that French influence went deeper into social life than simply a series of linguistic borrowings. The writer Theodor Fontane became the greatest observer of Berlin's Frenchified middle classes, which constituted a real *bourgeoisie*, on a Parisian model, rather than the citizenry (*Bürgertum*) of small-town provincial Germany. He himself pronounced his name with the stress on the first syllable in order to Frenchify it, and emphasized his own Huguenot descent: and – on special occasions – he even gave this pronunciation a more authentically French nasal intonation. In an essay on the character of Berliners, he described Berlin as a mixture of Brandenburg traditionalism and French (Huguenot) and Jewish influences. Huguenots and Jews had brought

Berlin humour (*Witz*) and self-irony to what had previously been a sullen peasant population.[22]

In Thomas Mann's novel *Buddenbrooks*, the greatest German epic of nineteenth-century bourgeois life, the second sentence is not in German. It begins in a colloquial low German dialect, and finishes in French: 'Je, den Düwel ook, c'est la question, ma très chère demoiselle' ('Yes, what the devil, that's the question, my dear young lady'). The older generation of Buddenbrooks characteristically drop into the French language.

The French behaviour that Thomasius had identified – that of the witty, urbane, rational, ironical *honnête homme* who was socially respectable (*salonfähig*) – in short lived on as an exemplar to the nineteenth-century educated German middle classes. This, the international 'bourgeois' style, was a distinctively non-aristocratic form of behaviour, and helped the urban notables (the German term is *Honoratioren*) to find their own style and establish their own identity. It contributed as much to civic pride as did the rather more romantic medieval fantasies about being a burgher which appeared in the first half of the nineteenth century. Without this style, the beneficent but socially exclusive liberalism as propounded by wealthy city notables would have been unthinkable.

The political impact of France is a more problematic subject. Educated Germans initially greeted the 1789 revolution with considerable enthusiasm. The poets Schiller and Klopstock, and the philosopher Fichte, felt deeply moved by 1789's promise of Enlightenment. However, most of Germany was untouched and unaffected until the French Revolution expanded to defeat and occupy, first parts of Germany, and then under Napoleon almost the whole of it. Some of the results were positive and long-lived. In Bavaria, the enlightened minister Montgelas introduced legislation styled directly after a French pattern. The French revolutionary law of 1791 provided the foundation for the principle of self-administration later adopted in German municipalities; though as actually applied in the Germany of the 1790s, this type of reform caused only administrative chaos. In addition, French constitutionalism left a deeper mark on German political theory than did radicalism or Jacobinism. Benjamin Constant, the liberal constitutional theorist of the Restoration (his most important political work, the *Principes de politique applicables à tous les Gouvernements représentatifs*, was published in 1815) had a significant following among German liberals. In this work he had set out an argument for limited constitutional monarchy and the division of power, and against the Rousseauist utopia of finding a general will. Karl von Rotteck, Carl Theodor Welcker, the

German State Encyclopaedists, as well as Robert Mohl and Paul Pfizer, acknowledged his influence.[23]

What benefits Germany received from France were only visible much later and from the long-range perspective of the historian who deals in broad sweeps of time. In the 1790s and 1800s, however, it was hard to think of France other than as the enemy.

France presented an obvious and direct threat, against which the German nation mobilized itself. The Rhineland suffered a brutal, physically destructive and economically crippling occupation as early as the autumn of 1792. Only in 1814 did the French armies depart. The occupation of Prussia was much shorter, but just as humiliating and costly. High levies and taxes to pay for the war ruined the economy, while many Prussian soldiers died fighting in Napoleon's Grand Army in Russia. Nationalism directed against France combined widespread popular support with an intellectual appeal. Former Jacobin enthusiasts now turned against France and began to speak the language of German patriotism. The previously radical Andreas Rebmann learnt from what he considered to be his earlier mistakes: 'I confess that I was once a warm supporter of the Rhine frontier, just as now, as a German, I am a vehement opponent of the same . . . I have never forgotten that I am a German.'[24] Joseph Görres as a young man had been an enthusiastic member of Mainz's Jacobin movement; by 1797 he had also taken up anti-French nationalism. In 1813 in Prussia a popular insurrection against French rule found recruits from all social classes.

France's role as an enemy outlived the defeat of Napoleon (1813–15), which produced an initial and short-lived united patriotic uprising (though one probably exaggerated in subsequent nationalist myth-making). In 1840 a war scare led to a new blossoming of patriotic sentiment. Max Schneckenburger's 'The Watch on the Rhine' ('Die Wacht am Rhein') was composed in 1840; Hoffmann von Fallersleben's 'Deutschland, Deutschland über alles' was written in 1841. The most popular Rhine song of all, Nicolaus Becker's 'They shall not have him, the free German Rhine', had between seventy and two hundred different tunes.[25] The *Songbook of the German Michael* (*Liederbuch des deutschen Michel*) appeared in 1843.[26] Michael, the new national type, stood in sharp contrast to the French symbol Marianne. He was strong, stern, and stubborn; she was womanly, wily, and wicked. The beginning of the completion of Cologne cathedral in 1842 was turned into a national response to the French threat. The new King of Prussia, Frederick William IV, who had come to the throne in 1840, briefly identified himself with the patriotic and anti-French wave of sentiment.

Subsequent framers of Prussian and later of German policy were more persistent in their exploitation of the French threat. War against France in 1870–1 provided the occasion for the creation of Bismarck's empire; and thereafter Bismarck still tried to exploit the fear of French revanchism to stimulate an artificial national unity in Germany – in 1875, and again in 1887.

France's main importance for nineteenth-century Germany was as a threat; but she also provided a refuge for non-conformists, radicals, and revolutionaries. In the 1830s, Karl Marx lived in Paris briefly, and so, for longer periods, did Ludwig Börne, Heinrich Heine and Richard Wagner. But the radical and democratic revolution of 1848 was as much a failure in France as in Germany, and after the mid-nineteenth century Britain, America and Switzerland exercised a greater attraction for Germany's political diaspora.

France as a political model – as opposed to France the social guide to bourgeois etiquette – consistently disappointed. The universal principles of reason and enlightenment had led in the 1790s and 1800s to a ferocious war against Germany. Even as an asylum, nineteenth-century Paris was less an inspiration than simply a meeting place for *émigrés* cut off both from their own countries and from the mainstream of French political life. All France could do was to give a notion of the bourgeois order and of bourgeois life. For political inspiration the Germans looked elsewhere.

A Passion for Greeks

It is far easier to identify with precision the origins of the cult of Greece than to find the beginnings of French influence over German life. Greece had a German rediscoverer. Johann Joachim Winkelmann developed a notion of a Greek ideal of beauty, harmony and balance while struggling with the miserable realities of life as a provincial schoolmaster in Brandenburg. For Winckelmann, Greece was always an unattainable ideal. He went to live in Rome, but in practice avoided an opportunity to visit Greece. Instead he urged Germans to construct their own Greece. As a step in this direction he wrote, in 1775, *Thoughts on the Imitation of Greek Works in Painting and Sculpture*. The book examined the Greek ideal of beauty and of the perfection of physical form.

The purest springs of art have been opened: fortunate the man who finds them and drinks at them. To search for these springs means to travel to Athens. Dresden will become from now on the Athens of artists [Winckelmann added in acknowledgment of the Saxon patronage of the arts]. The only way for us to become great, yes

19

even if it is possible inimitable, lies in the imitation of the Ancients. What someone said of Homer – that to understand him is to admire him –is true of the art works of the Ancients, and especially of the Greeks.

The Greeks had done more than simply lay down a model – they had devised the framework within which all artistic and political activity could be comprehended. The statues of Laocoön had become for Winckelmann a 'complete rule for art'.[27]

The work of Winckelmann and his successors in incorporating Greece into German culture rested on a very unstable foundation: they knew well that the Greek world they had constructed was unreal. Goethe, a great philhelline, portrayed this relationship in the second part of *Faust*: Faust summons up the ancient world in the shape of Helen of Troy; but Helen is an artifice and a phantasmagora rather than a real woman, and Mephistopheles takes delight in pointing this out. Greece was a world of illusion and escape – most clearly in the case of the tormented and finally distracted poet Friedrich Hölderlin. The antique gods haunted him by their denials of modern experiences:

> Whom does this terrifying glory of antiquity not uproot, as the
> hurricane uproots young woods when it seizes them, as it seized me;
> and when, as was my case, that element is lacking from which one
> might obtain strengthening self-confidence? . . . I loved my heroes
> as a moth loves the light. I sought their dangerous proximity, and
> fled it and sought it again.[28]

The political attraction of Greece was as much of a phantasmagora as the erotic attraction of antiquity for Winckelmann or the personal appeal of a liberating heathen antiquity experienced by Hölderlin. It provided a nicely opaque and ambiguous model.

Much of the yearning for Greece meant, as with Hölderlin, an escape from politics. Others, notably Friedrich Schiller in the *Letters on the Aesthetic Education of Man*, saw Greece as a model for how a society could create free citizens. Hegel's admiration rested on the same perception: for the Greeks freedom had meant freedom in society and integration with the concerns of other people, and not the damaging and destructive revolt of the individual against society or a self-indulgent romantic craving for eccentricity.[29]

At the most obvious level, modern Greeks gave encouragement to anyone who wished to see an old and civilized people reassert themselves in the face of foreign oppression. Moreover, ancient Athens gave a model of the harmonious functioning of a participatory democracy, which had enabled large numbers of educated citizens to reflect wisely and determine public events. In Greek society, arts were part of popular and political culture. The Greeks had, in short, set up the ideal of the 'beautiful and strong free man'.[30]

Beyond an identification with a collective community, the thought which lay at the heart of political Hellenism, little more systematic doctrine might be evolved. After all, Greek society depended on the institution of slavery, and nineteenth-century Germans concerned with freedom did not want to consider how this issue affected their political vision. To develop a more concrete set of prescriptions required highly strained analogies.

The political left could draw a simple lesson from the collapse of the Hellenic world. The early socialist August Becker explained that 'Athens had declined because it did not know communism'.[31] For others, Greece lent herself to a more authoritarian consciousness. The nationalist historian Heinrich von Treitschke even tried to argue a bizarre parallel with modern history in which the conflict between Athens and Sparta matched the struggle of Prussia against Austria: 'When we look at history dispassionately, we do not find the embodiment of the Hellenic ideal in the brutal warriors of Sparta, but in the undying loveliness of Athenian life.' Well-armed Sparta looked more like an obvious analogy to nineteenth-century Prussia, but Treitschke thought Austria a better historical fit: 'To belong to the Spartan party was as common in reactionary circles of Greece as Austrian inclinations once were in Germany.'[32] By the 1890s, the Athenian model had become so malleable that it could be applied to practically any vision of Germany.

Perfidious Albion

England was an attractive model because – unlike France – she appeared in the nineteenth century to be a political and economic success, and because she did not directly threaten Germany. Even during the naval race after 1897, the British threat to Germany was largely a product of German imaginations. Moreover, unlike ancient Greece, England was a modern reality. She was additionally attractive because – as indeed had been the case with the Greek example – her lessons were so ambiguous. Conservatives saw English history as composed of long stretches of continuity and a Burkeian observation of tradition. Constitutionalists admired parliament and the checks it imposed on the crown's prerogative and hence on the emergence of any absolutist rule. Liberals knew that progressive reforms were under way. Many socialists believed an

English-style parliament would assist their cause. In fact, only out-and-out reactionaries (who did play an important role in Prussian affairs) as well as violent revolutionaries (of whom there were relatively few) were excluded from the general Anglophilia. England also had a role as a practical exemplar. For the first half of the nineteenth century, England showed the way for economic development. At the end of the century, she had the model overseas Empire – which many Germans hoped and wished to imitate.

Leopold von Ranke believed England to be the embodiment of a sensible and flexible but slow and unideological change in domestic politics, and the upholder of the principle of balance in international relations. The Hanoverian historian Friedrich Dahlmann took the English constitution as his model. During and after the revolution of 1848 this constitutionalist doctrine came to be associated with a loose aristocratic and Whiggish reform movement, often called the Saxe-Coburg party. In 1858, when the Prussian King Frederick William IV's madness required a regency and Prince William summoned a so-called 'New Era' ministry, it even looked for a brief while as if Prussia might adopt the moderate English constitutional position. The growing conflict between King and parliament destroyed the chances of the New Era, but the hopes remained, and remained attached to the royal house.

William (who became in 1861 King William I of Prussia and in 1871 German Emperor) became less flexible as he grew older, and more attached to the expansionist and hardly constitutionalist line of his Minister President Otto von Bismarck. But his wife Augusta wanted more liberalism and less of Bismarck. More importantly, there was a reversionary interest. William's son Frederick had married Queen Victoria's daughter Princess Victoria, and the court of the Crown Prince encouraged Anglophile and liberal sympathies. The Austro-Hungarian Ambassador to Berlin wrote about the danger this represented to future German policy: 'The future Queen of Prussia and Empress of Germany has remained so completely an Englishwoman in all her feelings, thoughts and strivings that she regards all steps taken here in defence of German interests against English presumptions as an offence personally inflicted upon herself.'[33] But when Frederick came to the throne, he was already dying of throat cancer; and his reign lasted only ninety-nine days.

The possibility of following an English path now appeared to be slighter. William II preferred his grandfather's views to those of his father. German liberals still hoped to learn from England, however. The economist and sociologist Max Weber still took his ideas about how Germany might develop from England. English governments were responsible to parliament, and not to the crown alone. Weber concluded that parliamentary rule was a well-balanced and appropriately ordered self-selection process through which a power elite might continually regenerate itself in line with the requirements of a modern age. Other parts of the Weberian analysis of modern politics came from English inspirations. The concept of 'charismatic leadership' – a key part of Weber's typology of legitimacy – took as its model Gladstonian populism. Admiration for England did not, of course, make Weber – or any of the other liberals who accepted these arguments – less committed to German nationalism.[34]

Liberal nationalists drew foreign policy lessons from their constitutional views. Germany should not only come to be more like England, she should also come to like England more. The liberals pointed out that a rivalry between the two states would hurt the trade and commerce of both, and thus erode the foundation of their liberal worlds. Both, as political units dependent on a high level of world economic integration, should have an interest in world peace.

Prussian reactionaries disliked this theory, well before their economic interests drew them away from the principle of free trade in the 1870s. They also had an ideological foreign policy which hinged on rapprochement with autocratic Russia: a common aversion to revolution in Europe as well as to the particular menace of rebellion in the Polish territories ruled by Russia and Prussia. Since 1815, Russia had been the principal guarantor of the cause of legitimacy and opposition to revolution throughout Europe. Even when in 1850 Russia intervened to force the humiliatingly pro-Austrian Punctation of Olmütz on the Prussian monarchy, its actions were regarded as fortunate by many conservatives. Otto von Bismarck, not untypically for Prussian reactionaries, saw the Olmütz agreement as desirable in that it prevented the King of Prussia from entering into a 'shameful alliance' with popular and liberal nationalism.[35] In addition, conservatives hoped to imitate some of the forms of the Tsarist autocracy, and looked to the east with a nostalgic longing. The Russian model influenced the conservative style. The most distinguished Prussian Guards regiments had as their honorary colonels-in-chief Tsars and Grand Dukes. Potsdam, the military heart of Prussia, had a log-hut Russian colony, Alexandrowka, built in 1826 for the Russian musicians employed by the First Guards Regiment.

On the other hand, it was not necessary to look east or to Tsarism to find an ideology of tasteful nostalgia. Many conservatives saw in England an attraction that did not depend on constitutional doctrine. England was the source of the Romantic movement, and of the Medieval Revival in literature and architecture. Germans often found their

Middle Ages in the pages of Walter Scott. Scott's *Minstrelsy of the Scottish Border* (1802), which rediscovered folk songs and tales, directly inspired Joseph Görres's story book (*Die teutschen Volksbücher*) and the immensely influential collection of German songs published in 1805 by Achim von Arnim and Clemens Brentano, *Des Knaben Wunderhorn*. Even the most German of the Germans looked to England. The heavily romantic composer Carl Maria von Weber embodied in *Der Freischütz* the folkloric, picturesque and demonic forces that went into romantic nationalism. Richard Wagner, whose own nationalism was infinitely more complicated, saw in Weber the great German musical master, and began his own experiments in patriotic composition with music composed for the reinterment of Weber's remains in his native soil. In 1817 Weber explained the need to create a new German style from the beginning: 'No people has been so slow and so uncertain as the German in determining its own specific art forms. Both the Italians and the French have evolved a form of opera in which they move freely and naturally. This is not true of the Germans, whose peculiarity it has been to adopt what seems best in other schools, after much study and steady development.'[36] Nevertheless, he felt attracted by Scott as mediated by Brentano and Arnim's *Wunderhorn*. Weber died in London in 1826, having travelled there as a very sick man. Shortly before his death he wrote to his wife about the appropriateness of the English romantic: 'The whole English way of life is very sympathetic to my nature.'[37]

Alternatively, conservatives could attempt to blend the romantic with the conventionalist constitutional arguments. This mixture produced some fiery results: the most explosively demagogic patriots of the nineteenth century had an attitude towards England which swung between violent hatred and strong attraction. Love-hate is the only appropriate term for this relationship. Neither Heinrich von Treitschke, the most famous of Prussian-German nationalist historians, nor Kaiser William II, was given to balance or moderation.

Treitschke began as a typical Anglophile of the mid-century. He was stating nothing more than a commonplace when he wrote in his first article for the *Preussische Jahrbücher* in 1858: 'Admiration is the first feeling which the study of English history calls forth in everyone . . . Each of our parties again and again uses the English example to prove its program, and it seems the [English] constitution exercises an irresistible and inevitable power of attraction.'[38] In later life, Treitschke fell away from this devotion to things English, and came to worship a nationalism that he identified as more Prussian than German. England was fickle and treacherous, and guided only by commercial advantage. In 1871, at the height of Prussian military success, and when he was most outraged by what he held to be English inconstancy, he could still sign an autograph for some English ladies with the words: 'England, with all thy faults, I love thee still.'[39]

The Kaiser was proud of his English parentage. He grew up speaking English, and took pains to educate his children in the same way – so much so that his wife was worried about the effect on young minds of 'the strong English sympathies of the Kaiser'. Philipp Eulenburg, who was once an extremely close friend of the Kaiser's, wrote: 'It sounds ghastly to a German ear when I say the German Emperor is not a German at all, but actually an Englishman.'[40] But William also believed that England was directly responsible for his personal misfortunes. He blamed English physicians for his defective appearance – for his arm deformed at birth – and perhaps also for the death of his father (through an initial misdiagnosis of Frederick's throat cancer).

Part of the Kaiser's subsequent political irresponsibility lay in provocative anti-British gestures – such as the telegram of congratulations after the South African Jameson raid. But he did just as much damage when he tried to be sympathetic: when for instance in the *Daily Telegraph* interview (1908) he made the improbable revelation that it was really he who had designed Britain's strategy against the Boers. It is at least plausible that one of the reasons William II came to loathe the English so much was that he felt himself to be so much more an Englishman than the pathetic examples of that race that he actually encountered: than King Edward VII or the limp Whig aristocrat Sir Edward Grey.

The Kaiser's son was if anything even more aggressively nationalistic than his father, and he became a notoriously irresponsible parody of the reactionary Prussian feudal aristocrat; but he had the same love of English style as his father. He insisted on the construction of an English country house for his use in Potsdam – the Cecilienhof, whose construction (1911–17) coincided with the Great War and a general outburst of Anglophobia.

The association of extreme nationalism with love of England did not even end with the Great War and with Germany's defeat in 1918. It was a commonplace of German political argument in the 1920s that the war against England had been an accident or a mistake. In the 1930s, Hitler consistently believed that he had a particular insight into how English minds worked, and that Germany naturally had a special relationship with Britain. Even England could be all things to all Germans.

An American Dream

For most of the twentieth century, the USA played the role that had previously been performed by England. But the American model had a long history. German admiration went back to the American Revolution, which had been a source of inspiration to Germans looking for a national revival and, in particular, for a rational constitution. Poets like Klopstock and educators like Pestalozzi admired the spirit of American liberty. Though many Germans misunderstood the American emphasis on equality, the New World remained an ideal and shone across the ocean. The legal writer Johann Christian Schmohl discussed the model America offered to despotically ruled Europe: 'Europe on its own does not have enough strength to reform itself. But examples and help from others may yet effect something. It is America that will be Europe's saviour. America will nobly repay the tyranny and devastation it suffered at Europe's hands with liberty and affluence instead.'[41]

In the early nineteenth century, Germans went to America to learn about politics. America gave a solution to one of the thorniest problems of German political life – how to integrate many states with quite separate political traditions, institutions, and laws into a larger entity. Unlike the two European examples of the nation-state, France and Britain, the United States could attract interest as a nation that was not a state but a federation of states. The economist and economic promoter Friedrich List also thought that America showed the way for economic development. After the failure of 1848, there was a political emigration to the United States: Carl Schurz was the most famous exile. Schurz's attitudes resembled those of 1848ers who had stayed in Europe. Richard Wagner, for instance, believed that the musical future lay in a classless America rather than in an outdated, hidebound, reactionary Europe.

At the end of the nineteenth century, it was the vigour and power of America's economy which attracted the Germans' imagination. German businessmen crossed the Atlantic in order to learn how the concentrated economic power of the new 'trust' worked. American ideas about scientific management came in German versions. The most famous of these handbooks, F. W. Taylor's *Principles of Scientific Management*, published in 1911, was already available in a German translation in 1913.

The German obsession with America reached a first peak in the 1920s. In 1918–19 Woodrow Wilson's vision played a major part not only in shaping the peace treaty but also in creating German democracy. During the final weeks of the war, Germany's military leaders pushed democratization in order to respond to Wilson's call for the 'destruction of any arbitrary power that can separately, secretly, and of its single choice disturb the peace of the world'. The US government's role in making German politics fell away after Wilson's failure to secure Congress's support for the peace treaties and the League of Nations covenant. But a substantial flow of private capital across the Atlantic kept alive the American involvement in Germany. That participation found a reflection in cultural life.

George Grosz's painting *Eclipse of the Sun* (1926) showed the dollar blocking the light. Fritz Lang's film *Metropolis* (1926) depicted the Americanized skyscraper world of the future, in which individuals could lose their identities and become merely slaves to a colossal machine. Kurt Weill introduced jazz elements into German music. Politically, socialists modified traditional doctrines about class conflict in the light of harmonious lessons they believed they could learn from America.

Even in the Third Reich, there were attempts to make parallels with America. Hitler sometimes liked to argue – though this was usually before foreign audiences – that he was simply being a German Roosevelt. Motorization – the building of the *Autobahnen*, and the launching of the people's car, or *Volkswagen* – used an American model, taken directly from the example of Ford. At other times, Hitler likened the drive for more territory in the East to the American ideal of the 'frontier' and the West.

The extensive Americanization that followed the political settlement of 1945, and the direct involvement of the US government in European politics, thus had many precedents – some distinguished, others less salubrious. Post-Second-World-War Americanization was not an immediate success. There was, for instance, in 1952 disappointment among those who wanted to democratize German popular culture that a tour by the jazz musician Louis Armstrong had had such a poor reception. The American impact came through economic ties: the massive export of American capital – first in the form of government aid (the Marshall programme), and then in the 1950s more and more direct investment. The second foundation was political and military: the constitutional reordering along democratic lines between 1945 and 1948 and then, subsequently, the inclusion of West Germany in the Western defence system (she joined NATO in 1955); and also the stationing of large numbers of US troops in Germany.

The most superficially apparent manifestations of US influence on Germany were, however, cultural and material. Where Americaniz-ation worked most obviously, it took the form of the introduction of new machinery, and particularly of new consumer goods. Nylon stockings, Coca-Cola, and Walt Disney cartoons in the 1950s, and the fast-food chains in the 1970s (McDonald's opened its first German branch in 1971) set the tone for Germany's American experience. The cultural side of American influence offered the easiest target to those who wanted to criticize the profounder political links.

Other Models for German National Life

If France, Britain, and the USA provided the major models of modern national existence, and classical Greece encouraged speculation about political theory, other templates of nationality briefly pressed and left their shape on the German political imagination. Holland in the 1780s, Italy in the 1810s and 1820s, Poland in the 1830s, after that the Swiss: all could inspire the German soul.

In the 1780s, the Netherlands had been the principal model for a patriotic and German uprising against tyranny. In Schiller's *Don Carlos* (1787), Marquis Posa explained to King Philip how the Netherlands would bring a 'general spring' to 'rejuvenate the shape of the world'. Goethe's Egmont led a similar revolt for the sake of 'Freedom' (the play was published in 1788). Schiller wrote a history of the Dutch revolt (again 1788) as a moral tale for Germans. It was the story of 'the most beautiful monument to the strength of citizens', which would 'create in the hearts of my readers a happy feeling about themselves'.[42] The United Netherlands showed how a hard-working people could create their own state and their own society without needing heroes. Posa's insistent plea to the King of Spain presented him as only one of many people demanding the freedom of thought everywhere: the Netherlands had 'thousands better' than he. This was a nicely bourgeois freedom – unaristocratic and unheroic.

Italy came to German attention as both areas were occupied by Napoleon's armies. By the 1810s a stock picture of Italy had emerged in Germany. Poets followed Goethe and knew it as 'the land where the citrus blossoms'. At the beginning of the nineteenth century, in the tense political atmosphere of French-dominated Italy, a group of German painters who called themselves the 'Brotherhood of St Luke' went to Rome. Many converted to Catholicism. This school, also known as the 'Nazarenes', tried to link early Italian Renaissance styles, religious revival, and German patriotism. The painters included Friedrich Overbeck, Peter von Cornelius, Ludwig Vogel, Joseph Wintergeist, Friedrich Wilhelm von Schadow, and Julius Schnorr von Carolsfeld.

Germany and Italy after 1815 shared political division and partial subordination to the multinational Habsburg Empire. Mazzini's Young Italy movement looked for other 'young nations' throwing off their shackles, and indeed for a Young Europe. Overbeck depicted the links – religious, romantic, cultural and political – between Italy and Germany in a painting of 1828, *Italia und Germania*. He explained that his painting 'represents . . . the yearning which constantly draws the North to the South, to its art, its nature, its poetry; and this in bridal costume – for both, the longing as well as the object of her love, for both continually renew each other as ideas'.[43]

From the time of Winckelmann and Goethe's journeys to Italy, the *Italienreise* represented an important ingredient of German identity. It expressed the romantic longing for a freer, more imaginative world permeated by the presence of antiquity. Even at the beginning of the twentieth century, the *Italienreise* was still a cultural pilgrimage that marked a decisive step in the lives of middle-class Germans. They usually went there on honeymoon. Sometimes they encountered profound experiences. Thomas Mann had an excited vision of the glory of Germany when he heard an Italian band play Wagner, while his brother Heinrich offered a satirical version on the same theme. It is in Rome that His Imperial Majesty's loyal subject – the hero of *Der Untertan* (published 1918) – sinks to the ground before Kaiser William II.

Poland provided lessons in romantic and messianic nationalism for a brief while: after the November Insurrection against Russia of 1830, and before 1848 brought out the conflicts of the Polish and German nations. The rising of 1830 lasted almost a year, and inspired great sympathy. Polish refugees flocked over Germany, and were lionized as the suffering face of a doomed romantic people. Even before the Polish national poet Adam Mickiewicz in *Dziady* ('Forefathers' Eve', 1832) compared Poland to a Christ suffering sacrificially on behalf of other nations, the German poet Harro Harring wrote a poem with the title 'Freedom's Salvation' ('Der Freiheit Heiland'). In this, freedom depended on the sacrifice of a life, and Poland played the part of John the Baptist in preparing for this sacrifice. Then freedom would appear:

> Like a Christ, he'll love the poor,
> Will show pity, mercy more
> For the humble weak; but being ever just
> Driven on by holy flames of dreadful rage,
> He'll war against the people's traitors wage
> And turn every prince's lackey into dust.[44]

So Germany would learn and benefit from the experience of suffering Poland.

Switzerland, whose small-town society at the outset of the nineteenth century closely resembled that in Germany, could give a German-

language version of the Polish quest for freedom. The Swiss drama of liberation was stolen by the Germans: it was Schiller who in 1804 told the story of Wilhelm Tell and the oath to freedom on the Rütli. After 1848, Switzerland – together with Britain and the USA – attracted political *émigrés*, and had the obvious advantage of greater proximity. The revolutionary poet Georg Herwegh as well as the composer Richard Wagner and the economists Karl Knies and Bruno Hildebrand lived in Switzerland.

Throughout the nineteenth century a two-way influence operated. The Swiss had low taxes and little bureaucracy. They participated actively in local government. They had a romantic, wild, Germanic landscape that contrasted with the elegiac classicism of Tuscan scenery. Swiss constitutionalism was translated into German liberal terms by the Swiss lawyer Johann Caspar Bluntschli, who worked as a professor in Munich and Heidelberg. On the other hand, the Swiss-German community felt a powerful pull from the vigour of mainstream German nationalism – an attraction that at least until the 1870s caused great political difficulty within Switzerland.

Germans who felt and thought about, and rejected or imitated, all these different models were confronted by a bewildering amalgam of ideas, social organizations, and patterns of behaviour. The confusion increased because of the linguistically mixed character of the Central European population. In practice, no one could draw neat lines on a map delimiting one linguistic area from another. There were enclaves, areas of mixed population, and regions where different dialects constituted nearly different languages. Even at the end of the nineteenth century, after a few generations of authoritarian schooling had attempted to bring system and order to this linguistic chaos, and succeeded in making people highly conscious of the problem occasioned by the sounds that they spoke, the difficulty remained. Where were Germans and what was Germany? Apart from the territories which in 1871 became part of the German Empire (*Kaiserreich*), and which included a substantial non-German population, there were German speakers in Switzerland, Austria-Hungary, and the Russian Empire. In 1910 in Switzerland 2,599,154 out of a population of 3,741,971 spoke German as their first language; in the Austrian part of the Habsburg monarchy (Cisleithania) 9,950,266 out of 28,571,934, and in the Hungarian lands 2,037,435 out of 20,886,787. In the 1897 census in Russia, 1,813,717 German speakers out of a population of 100,331,516 were registered.[45]

The combination of uncertainty about where Germans lived, and of what – apart from a fictitious linguistic group – they were, led to an unstable sense of national identity. Germans learnt bourgeois manners from the French, politics from the Greeks, economics from the British, and consumerism from the Americans. It is not surprising that the rich diversity of German borrowing produced some very confused reactions.

The mix of models made the language of nation into a perfect vehicle of expression for disagreements about how German national life should be conducted. Anything perceived as threatening or unpleasant could be denounced as alien – liberalism as English, classical education as Greek or French, conservatism as Russian, commerce as English or Jewish, and modern capitalism as American.[46] So many ingredients went into the German national identity and became partly but never completely submerged in a German synthesis as to give Germans the chance of always denouncing as foreign what they disliked in themselves.

Many of these features are not peculiar to Germany or the development of a German identity. In later developing nations, which historically followed the Western nation-states, a greater fictional and inventive aspect, but also a substantial amount of imitation, enters into the language of national politics. Both the fiction and the imitation help to make nationalism an unattainable ideal. In terms of the domestic organization of politics, the generous use of models from the past and present creates all manner of new alternatives. Nationalism generates visions of idealized societies in which justice might be realized for all members of the national community. The appeal to broader social groups envisages a successful integration. In this way nationalism projects a utopian vision, and creates expectations and hopes that are bound to be disappointed. This is one reason why it has been important to nationalist theoreticians not to reach the end of the nationalist journey, and to continue to see the attainment of national goals as a remote, shimmering possibility.

Nations are striving to become something else, to transform themselves. In the early nineteenth century they were characteristically described as 'young', as if they were living a life of perpetual adolescence. 'Young Germany' and 'Young Italy' went alongside 'Young England'. One recent writer has suggested that 'nations which are independent, territorially satisfied and deeply nationally conscious have no need to be nationalist any more'.[47] But in practice, such a point is never achieved. The nation – like Peter Pan – cannot grow up. In reality, nations rarely regard themselves either as entirely independent or as territorially satisfied; and even if these conditions are met, the national consciousness can never, at least in the vision of the propagators of national doctrine, go deep enough. For political romantics (and nationalism is almost always associated with a kind of romanticism), the

complete accomplishment of the nationalist ideal is set in a future so distant as to be incapable of present realization. Fichte, the most famous of the German exponents of national development, saw the final point as lying in a very remote and hazy future: 'This generation [that would be completely educated in national consciousness] is not yet present, and still needs to be reared; and even if everything goes better than we can expect, nevertheless a substantial time is still needed in order to move into that new age.'[48]

Nationalism depended on arousing expectations unfulfillable in the present. But it also needed to provide answers to the question why its aspirations had been blocked. The failure of nationalism to realize the hopes it awakened could in many cases be told quite simply in terms of stories of oppression: the Hungarians had been trampled by the Austrians, the Slovaks by the Hungarians, the Poles by Russians and Prussians. National humiliation is blamed on foreigners or on foreign influence. Even after the attainment of national independence, stories of oppression could still be told as a way of relieving discontent and disappointment. In the aftermath of 1919, the peace treaties imposed by the international system were widely blamed for any political malaise: they had been (depending on the standpoint) either too harsh (for the losers) or over generous (for the victors).

Small states such as Switzerland, which could not tell the tale of national oppression, could still see their position as a small country constrained by international power realities. Where national oppression failed to give a good account of the difficulties and inadequacies of the nation-state, and where the united and independent nation was not obviously a constrained small state, the tensions between the myths of nationality and the failure to realize them, or between the desire for equality with other states (or even superiority) and the realities of international power politics, might be very explosive.

We might be tempted on the basis of the analysis of this chapter to believe that Germany fits well into a standard central or eastern European model of national development. Such a model has the following characteristics: the elaboration of a doctrine of nationality preceded the institution of a national state. The doctrine depended on building and synthesizing identity out of a jumble of historical traditions and eclectic observation of the realities of the contemporary world.

There is indeed nothing very singular or peculiarly German about the concept of an invented nationality: but what is unusual about Germany is that a nation-state generated in this 'eastern' way developed into a Great Power on the European and world stage.[49] (Japan may have experienced a similar evolution.) On this stage, all the other Great

Powers had evolved their doctrines of nationality in a rather different way. Britain, France and the United States were examples of the modern 'western' nation-state, in which the state did not have to be generated by a nationalist movement. Russia was first a traditional *ancien régime* empire, and then a revolutionary state that claimed to have transcended nationalism (and which indeed even stopped calling itself Russia). After 1871, when the German Empire was established, Germany alone played Great Power politics with all the unfulfilled ambitions and romantic expectations of a movement for national awakening.

2

The Origins of German Nationalism

German nationalism emerged out of a crisis of values. In the eighteenth century there was in Germany no agreed way of presenting any political case, no rules on how to play a controversy. There were over three hundred separate states (not counting the nearly one and a half thousand knights' estates), and their mutual relations inevitably were not always harmonious. Sometimes these states tried to mobilize patriotic sentiment when they fought against each other, or against non-German powers –France, Sweden, Russia or Poland. The larger states accumulated considerable local loyalty. Prussia, one of the two largest, managed to build up a specific Prussian patriotism. Alternatively, German states could argue the justice of their cause by appealing to universal values – to the principle of dynastic legitimacy in disputes about inheritance, to the laws of the ancient Holy Roman Empire, to a principle of justice (if the legitimacy claim let them down), to the theory of the balance of power if they felt vulnerable. To a century which wanted to look for rationality and clarity, these highly heterogeneous principles were confusing. Looking back, the radical nationalist Johann Gottlieb Fichte described these mixed claims of the German states as 'national pride without a nation'.[1]

The idea of a political nation offered a powerful alternative to the bewilderingly diverse assertions of different sorts of legitimacy. But because of the fragmented state of Germany, because of the territorial multiplicity, *Kleinstaaterei*, doctrines of nationalism were at first scarcely convincing guides to political action. They began, not as political theories, but rather as a belief in a shared culture and a shared history. Cultural unity and political diversity stood in sharp contrast to each other.

Nationalist theory was more than simply a development internal to German history. The political complexion of Europe played a crucial role. Two extraneous considerations shaped the future development of German nationalism. It developed as a response to two contrasting international systems: first that of Napoleon, then that of Metternich. One was the extension of the practice of the French Revolution; the other the application of the principle of legitimacy across all of Europe as a bulwark of counter-revolution. As political structures, the European and the German state system were clearly interdependent. Napoleon turned Germany into a buffer zone against the Habsburgs in Austria and against Russia. Metternich in turn wanted a fragmented Germany as a protection against any new threat that might emerge from France. This was the purpose of the German Confederation created in 1815 at the Congress of Vienna.

One of the strongest arguments of German nationalist writers was that the need for a German nation had arisen as the consequence of the breakdown of European society and *civitas*. Nations had no function as long as a genuine international order existed. Specifically, the rights of Germans had been well protected as long as there was a universal emperor, but once this general security framework had collapsed, Germans had become vulnerable. Germans believed that at least since the sixteenth century they had been the victims of the European Great Powers.

The French Revolution and Napoleon ended any illusions there might have been about the effectiveness of the old Europe-wide *civitas*. The Holy Roman Empire disappeared after the imperial dynasty, the Habsburgs, were defeated by French armies. The battles of Marengo and Hohenlinden (1800) led to the Peace of Luneville. In the aftermath of Luneville, hundreds of smaller German states, kingdoms, ecclesiastical principalities, and Imperial Free Cities were distributed to the larger states as territorial compensation for losses to France. In 1805 the Emperor was defeated yet again at Ulm. He decided to call himself plain Emperor Franz of Austria and Napoleon then decreed the end of the Holy Roman Empire. In 1806 Prussia belatedly joined the war against France, lost the battles of Jena and Auerstädt, and had to suffer a French occupation.

In both Austria and Prussia patriotic rebels set out programmes of administrative reform, military renewal, and national uprising – sometimes with the veiled acquiescence of the ruling dynasties, sometimes in defiance of the monarchs. The Austrian plans were put in patriotic language in the writings of Friedrich Schlegel and Friedrich von Gentz. The Habsburg Archduke Johann began to organize a people's militia

35

and led a popular revolt in the Tyrol. Count Philipp Stadion tried in 1808–9 to put a package of reform proposals into practice – until yet another defeat at the hands of Napoleon drove him out of office. The consequence was that Austria's German nationalism faded into more or less complete historical oblivion, although in 1848 the Frankfurt Assembly recognized Archduke Johann's patriotism by electing him as Imperial Vicar or Governor (*Reichsverweser*).

Prussia's patriots performed better historically and generated a powerful and long-lived mythology of national awakening.[2] The reformers Stein, Hardenberg, Humboldt, and Gneisenau produced a new army, a new administration, a new education system, and a far-reaching land reform. They removed guild restrictions on manufacturing and trading, and in theory opened up all occupations to all. They prepared the way for a patriotic war against Napoleon, a war begun initially by a Prussian commander, General von Yorck, who in defiance of the King of Prussia's orders went over from the French to the Russians during Napoleon's winter campaign against Russia. The subsequent 'War of Freedom', as it was known at the time, or 'war of liberation', as it was later called, thus began with a defiance of dynastic authority. In a 'Short Catechism', the patriot Ernst Moritz Arndt explained that the German soldier was 'a German, before he knew of kings or princes'.[3] The poet Heinrich von Kleist in *The Prince of Homburg* depicted sympathetically a general's rebellion against his monarch for the sake of his country. Reichsfreiherr vom und zum Stein drew on his status as a Knight of the Holy Roman Empire, independent of princely authority: since the German princes could not make free decisions – because of the French occupation – the people instead should represent the nation in the interest of freedom. He told Count Münster:

> I am sorry that Your Excellency presumes a Prussian in me and finds a Hanoverian in Himself. I have only one fatherland, and that is Germany, and since according to the old constitution [of the Holy Roman Empire] I belong only to Germany and to no particular part, I am devoted with all my heart only to that whole and not the parts. Dynasties at this moment leave me untouched, they are only instruments. My wish is to see Germany great and strong, in order to assert her role between France and Russia and to regain her autonomy, independence and nationality.[4]

Stein deduced that if the King of Prussia wished to avoid a popular rising against his throne, he should himself lead the revolt against the French.

By August 1814 around 30,000 Prussians had volunteered for the war against France. They came from every social class, although students

joined the national banners with a special enthusiasm. Though these
volunteers formed only a relatively small fraction of the total of 279,000
Prussian soldiers fighting against Napoleon, they show the pervasiveness
of hostility to France, and of Prussian patriotism. Probably a Prussian
patriotism, however, and not a German one – that remained the
property of a relatively small number of leaders and visionaries, the
Arndts and the Steins.

The war of liberation, however, laid the foundation for a myth:
Germany, guided by far-sighted statesmen, fought a war in which all
social classes participated. Genius-statesmen took up the cause that the
princes had abandoned. A new style of leadership was needed by the
nation. For instance, the Prussian officer Carl von Clausewitz associated
the national mobilization and victory with the triumph of a romanticized
conception of genius. In his posthumously published *On War* he wrote:
'Genius consists in a harmonious combination of elements, in which one
or the other ability may predominate, but none may be in conflict with
the rest.' 'What genius does is the best rule, and theory can do no better
than show how and why this should be the case.'[5] Germany won, while
the territorial states and Prussia and Austria had earlier been defeated,
because in the aftermath of the French Revolution national wars had
replaced the cabinet battles of the eighteenth century. October 18, the
day of the battle of Leipzig which marked the conclusive defeat of
Napoleon in Germany, became a day of festive celebration for
nineteenth-century nationalists.

In 1815, however, there could be little doubt that the Germany of the
princes had returned decisively. Germany was now divided into 38
states,[6] and dominated politically by Prussia and Austria. The new
German Confederation was a loose alliance of independent states with a
federal diet – which coordinated the independent policy of the 38 or 39
states, and which did not legislate or create a uniform system of law, or
make economic policy or church policy. The central institutions of the
federation came nearest to exercising effective authority only when it
came to imposing a black reaction: in 1819 with the Carlsbad decrees
(against freedom of the press); and the 'six articles' of 1832 (which
reimposed the 1819 decrees). Austria's interest lay in maintaining
Germany as a block against French power: keeping her divided so as not
to increase the power of Prussia, and keeping her reactionary as a
bulwark against the revolutionary impulse.

The hopes of the era of liberation vanished. Caspar David Friedrich
provided a powerful visual symbol in his painting *Ulrich von Hutten's
grave* (1823) (see plate), in which the names of the heroes of the war of
1813–14 appear against a gothic ruin and overlooked by a statue of Faith

– with her head broken off to demonstrate the betrayal. Germany had once again been frustrated by the system of international politics.

In consequence, German nationalism survived 1815, the final surrender of Napoleon and the Congress of Vienna, as a doctrine of opposition to a new principle of the international order. Congress Europe relied on dynastic legitimacy and the denial of the principle of nationality. It aimed to be an international order based on a conservative international political doctrine. Nationalism aimed at the subversion of that order.

At this stage German 'nationalism' (rather than the more widespread xenophobia and hatred of the French) is better described as a national awakening that took place among a relatively limited cultured class. The nation as a cultural community was partly the creation of the German Enlightenment, and partly a reaction against French Enlightenment. That is to say that it was shaped by rejection both of theological ideas and of the universal doctrines of human emancipation as preached by the *philosophes*.

There had long been propagandists for a linguistic Germanness: Thomasius in the eighteenth century, or Martin Opitz in the seventeenth, and even Martin Luther in the sixteenth. Its most important and famous exposition was, however, that given in Johann Gottfried Herder's *Essay on the Origins of Language*, published in Berlin in 1772. Herder's primary aim, consistent with Enlightenment thinking, was to refute the theological view of language as God-created. Instead, he said, language had been the product of man's need for sociability. Men lived in communities, which depended on language to bind them together.

Nor, Herder believed, could language have been the invention of any one man. It required transmission through generations by means of education or a more general acculturation: 'I came into the world and was subjected to instruction by my family: and so was my father, and so was the first son of the first father of the tribe.'[7] This cultural transfer over long periods of time occurred by means of communities or groups. The groups developed their own languages in order to affirm their identity, to use history as a necessary and integrative myth: 'by making the deeds of their forefathers into songs, by issuing appeals, by constructing eternal monuments, the thought of the language is kept more and more patriotic.'[8]

Consciousness depended on long historical continuities; but history by itself could not suffice to construct nationality. The group became a nation only when it started to define itself by observing other groups or nations. A nation required something external to it in order to realize an identity. One nation, cut off from others, would become isolated and would lose the need to develop a personality: 'Small and so-called barbaric peoples illustrate this principle. They are shut off with only the necessities of life and can remain for hundreds of years in the strangest ignorance: like those islands where there is no fire and like some other peoples without a trace of mechanical skill.'[9] Nations, on the other hand, confronted other nations, and saw themselves by seeing what they were not.

Two consequences followed from Herder's analysis, one concerned with history and its uses, the other with strange nations and their lessons. In the first place, there could be no universally valid picture of how a nation should conduct its affairs. Each country had its own unique quality because it had its own history. Herder was savagely sceptical of the notion that modern times demonstrated a continuing progress towards ever greater felicity. In *Another Philosophy of History*, he mocked the universal claims of the Enlightenment's doctrine of emancipation: 'Ideas of a general love for humanity, for other peoples and for enemies are exalted, and the warm feeling for fathers, mothers, brothers, children, and friends is endlessly weakened.'[10]

The education that Herder saw as central to the creation of national identity thus required something rather different than the schematic presentation of a 'few bright ideas': 'ideas', Herder explained, 'really only yield ideas'.[11] Instead, it would be better to use history and revert to the beliefs of an earlier age – of the Middle Ages or of ancient Greece. 'How differently those peoples and those ages once thought when everything close at hand was still thought to be National. Every acculturation and education [*Bildung*] arose out of particular and individual needs, and went no farther than that – nothing other than experience, action, and the practice of life in a limited sphere.'[12] In *Ideas for a Philosophy of History*, he was even more decisive in the rejection of the view that there might be a textbook answer to the problems of a nation:

> Do not believe, you men, that a premature and intemperate education means happiness or that the dead nomenclature of all sciences and the precariously balanced use of all arts can provide the knowledge of life to a living being . . . Let us once more thank Providence for not making the whole of mankind too sensitive, and for not turning the entire globe into a lecture theatre for learned scientists.[13]

How else apart from through the application of a schematic design could the cultural education of a nation take place? It was not sufficient to be merely practical, limited and self-sufficient. That course would lead merely to cultural decline. Instead other nations should provide a pattern for a healthy spiritual life. This was Herder's second great doctrine. Cultural transmission meant learning from other people – from members of the same nation, and from ancestors; but also from other peoples:

> Here nature has made a new chain, the transmission from nation to nation! Arts, sciences, culture and languages have in a long procession refined themselves and have defined nations – nations which are the first link of the progression provided by nature . . . Let some nations move forwards and others backwards: thus everything is . . . as it was in the ancient world. Egyptians and Greeks, the Romans and modern peoples have done nothing more than carry on traditions. Persians, Tartars, Goths, and priests come in between and destroy, but it is all the easier to go on building on the basis of the old ruins.[14]

Each culture had a particular moment when it reached a zenith: 'Each state has a period of growth, maturity and decline, and the sciences and arts accompany this progression.'[15] After nations had reached the peak, they disappeared once they had nothing more to offer to the development of the universal culture. 'The genius has spoken what it had to say! Its imprint on the ages has been made; the sword is blunted, the scabbard lies in pieces.'[16]

That was why it was foolish for Germany simply to attempt to imitate the Greeks: 'We can never achieve the purity of the Greek national character, with its simplicity in science and in learning. So let us be what we can be and attempt to copy from the Greeks only in so far as our constitution allows us – and in this way we may become what they could not be.'[17] Of all modern countries, France had most clearly passed the point at which it might serve as a model for other nations. French decline had already set in. Herder's work is filled with attacks on the over-generalized conceptions of the French Enlightenment – with refutations of Montesquieu and condemnations of Voltaire. French culture had lost those essential roots in more popular existence. 'How have they become the people of *honnêteté*, of manners, of the art of living, and *amusements*? What have they lost in this process? And what have they robbed and what are they robbing from other peoples by spreading to them their follies!'[18]

Learning from others was a salutary shock to a national culture; but if the shock were too great, if too much was learnt too slavishly, it might kill. 'The age in which we long for the distance, in which we pine after things foreign is already the age of sickness, of flatulence, of unhealthy fullness, and of the premonition of death.'[19] Nationalism had to be at least partly self-sufficient and self-sustaining. Even the history of barbarous epochs offered to nations an alternative way of building national identity. The historical and the imitative aspects of nation-building required bonding together.

Herder was inspired by ancient folk stories: he delighted in the stories of Fingal and Ossian as evidence of the multiplicity of cultural developments. 'The crude anticipations of Mengs's and Dürer's paintings already glistened on the red painted shield of Hermann [the Cheruscan].'[20]

The medieval enthusiasm of Herder formed a central component of the German Romantic movement and of German nationalism. The most famous convert to medievalism was Goethe, who as a young student developed a passion for Strasbourg cathedral. Gothic architecture had previously had a poor reputation. It was chaotic and gloomy, and looked over the crowded, insanitary, smelly, and dark streets of small-town Germany. The old imperial cities, where many of Germany's gothic monuments were sited, stagnated in economic and social decline, the buildings themselves usually poorly maintained and threatened with ruin.

In Strasbourg, instead of finding over-complex and ornate decorations flung thoughtlessly together, Goethe saw to his astonishment a carefully coordinated and proportioned work. Its proportions, but also its history, intrigued the young student: 'Since I found this building constructed on an old German site and built in the real German age, and since the name of the master architect on his modest grave had a patriotic ring and origin, I dared to change the previously despised appellation Gothic and to vindicate it as the German architecture of our nation. I was inspired by the worth of this work of art.' Goethe laid down this challenge in a sixteen-page brochure, published in 1782 and entitled *Von deutscher Baukunst* ('On German Architecture'). This pamphlet combined extolment of the German with the assertion of a romantic notion of the individual – and German – genius of the cathedral architect Erwin von Steinbach. But Goethe did not really sustain his gothic passion of 1782, and reverted to the world of Italy and Greece. He only came back in the 1810s under the influence of a young architect and collector of German art, Sulpiz Boisserée.[21]

Appropriately, Goethe went on from his encounter with the gothic to an association with Herder, who also used the example of Strasbourg Cathedral in another patriotic brochure, *Of German Nature and Art*. Herder's main discovery, and his principal legacy for nineteenth-century nationalists, was the insistence on education and culture as the distinguishing mark of national existence. In education, Germany could learn from her own past and from other cultures without being simply imitative.

Cultural community developed out of an exclusive language, which called by name, and in this way set up a series of identities. Education and acculturation (*Bildung*) transmitted names and thus also national identity. In German society as it existed in the late eighteenth century, *Bildung* was the prerogative of a relatively small elite who underlined their status by defining it in terms of education. In the historical literature, they are known as the *Bildungsbürgertum*, the educated middle classes. They believed that they formed an aristocracy of the 'spirit' (*Geist*). Sometimes they could be found in state service (particularly in highly enlightened states such as Baden or Weimar), and sometimes in free professions: in the law, in medicine, or – though only very occasionally – in writing. Though it was not an elite which thought of itself primarily in financial terms, money was important. The survival of the *Bildungsbürgertum* across generations depended on financial independence, if only because of the cost of education, or of the income forgone by participating in education.[22]

On the other hand, the identification of culture and nation envisaged by Herder and his successors required a continual reaching out to new social groups. Education into linguistic awareness and national sensitivity meant a continual broadening. A widely available education would have revolutionary consequences. It was not just the *Bildungsbürgertum* that defined itself by education. The restricted availability of knowledge had been one of the chief defining characteristics of *ancien régime* society. A society of craftsmen is full of craft and guild mysteries, of transfers of skills which had been kept as closely guarded secrets. Breaking apart this closed and inaccessible world would transform social relations. Herder realized this, and argued for the wide availability of practical as well as theoretical knowledge. His emerging nation eroded all kinds of monopolies on information and education.

Fichte continued the logic of Herder's argument. In all the apparently opposed political stances that he adopted – from fiery Jacobin to German patriot – he remained obsessed by education. 'Culture' meant for him nothing more or less than a total external and internal freedom: 'Culture means the exercise of all forces for the goal of complete freedom – the absolute independence from everything which is not ourselves or our pure self.'[23] This pure self would be guided solely by reason.

Fichte originally welcomed the French Revolution because of its promise of social emancipation and political liberty. When he found that the revolution meant French nationalism and the exploitation of Germany rather than her liberation from the rule of the petty princes, he turned to a specific patriotism rather than a universal doctrine of liberation. The main theme expounded in the 'Addresses to the German Nation', delivered in Berlin in 1808 during the French occupation, was how a state-directed education could create a German character.

Character was not the product of institutional arrangements, but of the passing of values from one generation to another. Fichte used the Burkeian image of a continuous chain linking mankind over time. In order to develop a self-sustaining national culture what was required was 'not the spirit of a peaceful civic love of the constitution and the laws but the consuming flame of a higher love of the Fatherland, which conceives the nation as the mantle of the Eternal, for which the noble soul sacrifices himself with pleasure and the ignoble, who only exists for the noble, should simply sacrifice himself'. He set himself quite deliberately against the view that patriotism should be searched for and located in institutional realities. This is how he arrived at his famous conclusion about the Germans and their nation: 'We must, to put it in one word, find character: for to have character and to be German is without doubt the same thing.'[24]

The 'Addresses' were directed at the German people under French occupation. A nation could be reached, even if it were politically unfree, through the printing press; but general education offered the most hope for the German future. All children – with both sexes mixed – would be trained in practical things, roughly in accordance with the programme suggested by the Swiss educational reformer Johann Heinrich Pestalozzi. The particularly adept scholars should be set to learn 'sensibility', 'without exception and without distinction of birth'. Nowhere was the theory of a *Bildungsbürgertum* as a new social elite, not dependent on traditional social arrangements, more clearly enunciated than by Fichte. 'The majority of citizens must be educated in this patriotic way; and, in order to make sure of this majority, the education should be tried on everyone.' A utopia of universal civilization opened up: 'before, the majority of the population just lived for the flesh, for matter, for nature; the new education will ensure that the spirit alone lives in and guides the majority, and indeed soon the whole population.'[25]

The state's educational mission to create a national consciousness was the obvious answer to the problem of absent national identity. The state might consciously shape a new political class in its own image. Education could make citizens. The humiliated and defeated King of Prussia himself embraced this message. Intellectual revival was a first step to a general national revival in the face of the French occupation: 'The state must replace through mental forces what it has lost in material forces.'[26]

Destroying the *arcana*, the secrets of the old guilds, belonged as part of this programme for the mental regeneration of Prussia. It would also bring practical benefits: a widespread freedom to practise manufacture and commerce (*Gewerbefreiheit*) would make Prussia stronger, and allow her to recover her material as well as her mental forces.

The fundamental pattern for the reconstruction of Prussian life was a classical one. After the Napoleonic defeat of Prussia, educational reforms made classical training the central part of the new curriculum. Ancient languages formed the basis of teaching in the new *Gymnasium* (a selective secondary school which prepared for university entrance through a certificate of maturity), and also of the universities.

Wilhelm von Humboldt directed Prussian educational policy for only a year and a half, but his vision came to shape German schools and universities for at least the rest of the century. He believed that the provision of specific skills of practical information was less important than the formation of character and independence in his students. They were to become the citizens of a new commonwealth. Generally educated scholars would be more flexible but also more humane. The Ancients provided the best model for this kind of education, and thus their languages should dominate curricula.

Classical languages were far more than merely the symbol of social apartness, or the hallmark of an expensive education. They offered the key to unlock the full moral and political persona as it had – until then – only been realized in the ancient world. It is not surprising that this ancient vision covered all aspects of life.

Classicism in education corresponded to classicism in architectural representation. Berlin's layout and appearance was transformed by Karl Friedrich Schinkel (1781–1841). His case is a central part of the story of the emergence of a new national iconography and the struggle over its form. Part of Schinkel's vision derived not from classicism but from the gothic and from its national connotations. In 1810 he had prepared a design for a mausoleum for the romantic Queen of Prussia, Luise, who had come to incarnate the spirit of Prussian defiance of French occupation in the years after Jena and Auerstädt. Gothic, Schinkel explained in developing his plan, embodied the national spirit and was in consequence 'higher in its principles than antiquity'.[27] In 1815, for similar reasons, Schinkel planned a gothic National Cathedral as a monument to the German liberation from Napoleon.

In practice, almost all of Schinkel's actually realized buildings embodied the principles of neo-classicism. This became the 'Berlin style'. Schinkel did make a joint design with another architect for a mausoleum for Queen Luise in the gardens of Schloss Charlottenburg, but it was a simple, sober and elegant Greek doric building (1810). On Unter den Linden in Berlin, the New Guard House (Neue Wache, 1816–18) was again a rather restrained classical doric monument to Prussia's victorious army. The Berlin Schauspielhaus (1819–21) and the Altes Museum (1824–8), both with ionic colonnades, were to be temples to the modern muses. The new Berlin in Schinkel's conception exhibited symmetry, austerity and purity in the national cause. It put Humboldt's programme in a visual form.

Schinkel's Berlin competed with a Bavaria extensively rebuilt under the aegis of Crown Prince Ludwig (1786–1868, and who reigned as King Ludwig I of Bavaria from 1825 to 1848) by Friedrich von Gärtner and Leo von Klenze. The Bavarian neo-classical architects were far more consciously imitative than Schinkel, partly through choice and partly as a consequence of Ludwig's dictate. Klenze was an archaeologist fascinated by Greece as well as a painter and an architect. His lifelong programme was the adaptation of Greece for Germany:

> Never has there been, and never will there be, more than one art of building, namely that which was brought to perfection at the epoch of the prosperity and the civilization of Greece . . . Grecian architecture can and must be the architecture of the world, and that of all periods; nor can any climate, any material, any difference of manners prove an obstacle to its universal adoption.[28]

Ludwig's Hellenism was no less enthusiastic. He drew a political parallel between modern Greece, fighting a war of liberation against the Turks, and the German national awakening in the face of the French armies. In 1832, Ludwig's own son Otto became the first king of an independent Greece, thus expressing in dynastic terms the sentimental link between Bavaria and Greece.

Ludwig became a compulsive builder of public monuments expressing German nationality in a Greek style. He conceived the idea of a national pantheon in 1807, when he visited Berlin at the low point of Prussian humiliation. In 1814–16 he held a prize competition for a 'Walhalla', a Nordic version of the pantheon. There were some who criticized Ludwig's narrowly classical view of how a German monument should look. 'Are we not', wrote one critic, 'being inconsistent when we try to glorify our nation by the erection of a great building while ignoring the great and splendidly original German style of architecture?' The Walhalla was, however, built high above the Danube at Regensburg between 1830 and 1842 on the classical design of Klenze. Ludwig explained that 'the Walhalla was erected that the German might depart from it more German and better than when he had arrived'.[29] From 1846 to 1863, after Ludwig had been obliged to abdicate the Bavarian throne, yet another great monument was created not far from the Walhalla in order to commemorate the liberation of Germany from France. The plans for the Liberation Hall (Befreiungshalle) at Kelheim on the Danube were drawn up by Gärtner and modified by Klenze. The building had a characteristically doric colonnade above a building overladen with numerical symbolism. Eighteen sides marked the fact that the battles of Leipzig and Waterloo had both been fought on the eighteenth day of the month.

Ludwig's desire to replace French rule by Greek style combined political and aesthetic argumentation. Long before Napoleon, Bavaria had been a political satellite of France and an enthusiastic importer of French tastes and fashions. In the eighteenth century, French tyranny over Germany had been cultural and not simply military. Now, in the nineteenth century, the classical revival put Germany on the right course to becoming a universal people – such as the Greeks had been.

German classicism left a lasting legacy – not simply as an experiment in artistic styles but also as a programme for social change and renewal. It is true that it claimed more than it could fulfil. Classical education in practice was exclusive and elitist. Its boundaries were marked by a knowledge of classical languages that was expensive to acquire – even free schools meant the loss of income that a scholar could have earned had he been working. But German schools were more accessible to a wider social range than those of any other European country. They created a considerable social mobility.

The cult of the gothic and the medieval always represented an alternative to the classical and one which purported to be less exclusive and more in accordance with the character of the 'people'. The gothic and the romantic acquired popular and national associations during the war of liberation: as in Friedrich's painting of 1814 depicting the romantic wooded landscape surrounding the 'Grave of Arminius' (or Hermann the Cheruscan). Stein's memorandum of September 1812 called for the restoration of the medieval and pre-Habsburg Holy Roman Empire in place of the decayed and atrophied regime of the Habsburgs (who had occupied the Imperial throne since the fifteenth century – with only a short interruption in the eighteenth). The poet Max von Schenkendorf invoked the myth of Barbarossa – the sleeping Emperor lying under the Kyffhäuser mountain who would awake to save Germany in her hour of need.[30] It was also during the French occupation that Schinkel began his experimentation with gothic cathedral design.

Schinkel did eventually design gothic as well as neo-classical buildings (the Werdersche Kirche in Berlin in 1825 was the first, though gothic had always been recognized as peculiarly appropriate for church architecture). He liked the idea he had encountered in England of factory architecture in a gothic style. The gothic did not need to be associated so unremittingly with thoughts of moral improvement and cultural ennoblement as did the classical.

In later buildings Schinkel tried to make a synthesis of gothic and classical principles. The Bauakademie in Berlin (1831) used gothic piers. The palace for Prince William at Babelsberg (1834–5) was an English-style gothic fantasy construction, though here again there were particular considerations: the English tastes of William's wife. At the end of his life Schinkel designed the gothic-style spiked helmet (*Pickelhaube*) that came to be the emblem of the Prussian army and police. The gothic began to take over Munich even during the reign of the very classical Ludwig I. From 1831 to 1839 a neo-gothic church, the Mariahilfkirche, was constructed in the Au outside the old city walls by the architect Daniel Joseph Ohlmüller.

But admiration for the gothic as a historic style was concentrated – remarkably, in the light of Germany's rich inheritance of gothic architecture – on only two buildings. Strasbourg cathedral had been made famous by Goethe and Herder. Cologne cathedral was incomplete. After 1560, the twin towers in the south-west and north-west corners were left truncated for the next three centuries: the south-west tower was only one-third of its intended height, and that in the north-west even lower. The Catholic novelist and cultural philosopher Friedrich Schlegel – originally a convinced Winckelmannian – was responsible for the discovery of Cologne as not only a monument to the Christian faith but also an artistic expression of the infinite.

Cologne became such a powerful symbol because of its unfinished state: it represented perfectly a vulnerable and fragile nation. During the secularization of the Napoleonic era the shortage of funds for the maintenance of religious buildings even meant a danger of collapse. In 1814 the former Jacobin Joseph Görres presented the maintenance and the completion of the cathedral as a national task of pre-eminent importance. 'Long shall Germany live in shame and humiliation, a prey to inner conflict and alien arrogance, until her people return to the ideals from which they were seduced by selfish ambition, and until true religion and loyalty, unity of purpose and self-denial shall again render them capable of erecting such buildings as this, which in their degenerate state they now abandon.'[31] In 1823–4 Sulpiz Boisserée published 'Views, Sketches and Individual Parts of Cologne Cathedral' (*Ansichten, Risse und einzelne Theile des Doms von Köln*), a series of meticulously engraved plans and drawings for a completed cathedral.

There was a substantial amount of rebuilding and restoration work in the 1820s and 1830s, but the extension of the building only began in 1842. The cathedral completion required a whole artillery of patriotic phrases. It represented the German response to the French military threat of 1840. It demonstrated the integration of Prussia's previously neglected Rhineland Catholics into the national community. And, in addition, it was a vehicle for the medieval passions of the energetic new King of Prussia, Frederick William iv. He spoke at the laying of the foundation stone, declaring: 'The spirit which builds these portals is the same which broke our fetters twenty-nine years ago, which brought to an end the humiliation of the Fatherland and the alien occupation of this province. It is the spirit of German unity and strength.' The thought behind Cologne had in reality been the idea of the German national war against Napoleon. Görres explained that the completion occurred 'in order that the vows of our forefathers may be truly fulfilled and the cathedral become in very truth a monument of liberation: liberation not only from foreign oppression, but also from our own delusions, prejudices and contentions which alone have brought this oppression on us.'[32]

The building of the complete cathedral represented the extension of the nationalist idea to a broader group. A similar idea of linking nation and church lay behind the historicizing frescoes commissioned from Alfred Rethel in the Council Chamber of the Holy Roman Emperors in Aachen (Aix-la-Chapelle).

In the 1840s, nationalism started to involve more people. Before, it had been confined to a relatively small number of writers and thinkers. The story of the widening of nationalism is evident in the history of the gymnastic societies.

The first movement of a popular nationalism had been generated during the German response to the French Revolution and Napoleon. There were popular protests and riots, but also a more systematic patriotism built around societies and associations. Whereas the general national language of opposition was widespread throughout Germany, membership of the patriotic clubs was narrower. There were student fraternities (*Burschenschaften*); and gymnastic associations (*Turnvereine*) composed largely of university and *Gymnasium* students. 'Old Man of Gymnastics' (*Turnvater*) Ludwig Jahn began exercising with about two hundred *Gymnasium* students just outside Berlin in 1811. The *Turnvereine* emphasized solidarity and uniformity: the gymnasts wore identical clothes for exercising, and they called their fellows by the familiar *du*. Jahn worked out a crude and vigorous patriotic language.

Popular nationalism had wilted in the 1820s under the police supervision and the press regulations imposed by the Carlsbad decrees (1819). The revolutions of 1830 in France and Belgium began a new wave of German imitation, a wave which crested in 1832 at the Hambach festival. Between twenty and thirty thousand people assembled in a ruined castle. The new movement was a revolt of youth against the values inherited from the generation immediately before. The protestors looked back to an older, legendary Germany – the land of the ruined fairy-tale castles – that they could contrast with the bleak realities that they saw. At Hambach, there was singing and gymnastics. Dress played a major role: the demonstrators urged German princes to cast aside aristocratic 'ermine' and wear instead the 'manly toga of German national honour'.[33] Young Germans burnt corsets: a rejection of French dress and of formality, and an assertion of freedom in the spirit of the *Turnvereine*. Hambach was followed by a sharp reaction, with restrictions on the freedom of speech and assembly. From 1833, membership of the *Burschenschaften* was proscribed. The consequence was simply that a new and much more popular form of nationalist organization emerged.

In the 1830s and 1840s a new wave of nationalist feeling swept in to attack Metternich's Austria. The *Turnvereine* attracted a much larger membership in the 1840s, from a wider social background. This was the pattern of German nationalism for the nineteenth century. The gothic nationalists had imagined that they could appeal to a wider German sentiment than the classical educationalists had been able to do. Each successive generation of patriots believed that their predecessors had not been sufficiently near to the people (*Volk*) – not sufficiently *völkisch*. The previous group's absence of a genuinely *völkisch* character had condemned it to political impotence. The debate about *völkisch* nationalism became a discussion of the role of intellectuals in the formation of national consciousness. Each wave of intellectuals accused its predecessors of being over-intellectual and over-rationalistic. The newer the wave, the more anti-intellectual the stance adopted.

The newer nationalists wanted to set a distance between themselves and the older style of classical emancipatory patriotism. The 'people' and the gothic were to replace education and the classical. Freedom – the Greek ideal – now came to matter less than proximity to a national spirit. This new nationalism found a brilliant caricaturist in the poet Heinrich Heine, who wrote:

It cannot be denied that the Germans love freedom. But in a different way from other peoples. The Englishman loves freedom like his legitimate wife, he possesses her, and even if he does not

treat her particularly delicately he defends her against the red-
coated soldier who tries to enter her bedchamber – whether as a
gallant or as the constable of the law. The Frenchman loves
freedom as his chosen bride. He is full of flaming passion, he throws
himself at her feet with the most exaggerated declarations, he will
commit a thousand follies in her name. The German loves freedom
like his old grandmother.[34]

We respect old grandmothers, but above all we hope that they will die
soon and leave us a rich and unencumbered legacy.

The ambiguities of the nationalist position became ever clearer as
each nationalist wave broke on the rocks of German reality. The
problem was pointed out forcefully and influentially in Paul Pfizer's
Correspondence of Two Germans (published anonymously in 1831).
Pfizer was a Württemberg liberal and a judge. He used an epistolic
exposition for his analysis of the German problem (it was based very
loosely on an exchange he had had with another South German liberal).
Friedrich and Wilhelm corresponded about the state of Germany. Both
deplored the present condition, but offered different diagnoses, different prognoses, and different cures. It is tempting to see Wilhelm as a
cautious conservative and Friedrich as a starry-eyed liberal. Wilhelm
concluded that unity should go before freedom, while Friedrich thought
that 'Germany should free herself through her own strength'. Friedrich
wrote that German philosophy could regenerate the nation through the
strength of an idea. Wilhelm countered that 'we need common interests
for our future, common institutions for our present, common memories
for the past, in a word, instead of our previous particularism, a place in
world history'.[35] Wilhelm saw in Prussia the germ of future unity,
whereas Friedrich wanted to reassert the South German tradition of
constitutional reform. He defended the culture of southern peoples,
while Wilhelm thought that Germans were Nordic, and that the north
was more industrious and inventive.[36]

Above all, both correspondents were confused and uncertain about
their nation. 'One demands love for the Fatherland and doesn't even
know where to look for our real Fatherland.' Nationalism had been
whipped up by 'all kinds of artificial stimulants'. 'Germans have a deep
soul and a rich spirit, but lack the real substance – a Fatherland and a
home.'[37]

Wilhelm – notionally the conservative – lamented the absence of a
'popular spirit', and argued against Friedrich's insistence on the
centrality of philosophical speculation. 'In vain have we exploited all the
literatures of the world from all ages – even before Adam – in vain have
we constructed a universe through natural philosophy, taken it apart and

built it up again, dreamt an ideal world in art and poetry in place of the world we lack, intoxicated ourselves in a flood of mysticism, sunk into the depths of the absolute as Empedocles plunged into the volcano of Mount Etna!' Constitutional liberals ignored the realities of early nineteenth-century Germany: these were the concrete expression of misery, pauperization and emigration, as well as the more spiritual question of the loss of national identity.

The contrast that Pfizer tried to develop between the advocate of Prussian rule and the federalist was at the same time a clash between an idealist and a practical man, between a philosopher and a social reformer, and in the end between the South and the North of Germany.[38] One of the paradoxes that emerged from Pfizer's exposition was that the conservative Wilhelm expounded the more popular and the more real nationalism, and Friedrich remained with a nationalism of the mind. Throughout the nineteenth century, conservatives and radicals both went round the sides of the philosophical and liberal constitutionalist position in appealing for a broader national movement.

Pfizer attempted to escape this dilemma by integrating all sides of all arguments into a national consensus, though he did not show how that could be achieved in the light of the 'jealousy verging on national hatred'[39] between North and South Germans. Like the architect Schinkel, or the philosopher Hegel, or the aesthetician Friedrich Theodor Vischer who developed a theory of how medievalism could be mixed with classicism,[40] Pfizer was stating a case for the fusion of old traditions and for the invention of new ones. For Fichte and Hegel, the Germans had been the universal people; for Pfizer they were the 'cosmopolitan nation'. German nationalism was defined as an amalgam of all the traditions – of the classical and the gothic. It represented a grand-scale synthesis, and was permeated by the belief that it drew together the threads of the world's past.

It also defined itself by reference to other, not yet fully fledged, nationalisms. Other emerging nations queued behind Germany to make their entrance on the stage of world history. Herder stated that the future lay with the Slav peoples. But to most Germans, because German nationalism was first – the first romantic nationalism that depended on the power of the intellect to provide a synthesis of the world's previous development – it had a superior claim.

1848, the year of the revolutions, was critical in this respect. In eastern and Balkan Europe relatively small numbers of intellectuals had developed their own romantic nationalisms, often with a heavy Hegelian content borrowed from Germany. Though these nationalisms were directed in part against the old political structures of *ancien régime*

Europe – against Habsburg or Ottoman control – just as frequently they were aimed also against the assertion of German nationality. In a number of instances, eastern and south-eastern European nationalism formed alliances with the Habsburg dynasty against Germans.

South Slav nationalism was in fact encouraged by Metternich, who saw in it a counterweight to German liberalism. In 1848, his calculation proved correct. Czech nationalists did not form any alliance with the Habsburgs, but they also refused to participate in the Frankfurt Assembly of 1848, the body German liberals believed would give birth to the new Germany. After the Czechs attempted their own revolution in June 1848, some Germans argued that the Czechs needed to be defeated by political force. The Hegelian poet Wilhelm Jordan – who began 1848 on the political left – explained to the Frankfurt parliament: 'I conclude that we are leaving at last the misty summits of cosmopolitanism from which one's own Fatherland is no longer visible. I can see that at last we mean to proceed against the attempts of puny nationalities to found their own lives in our midst, and like parasites to destroy ours.' The Prussian Catholic deputy Radowitz attacked the 'one-sided and exclusive conception of the principle of nationality' which defended other national rights – 'as if a great nation could confine its most vital needs, on which its existence depends, within its own linguistic territory'.[41]

Germany's superiority derived from her role as the 'bearer of historical development' in the sense of Herderian or Hegelian evolution. This theme was as popular on the left in 1848 as in the political centre and right.[42] Friedrich Engels complained about the damage done by the revolutionary movements of the Habsburg Empire: 'all these peoples are at the most diverse stages of civilisation, ranging from the fairly highly developed (thanks to the *Germans*) modern industry and culture of Bohemia down to the almost nomadic barbarism of the Croats and Bulgarians; in reality, therefore, all these nations have most antagonistic interests'. Whereas the Germans and the Magyars 'represent the revolution', the Slavs were condemned by history to 'represent the counter-revolution'. This survey ended on a bloodcurdling note: 'The next world war will result in the disappearance from the face of the earth not only of reactionary classes and dynasties, but also of entire reactionary peoples. And that, too, is a step forward.'[43] History stood against the Slavs since, 'apart from the Poles, the Russians, and at most the Turkish Slavs, no Slav people has a future, for the simple reason that all the other Slavs lack the primary historical, geographical, political and industrial conditions for independence and viability . . . Peoples which have never had a history of their own . . . are not viable and will never be able to achieve any kind of independence.'[44]

A central debate in the Frankfürt Assembly took place over the armistice of Malmö concluded between Prussia and Denmark. German liberals wanted to incorporate the Duchies of Schleswig and Holstein (which had a partly German-speaking population) into Germany and to block the Danish claim to the Duchies. At Malmö, Prussia abandoned her opposition to the Danes and bitterly disappointed the hopes of German nationalists. Since the Frankfurt parliament had no army of its own, it seemed that there was little choice except to accept the armistice, or – as the radicals wanted – to wage a people's war over future of the Duchies. In explaining why Schleswig should be part of Germany, Engels argued that Germany had the 'right of historical evolution'; 'the right of civilisation as against barbarism, of progress as against stability'.[45]

German nationalists argued the same case of cultural superiority when they were confronted by Polish nationalism. Polish nationalism had initially appeared as a highly attractive romantic nationalism, additionally appealing because it was directed primarily against autocratic Russia. The Frankfurt left took up the Polish cause. A disintegration of Russia would open up a power vacuum in eastern Europe which might allow a new and strong German nation-state to step in. Pfizer, for instance, had argued that the Poles were a model for the arousal of national self-awareness. But at the same time they posed a challenge to the more cultured and thus historically significant Germans: 'Or are not the Germans more important and more difficult to replace from the perspective of the progressive development of the human race than the Poles?'[46] In 1848 Wilhelm Jordan again put the same case, but more forcefully, and now associated himself with a highly aggressive nationalism. He attacked the notion, once almost universally accepted by German liberals, of using Polish nationalism against Russia. Nothing should be done to aid the Poles. 'The preponderance of the German race over most Slav races, possibly with the sole exception of the Russians, is a fact . . . and against history and nature decrees of political justice are of no avail . . . Mere existence does not entitle a people to political independence: only the force to assert itself as a State among the others.'[47]

In most cases during 1848, the claim to be nationally superior rested simply on *assertion*. The Germans as a historic nation had a cultural complexity that other would-be nations lacked. This was barely plausible as an argument when used by Marx against the Czechs, and against Professor Palacky's well-reasoned panegyrics on the history of the Czech people; but it failed entirely to deal with the problem of German–Polish conflicts.

In Frankfurt, a few nationalists such as Jordan used an alternative strategy of arguing that German superiority was demonstrated by military might. Unfortunately for those who pursued this argument, the nationalists in Frankfurt had little force that they could call their own; and by 1849 they were only too well aware that neither Austria nor Prussia was willing to make a commitment to the German cause. There was another, alternative justification of national supremacy: one which had the superficial attraction of being scientific, statistical, and measurable.

As German nationalism became more anti-intellectual, the case about a German superiority in things of the mind ('*Geist*') was replaced by a doctrine about a German ascendancy justified by the material facts of economics.

National Economics: Mars and Mercury

The Nation and the Social Question

German nationalism and the 'social issue' developed together. Though neither was in any sense a product of the other, by the middle of the century the 'social issue' shaped the way the politics of nationality were fought out. At the same time as the political struggle against autocracy and particularism emerged in the 1830s and 1840s, and as liberals began to debate the relationship between practical reform and national unity, they were obliged to confront another problem. Many Germans had become pauperized. High rates of population growth, in association with local or regional dependence on single trades or industries, made Germany profoundly vulnerable to economic crisis. Social cohesion crumbled and national morale was sapped. The coincidence of national and social issues created fears and hopes.

There was the fear that Germany would develop the same industrial illnesses as the more advanced Western countries. A process of learning from abroad similar to the one we have observed in the case of the conception of nationhood occurred in relation to social issues. Indeed, the two most extensive, compelling, and frightening accounts of the problems of the new industrial societies dealt with France and England: Lorenz von Stein's account of *Socialism and Communism in the France of Today*, published in 1842, and Friedrich Engels' *Condition of the Working Class in England*, published in 1845.[1]

Germans could begin to see in their own country the dangers described by Engels and Stein. The rising in 1844 of pauperized Silesian weavers was a reaction to a dramatic impoverishment. The income of handloom weavers had fallen, less as a consequence of competition from factory produced goods than because of the growing population pressure. Wages for domestic outwork went into a long-term decline as the supply of available labour working at subsistence levels rose. But the revolt was interpreted in terms of much more general significance. It was – many contemporaries believed – less a popular disturbance of the kind typical of the old Europe, than a first flaring-up of a general revolt in the name of justice and equality. Heinrich Heine's famous poem pointed out the universal implications of the weavers' rising:

> From darkened eyes no tears are falling;
> Gnashing our teeth, we sit here calling:
> 'Germany, listen, ere we disperse,
> We weave your shroud with a triple curse –
> We weave, we are weaving!
>
> 'A curse to the Fatherland, whose face is
> Covered with lies and foul disgraces;
> Where the bud is crushed as it leaves the seed,
> And the worm grows fat on corruption and greed –
> We weave, we are weaving!'[2]

Germany's poverty appeared striking when presented relative to other European countries. In the first half of the nineteenth century, Germany fell behind England. This was a subjective feeling of contemporary Germans, struck by the speed of British industrialization; but the figures guessed by modern economic historians bear out this hypothesis of a relative lag. Whereas, in 1820, Gross Domestic Product per head of population was 68 per cent of the United Kingdom's, in 1870 – even after the dramatic spurt in Germany of the 1850s and 1860s – it was only 55 per cent.[3] The most spectacular and humiliating consequence for national feeling that resulted from economic stagnation was a high, and rising, emigration. In the 1820s an estimated 8,500 Germans left, in the 1830s 167,700, and in the 1840s 469,300 (from a total population of around 30 million).[4] Though emigration in the 1840s was less than half the figure for some subsequent decades (the 1850s and 1880s), the unprecedented level of the 'hungry forties' provoked strong feelings about national decline – and was presented as a major political problem by commentators such as Pfizer or the economist Friedrich List.

On the other hand, there might also be hopes for a better future. Many observers believed that the politically fragmented condition of Germany after the restoration of 1815 had been one element in making the 'social question' worse. The small German states and the cities reacted to the growth of mass poverty by attempting to keep the problem out of their own confines. Harsher regulations made it more difficult for indigent strangers to settle. In this way, the problem was simply pushed away onto another political unit.[5] Nationally made policies stood a better chance of resolving the issues of vagrancy and poverty.

In the 1830s new technology also generated the hope that the breaking-down of distances and the cheapening of transport might produce national unity and at the same time create wealth and reduce poverty. Imitation again might come in handy. It was the English inventions of industrial manufacture and of the railway that promised Germany's salvation. The first great promoter of the idea of German economic nationalism was Friedrich List. Could not Germany simply solve her social problems by adopting British industry, and abolish her pauperism through the creation of new wealth? England's industrial slums may have been appalling, but Germany's non-industrial misery and poverty had caused her even more anguish. This was the theme of *The National System of Political Economy* (1841).

Economic advance depended on greater access to knowledge and scientific advance. In turn economic development allowed more national culture. At this point, in List's eyes, the romantic notion of *Bildung* and the practical concerns of businessmen came together. Only within nations as a framework for *Bildung* could education work effectively. Economists should not just assume an international system on the one hand and atomized individuals on the other: the nation's function was to mediate between the two. 'The civilization of the human race is only possible and thinkable by means of the civilization and education of nations . . . It is the duty of national economics to provide for the economic education of the nation and for her entrance into the future universal society.'[6] There were two obvious strategies for improving Germany's economic performance.

Germany could learn industry from Britain if her governments took steps to shelter the young and tender buds of manufacture. Protective tariffs could allow a developing country to build up manufacturing ('economic education'). But this meant that Germany should take pains not to learn economic theory from England at the same time as she imitated the manufacturing system. A tariff system went against the maxims of what List called universalist or cosmopolitan economics.[7] It was Britain alone, as the first industrial country, which had an interest in international free trade – because this stopped the emergence of rivals. It was as if, List said in a famous analogy, Britain had climbed up a fruitful tree, and then kicked away the ladder so that no one else could come up.

The second strategy involved transport to bring the country together. Again List made a plea for government coordination and assistance. His main business and commercial activity had been as a railway promoter. He had been in the United States and constructed a colliery railway in Pennsylvania in 1831, returning to Germany with the stated goal of improving transport. There his most ambitious plan was for a major Saxon line linking Leipzig and Dresden.[8]

List explained that 'the most important side of a general railway system for us Germans is not the financial, nor even the economic, but the political aspect. For no other nation is a railway of such incalculable value as a means to arouse and sustain the national spirit and to increase the defensive strength of the nation.' In a summary of the national benefits of the railway, he included the hope that it would destroy the evils of small-town and provincial 'obscurantism and prejudice', as well as that the train would be significant as a 'means of spreading culture': 'it speeds and facilitates the distribution of all literary, artistic and scientific products; it brings talents, knowledge and skill together'.[9]

The first German railway began operating in 1835 on the very short line between Nuremberg and Fürth (a distance of only six kilometres). But other lines followed, and by 1848 there were over 5,000 kilometres of track, and in 1870 18,810 kilometres. The train allowed people and ideas to circulate. The economic consequence of market integration increased interdependence and offered a practical way of binding together a nation. By 1870 – before the political creation of united Germany – the railway had been accepted as both the most striking embodiment of the idea of the modern world and the instrument of national integration. After the new wave of expansion in the 1850s, the historian Johann Gustav Droysen wrote in an essay 'On the Present Situation' about how the railway demonstrated the economic argument that private vices could work together for a public good. 'Transport and the railway and education are working silently but irresistibly to remove the rigidities and divisions within our nation. The small arts which are recommended by Christian-Germanic hypocrisy to create new divisions and tensions, new envy and new hatred, will only in fact speed up the already begun and now overwhelmingly powerful process.'[10]

The railway was digested into the symbolism of German nationality as well. The example of Cologne is very striking. Cologne's railway station was built next to the cathedral – the gothic symbol of the integration of the Catholic church and the Rhineland into the historic national tradition. As the trains crossed the Rhine over the great railway bridge (which was later named the Hohenzollern Bridge), they made a line straight for the cathedral choir. Allegedly this integration of church and railway design occurred at the instigation of the romantic Prussian King Frederick William IV in person.

Economic institutions also came to be crucial in the generation of a movement to political unity. However, we should be careful about anticipating this relationship in the early nineteenth century. Subsequently, in the second half of the century, it was an association which became central to the German perception of nationality, and in consequence produced many retrospective and perhaps erroneous interpretations of the history of early German nationalism.

One of the most firmly held beliefs about Imperial Germany after 1871 was that its roots lay in the Prussian-dominated Zollverein of 1834, a tariff union which included Saxony and the major south German states. As regards the origins of the Zollverein, there is now no doubt that this nationalist interpretation is somewhat misleading. The famous memorandum written by the Prussian Finance Minister Motz in June 1829 which explains how 'political unity' was a 'necessary consequence of commercial unity' treats the Zollverein less as a path to national unity than as a means of tying a strong and prosperous Bavaria to the Prussian and anti-Austrian cause.[11] In the 1820s, plans for a customs union certainly offered Prussia an opportunity to bring some movement into the German question, and strike at Austria's pre-eminence. That in turn raised general national issues. The economic diversity of Germany, and the difficulty of moving goods or people, gave a strikingly obvious indication of the absence of unity. In 1830, revolutionaries attacked and demolished customs posts throughout the country. The political debates of the 1820s made economic integration a key issue in the policy of the major states, though they did not mean that 1834 made inevitable the victory of Prussia and the creation in 1871 of the Small German or Prussian-German Empire.

After 1848 the Zollverein twice almost broke apart: between 1851 and 1853, when Austria tried to create a larger customs union which was intended to swallow up the smaller Prusso-centric association; and after 1860, when Prussia for internal and foreign political reasons wanted to lower the Zollverein's tariff level, and the South German states feared that this would lead to the ruin of the southern economy.

By the middle of the century, however, the Zollverein had generated a substantial political momentum in that its non-Prussian members had come to identify their economic interests with integration with Prussia. One liberal from Brunswick for instance commented in 1844: 'The Zollverein has become . . . in fact the nourishing ground of the idea of unity . . . We will have to get used to foreigners believing Germany to be principally the customs union.'[12] The economic drive frequently overrode political considerations: Hesse-Darmstadt, for instance, wanted to go with Austria, but its commercial classes believed this to be a suicidal course, and they eventually prevailed with a pro-Prussian line.

It is astonishing how rapidly a nationalist interpretation of the Zollverein grew up, which presented Motz and his successor von Maassen as the true progenitors of united Germany. This was the interpretation set out by Treitschke: nation-building was best examined through the history of the Zollverein. By the middle of the century, a view such as Treitschke's had an obvious and immediate appeal. 'The greatest act of national policy in that long period of peace [after 1815] was exclusively the work of governments and their officials, and was carried out without the participation – and even against the resistance – of the mass of the nation . . . Mars and Mercury are the stars which principally determine the destiny of states in this century of labour. The army and the trade policy of the Hohenzollerns form the two claims on which rests the Imperial dignity of our ruling dynasty.'[13] Treitschke discounted the patriotism of the eighteenth century and the nationalist enthusiasm of the Napoleonic era. Instead, fundamental political changes required the operation of real forces. Statesmen and not thinkers were responsible for political change and progress. Looking back, he concluded that 'the final result [German unification] was brought about by the very nature of things, and it produced a real Germany, united by economic interests, while Frankfurt [the 1848 parliament], like Regensburg [the former Imperial Diet from the Holy Roman Empire] in earlier days, was ruled by the mere phrases of politicians.' If the politically divided liberal movement had contributed little to the creation of the nation-state, then more credit was due to the Zollverein. The Zollverein, not liberal politics, brought Germans closer to each other – geographically and socially. 'The history of the Zollverein was a training of inestimable worth for Imperal policy, for its long years taught the Prussian official class, which was distinguished equally for its uprightness and for its disagreeable manners, the necessity of establishing friendly relations with their lesser associates – men free of all evil intentions, but vainer and smaller minded than they themselves.'[14]

Realpolitik and Determinism

How did the mythology of the railway and the Zollverein establish itself so quickly? When List died (he committed suicide in a lonely hotel bedroom in Kufstein in Austria in 1846) he was an isolated and neglected figure. Within a decade his view had become the German orthodoxy. Why did railways matter more than romanticism, and tariffs more than tales of the Fatherland? This change was a consequence of the collapse of the hopes of 1848. A re-evaluation of the course of German history took place. It was no longer a story of national awakening, but rather a more sober tale of institutional arrangements designed to promote prosperity.

In the 1820s, the political immobilism of Congress Germany had led to interest in a customs union as a weapon of diplomacy, and in the 1850s the political failure of 1848–9 also resulted in a revived interest in economic methods of integration. Economics also constituted a body of doctrine that might heal the social chasm revealed by 1848, and bind Germans together in a cohesive unit, the nation. The appeal of economics lay in its offering a blueprint for an imagined community of the future.

Nationalism now depended less on philosophers and literary men, and much more on historians (who made themselves into the high priests of 'realism') and particularly economists. The latter discipline began to call itself '*Nationalökonomie*'; while historians redirected their attention away from the concerns of the earlier generation of idealists.[15]

They became the preachers of a new national gospel. Heinrich von Sybel attacked the Austrian historian Julius von Ficker for offering too positive a view of the medieval empire. The Emperor had in Sybel's view really been in league with the Roman church in order to exploit the resources of Germany. The historians' debate very self-consciously carried into the medieval past the modern conflicts of Hohenzollern Prussia (whose apologist Sybel had made himself) and Habsburg Austria. Fighting about the old Holy Roman Empire became a way of propagandizing for the present.

For the seventeenth century, historians of the mid-century presented a new assessment in which economics figured largely. No longer did just religion or the force of arms determine the course of events. Gustav Droysen (the son of Johann Gustav) showed in a biography of the Protestant and German national hero Gustavus Adolphus how it was the expansion of trade and commerce that had made Sweden into a great power.[16] The German princes had learnt a lesson from Sweden, and so made possible the national revival of the eighteenth century. Sybel described the change – not as the discovery of a common language or a common culture, but in bureaucratic and administrative terms. The economy now mattered more in German accounts of themselves than the intellectual excitement of Goethe's Weimar: 'The new military and bureaucratic state made the common good its highest goal and material interests the most important object of policy. So it shattered completely the complex of estate privileges and particular interests, and replaced medieval excesses, the two swords, the protection of faith, and ecclesiastical states, with a completely realistic policy aiming at utility, rationality and the development and use of all forces.'[17]

The new hard-nosed approach to German issues was most powerfully expressed in relation to the circumstances of the post-1848 world by the journalist Ludwig August Rochau. He contrasted the amorphous cultural fantasies of old-style nationalists with the political hard-headedness to which he gave a new label, *Realpolitik. Realpolitik* caught on quickly as a slogan for mid-century Germany. It concerned itself with geopolitics, with armies, and with economics. According to Rochau, 1848 had failed because the Frankfurt Assembly had had no army and no realistic concept of foreign policy. A united Germany could only be formed on the basis of the possibilities offered by the European state system. But above all, the correct policy depended on its conformity with the 'spirit of the age'. Rochau was obsessed with the idea of a *Zeitgeist*. 'A policy contrary to the *Zeitgeist* carried on as a systematic policy and over a long period of time is not simply incapable of execution, it is also unthinkable.' This meant for Rochau that political institutions and assemblies could only work if they were properly representative – or, as he put it, if they were 'the correct expression of social forces'.[18]

According to Rochau, none of the conventional ideologies could match the challenge of translating the new social and economic order of the mid-century into political institutions and behaviour. For instance, political conservatism. The rapidity of economic change – the railways, urbanization, industrialization – made conservatism of the old variety a meaningless concept. Industry had established new social and economic links. As a result, what conservatives wished to conserve was rapidly changing. One way of reading *The Principles of Realpolitik* is as a demolition of traditionalist arguments. Rochau wanted to cut himself away from romantic reactionaries (such as the Catholic politician Radowitz, on whom Frederick William IV relied in the implementation of reaction after the upheaval of 1848). He also believed that a military autocracy, such as that envisaged by Radowitz's successor as Prussian Minister-President, Erwin von Manteuffel, was short-sighted. It could not hope to survive in the modern world. Conservatism was in addition self-contradictory because there existed too many different types of a doctrine that insisted that the political task lay in conserving one historical reality. Old-style liberalism, bureaucratic rule, Catholic ultramontanism, the economic interest of the Junkers (the Prussian landowning nobility) – all these tried to disguise themselves under the banner of conservatism. 'All these political factors have few common and many contradictory interests and purposes.' In fact, Germany lacked a genuine aristocracy of the sort needed to sustain an English- style conservatism: the German old order, according to Rochau, had already gone under. Only a rational and liberal economic system could stop the pauperization of the working class and create a new social solidarity in place of the collapsed feudal order. And to this problem, liberal economics rather than a liberal constitution supplied the solution.[19]

In 1869 Rochau wrote a second volume of the *Realpolitik*, after the institution in Prussia of Bismarck's regime, after the Prussian victory over Austria at Königgrätz, and after the formation of the North German Confederation around Bismarck's Prussia (1867) had apparently vindicated Rochau's original arguments of 1853. *Realpolitik* as a concept could clearly be applied to Bismarck's disregard for almost all the traditional conservative principles – in particular for the theory of legitimacy – and to his rapid formation and then destruction of foreign political alliances. In the 1869 version, Rochau's admiration for naked power politics appears without any moral figleaf. 'The test of political power is the struggle . . . The highest judgement in all cases of power against power is war.'[20] Prussia's victories alone showed that Prussia's cause was right. In few other places – even in the voluminous literature produced by the Prussian school of history, by Sybel and Treitschke and their followers – was there a more open demonstration of the presumption that for Prussia might was right.

The new version of *Realpolitik* also depicted with a new and brutal candour the basis of Prussia's might. Freedom, Rochau wrote, was not to be achieved through political change but only through the acquisition of property. Whatever progress had been made in the direction of national unity was a consequence of human self-seeking. A Fatherland was no longer a question of patriotic dreams; 'for Germans, unity is basically a pure business affair' [*eine reine Geschäftssache*].[21] On the basis of this supposition he could predict that the North German Confederation in its current form could not last, and that further institutional change was needed in order to carry Germany along with the spirit of the age and the spirit of the people – with the *Zeitgeist* and with the *Volksgeist*.

This doctrine amounted to an economic determinism of the type that became commonplace to German thinkers after the middle of the century. The most enduring expression of such determinism was Karl Marx's *Das Kapital*, the first volume of which was published in 1867. It was perhaps a less original work than we are usually tempted to suppose, for it rather echoed and then distilled many of the views circulating in contemporary Germany. It sought to demonstrate the necessity of events. In *Das Kapital*, Marx abandoned a Hegelian tradition of which in the 1840s he had formed an important part, and which had allowed greater room for individual actions and initiatives.

The work is a monument to the natural or ineluctable or iron laws of social action. 'It is not a question of the higher or lower degree of development of the social antagonisms that result from the natural laws of capitalist production. It is a question of those laws themselves, of those tendencies working with iron necessity towards inevitable results.' Marx's view of the purpose of economic science was very similar to that of List: to make through a process of productive social learning the operation of inevitable laws smoother and more harmonious; or to learn creatively from other countries. 'The country that is more developed industrially [i.e. England] only shows, to the less developed [Germany], the image of its own future . . . One nation can and should learn from others. And even when a society has got upon the right track for the discovery of the natural laws of its movement – and it is the ultimate aim of this work, to lay bare the economic law of motion of modern society – it can neither clear by bold leaps, nor remove by legal enactments, the obstacles offered to successive phases of its normal development. But it can shorten and lessen the birth pangs.'[22]

In setting out his argument, Marx was simply being more consistent than the majority of his German contemporaries; but they shared his view as to the importance of economics in an ineluctable determination of the historical process. In this, they responded to the striking transformation that followed the mid-century. The term 'economics' or 'industry' crept into almost all the new manifestations of the German nationalist movement. The free trader 'Economic Congress', set up in 1858, was closely intertwined with the National Association (National-verein), and became one of the key pressure groups in Prussia for national unification. It included bankers, merchants, industrialists, civil servants and politicians, as well as academics and journalists.[23] Patriotic journals now took titles such as 'The Patriotic Magazine for Information, Use and Entertainment, in particular for the Promotion of Knowledge of the Fatherland, Art and Industry'.[24]

Economics claimed to be a central science, in that it could change social and thus political structures. The economist now became the man who had an answer for everything. There were even jokes about the claims of political economy to a monopoly of the truth, and of economists to omniscience and omnipotence. The satirical magazine *Fliegende Blätter* in 1855 told its readers how an economist had tried to convince a beggar that he was really very rich, since 'time is money'.[25] It was a joke about the machine age and its pretensions.

In truth economics had become a central part of the vision of political liberalism. German liberals pressed the claims of the economists. The great influence exerted by liberals in the Prussian parliament, in the civil service, and in local journalism and politics – but also in the states of southern Germany – in turn affected policy. Prussia needed to win over the South German liberals for the sake of pursuing her power diplomacy in Germany effectively. The Prussian Minister-President Otto von Bismarck felt in addition that he should woo the Prussian liberals, since he did not believe he could fight a perpetual constitutional war against them. Rudolf von Delbrück as Prussian Minister of Commerce reacted to both the Prussian and the South German consideration in pursuing a free trade and liberalization programme for Prussia; he also believed this to be in the best interests of Prussia's economy. Economics and free trade allowed Prussia to follow a new German policy: they were the prerequisite for Bismarck's enlarging of Prussia and his creation of a new Germany in the 1860s.

Bismarck's story can be read as an example of how popularized economic determinism came to dominate the intellectual horizons of nineteenth-century Germans. Bismarck, it hardly needs to be said, did not set out to apply Marx's political and economic philosophy any more than he believed that he was implementing the elements of *Realpolitik* as formulated by Rochau. However, he shared many of their assumptions.

To begin with, the nineteenth century was, he thought, the age of 'material interests', in which the old theories of the *ancien régime* were redundant – whether legitimism or conservatism, devised as defences of the *ancien régime*, or liberalism, conceived as an onslaught on the old order. In this world, individuals were the prisoners of broader movements. They could not alter the inexorable march of historical determination. In 1869, the most powerful man in Germany wrote meekly: 'I am not so presumptuous as to believe that such as we make history. My work is to observe the currents and steer my ship in them as best I can. I cannot direct the currents, still less conjure them up.'[26]

Some of this is doubtless a carefully calculated duplicitous excess of modesty. Bismarck was in reality a very influential man, and knew this perfectly well. At the same time his vision was shaped by the austerely determinist Pietist theology of his wife and of the circle around her. Germany's new factory chimneys simply fitted into an already present, centuries old, and deeply pessimistic theory of the determination of human action. It meant scepticism about individual idealism and also about the belief systems to which that idealism attached itself.

If individuals had to swim with the tide of destiny, so did nations. National destinies were, if anything, more determined than those of individuals. External events – such as economic change or foreign political development – mattered much more than the longings of romantic nationalism. These belonged to invention: there was nothing special about territorial and national identities, or about the 'swindle of nationalities', as Bismarck termed it. In human affairs, all was subject to perpetual change.

As an illustration of this fluidity, Bismarck thought of the connection between Prussian and German identities. Were not both simply a matter of temporizing with external exigencies? Of bowing before an implacable God of history and destiny? In 1869, Bismarck wrote to Albrecht von Roon, the Prussian War Minister, whose sympathies lay with an older and specifically Prussian brand of conservatism. It was only two years after both of these men, because of the rapidity of political change and largely as a result of Bismarck's own strategy and actions, had become part of the North German Confederation. Only one year later both were to become subjects of a new German Empire. 'You will have to admit that both we and His Majesty are born *North Germans*, while around one hundred and seventy years ago our ancestors cheerfully allowed themselves – for the sake of higher interests – to exchange the glorious name of *Brandenburgers* for the then rather extinct title of *Prussians*, without really being Prussians.'[27]

'Higher interests' meant the concerns of the state, the pattern of foreign policy, and the development of the economy. The economy not only provided states with the weapons they needed in order to resist domination from the outside, but also made for internal pacification and satisfaction. It offered the wherewithal of political bribery. Bismarck based a highly successful political career on the insight that it was possible to buy almost everyone: foreign states (through promises of assistance or of territory), liberals (through German unification), conservatives (from the 1870s through tariff protection), and socialists (through welfare legislation).

The idea that ideas did not matter made Bismarck very happy. Intellectuals in politics were to him a relic of the past, of the obsolete world of the eighteenth-century Enlightenment. The liberal vision depended on altering the world on the basis of enlightened opinion and rational thought; Bismarck thought it better to direct politics according to opportunity and necessity. The liberals would be driven away by the logic of an ineluctable historical process; and history would become the history of the productive classes. Thus went his sneering argument in introducing the tariff legislation of 1879, which effectively broke the liberal hold on parliamentary politics: 'The wise men who are without a trade, without property, without business, who live by salaries, fees and [bond] coupons, will over the course of the years have to submit themselves to the economic demands of the producing people.'[28] The German Empire was, so Bismarck held, a political body carried on the wave of material success.

Economics could be used to stabilize a politically highly volatile state. The first institutional step towards a united Germany under Bismarck had been the customs union parliament of 1867, which was composed of members of the North German Confederation Diet, and elected representatives of the southern states (who had been excluded from the Confederation by the terms of the Peace of Prague imposed by Prussia on Austria after the military victory of 1866). Both northern and southern deputies were to be elected by universal male adult suffrage. It was better, Bismarck thought, for would-be German politicians to discuss tariffs and business than politics. In 1881 Bismarck proposed the creation of a second parliamentary chamber to supplement the Reichstag, the heir to the Zollverein parliament and likewise elected by universal suffrage. A new chamber, formed out of the professional and business associations of the big business groupings, would provide a counterweight to popular pressure in the Reichstag.[29] These pressure groups had already begun to play a prominent political role in the 1870s: the League of Mining Interests (founded in 1858); the League of German Iron and Steel Industrialists (1874); the Association of Tax and Economic Reformers (1876); and above all the Central Association of German Industrialists (1876). For agriculture, in addition, there was the Congress of North German Farmers (1868).

Bismarck believed that the discussions of these groups would make it easier to produce harmonious politics, precisely because politics would be left out. Instead politics would be reduced to a simple and calmly conducted balancing out of different interests. The 1881 proposal came to little, since it was rejected by the Reichstag (though a similar Prussian version operated, unsuccessfully, for a short time). Nevertheless, the Iron Chancellor took up the plan in 1883 again with slight modifications; and an economic and apolitical coordination and harmonization of interests remained in German life as a long-term ideal. It formed the basis of a proposal of the right in 1913 – to create a 'Cartel of the Productive Estates', directed primarily and very obviously against the socialist party. It also reappeared after the First World War in 1918–19, as a creation of the political middle against revolutionary threats. Business pressure groups and labour organizations pledged themselves to work together to preserve order.

Even the victims of progress could be absorbed into useful economic organizations, and their pain assuaged in this way. Members of the declining middle class (*Mittelstand*) – and particularly craft manufacturers – formed interest associations that worked with the major parties: especially with the conservatives and with the Catholic Centre party (Zentrumspartei). Some commentators believed that this integration had led to a greater social harmony. In 1915, a leading left–liberal explained why the protest of the *Mittelstand* had been so muted: 'In the German Empire the stream of protest against the new economic creed has for the most part died out, and has largely been absorbed into forms of association that are efficient for work.'[30]

Bismarck's conception of the Kaiserreich was, it may be argued, a mixture of anti-intellectualism and an idiosyncratic reflection of his religiously based belief on the limitations of individual action. If this were all, it might be discounted; but it was a view shared by academic economists, by the civil servants they trained and influenced, by a population that witnessed the dramatic social transformation, and indeed even by the critics of the Kaiserreich who deplored all these developments. Of these groups, bureaucrats mattered most in the making of policy in nineteenth-century Germany. Prussia had been created as a civil service state (*Beamtenstaat*), and the reforms of the early nineteenth century only helped to consolidate the dominant position of the civil service. Their views crucially determined the development of Prussia-Germany, and it was administrative reformers such as Rudolf Delbrück and later Johannes von Miquel who put into practice their concepts of a plan for rational economic development. The economic creed in consequence left its mark on German political conduct long after the dismissal of Bismarck, and indeed even after the collapse and military defeat in 1918 of the German Empire of 1871.

The Academic Impetus

The new German supremacy in business and especially in technical matters owed a great deal to the legacy of the administrative reforms of the early nineteenth century. Scientific education constituted a direct link between the era of humanistic reform and Germany's impressive economic performance several generations later. Wilhelm von Humboldt's vision had emphasized the centrality in academic life of research not directed towards specific goals. It led to a relative freedom and independence of academic activity which produced a German scientific supremacy long before, in economics, Germany could even think about catching up with her rivals. After the middle of the 1830s, Germans made more major discoveries in energy, electricity, magnetism and optical research than did Frenchmen or Englishmen.[31] A few years later it became apparent that the new ideas generated not simply intellectual excitement but also new productive possibilities: an unexpected by-product of the great classical humanists. Justus Liebig, an academic scientist with laboratories at the university of Giessen, applied his chemical knowledge to produce plant fertilizers. August Kelkulé von Stradwitz developed through studying the benzene molecule a whole new science of inorganic chemistry. By 1890 there were twice as many academic scientists in Germany as in Britain. Their activities had – among many other results – led to a virtual German monopoly on the world dyestuffs market.

Germany's businessmen quickly recognized the importance of scientific development. For instance, Werner von Siemens, the founder of the electrical firm, sent his son Wilhelm to study physics at Leipzig. He also set the pace in the foundation of a natural science research institute (Physikalisch-Technische Reichsanstalt, 1887), explaining that 'Research in the natural sciences always forms the secure basis of technical development and the industry of a country will never gain a leading position internationally and maintain it if the country does not at the same time stay in the lead in making advances in the natural sciences. Achieving this is the most effective way of promoting the industry.' Carl Zeiss and Ernst Abbé used optical science for commercial purposes. The industries that grew most dynamically at the end of the century – electrical, chemical, optical – depended on a high level of scientific achievement.

This became noted throughout the world as the German peculiarity. The English Darwinian T. H. Huxley enviously explained that Germany had won because she 'put her strength' in science. Science became the expression of a new national superiority and of economic triumph.[32]

Economists and National Economics

On an academic level, the fusion of politics and economics within a national framework was the task that the so-called 'Historical School of Economics' set itself. It had a great impact in training generations of parliamentarians and, especially significantly, of civil servants. Wilhelm Roscher's work *Sketch for Lectures on State Economy, by the Historical Method* of 1843 laid the foundation for the School's theoretical development.[33] The professors of this doctrine made very ambitious claims even before 1848, but the revolutionary year gave their argument an additional urgency. In an article of 1849, Roscher stated: 'I do not need to explain the importance of our science for the whole of our past and future. Before, this science was merely a means of enrichment, and then it became more generally a method of government. But now we agree that the successful development of our whole culture is conditioned by the correct foundation and the general distribution of national economic truth.'[34] In 1854, he began his textbook analysis of economics with the programmatic statement that 'our intention in this book is not to be practical, but to educate practical people. For this purpose, we attempt to develop *natural laws*, which men cannot master but at the most use.'[35]

The past could be used to generate laws applicable also to the present. For instance, there was the problem of economic crisis – a key political concern since it was a combination of an old-style agrarian crisis with the collapse of a modern business cycle which had led to the revolution of 1848. The development of the economy showed, Roscher thought, that as nations progressed to higher riches, crises would be more pronounced and more severe. 'Collapses of demand are the shadow side of higher culture.'[36] What could be done about these crises? Politicians here needed to draw a lesson from the past. States should not intervene to try to prevent crises. All they could do is maintain a steady policy. This required the government to be strong and independent, since there would be a substantial political pressure on the state to become involved in regulating the economy. It would be best simply to remove as many restrictions as possible – in particular the guild regulations and associated limitations on the exercise of crafts and professions. Roscher compared the removal of legislative restrictions in an economic crisis to a doctor loosening the clothes of a sick person.[37]

There were quite specific historical analogies which showed the right and wrong ways to deal with economic problems. If the past were studied sufficiently conscientiously, then objectively correct historical laws could be derived, which would make all politically inspired debates redundant. All past actions, measures and consequences had to be seen in a general perspective: 'the mistake is often that measures which are in certain circumstances beneficial and even necessary are applied in quite different circumstances. Here a complete understanding of the conditions of the regulations would settle the dispute to the satisfaction of both parties.'[38] Athenian democracy, for instance, Roscher thought – clearly with an eye on the contemporary demands of radical democrats – had been ruined by the excessive growth of welfare costs.

Karl Knies, the other founding father of the 'Historical School', was less obviously and directly political than Roscher; but he was equally haunted by the practical significance of the theory he expounded. His analysis *Political Economy from the Standpoint of the Historical Method* (1853) staked out the general claim. 'Whoever follows closely the fundamental drives and the laws of development of nations in recent times, soon notices that the most important questions of the past and of the immediate future are concentrated in the field of economics.'[39]

He did not follow Roscher in wanting to draw simple conclusions from the past. There were no eternal and static laws. At the heart of his system lay the wish to find laws of change, progress and development. This meant that observations and deductions, drawn for instance from an English example, could not necessarily be transferred wholesale to Germany. In economic phenomena, only analogies and never identities might exist.[40] Specifically this revision meant an acceptance of the view already advanced by Friedrich List – that Germany's development could not follow the same lines as English economic growth, but would need to take a new and individual course. Different policies might be required (though in the 1850s and 1860s the Historical School still believed in free trade).

The most far-ranging formulation of the view that catching up with Britain meant escaping the social problem in Germany came in 1848 from Bruno Hildebrand: *National Economics of the Past and Future*. He used a sophisticated range of statistics – emigration, mortality, wages and income – to demonstrate that England in reality did not correspond to Friedrich Engels' grim picture. Ireland, without any industry, had suffered from pauperization and proletarianization much more than had England – where rising wages were making life more comfortable for the working class. Hildebrand found wage rates six and even ten times the German levels. Germany, he concluded, should try to be like England and not like Ireland. The future lay with machines and industry:

The temporary sufferings produced by every mechanical invention of the human genius, the hunger and unemployment of workers competing with machines, are only the birth pains of a new epoch. Printing once put many copiers of books out of work. But they are necessary victims, with whose price the great progress of the human race is bought. Great Britain has the important world historical vocation to conquer for humanity this new future through her power and hard labour.[41]

Soon after the Historical School began to formulate the theory of economic prosperity as the key to national power, the first doubts arose. In the first place, the process of change was inherently ungovernable and unstable. Moreover, enhanced prosperity produced new social attitudes and stimulated the emergence of an excessive materialism. The laws of development could also lead to national destruction. Roscher began to use a historical form to express his reservations already in the 1850s:

> In over-cultivated, or in already declining epochs, a conscious over-estimation of material interests begins to be common. Here a short-sighted egoism sacrifices not only the higher things of life [*höhere Lebensgüter*] but also the future of life itself. Those mere slaves of mammon among economists and businessmen should see communism as the mirror of their own contrariness. We must not forget that whole nations develop in the same manner as an individual. The man who creates his own wealth usually reaches the zenith of his riches only after the blossom of his other life has faded. The richest period generally introduces a decline.[42]

So the state – whose own success was grounded on the emergence of national riches – should act to counter the extreme polarization of wealth that had been the consequence of economic development. This issue became more acute after the spectacular growth of the 1850s and 1860s, after the boom that followed the Reich's foundation (*Gründung*) in 1871, and after the crash of 1873 (the boom: the *Gründerjahre*; the crash: the *Gründerkrise*).

The Gründerjahre and the New Problem

The boom and bust demonstrated the rapidity of change in the new Germany: easy money was easily lost. The volatile trade cycle also threw up plenty of potent symbols of Germany's transformation. As the Swiss lawyer Bluntschli commented, 'the German Empire has the ambition of being a modern state in every sense of the word'.[43] The new political system proclaimed on 18 January 1871 in the Hall of Mirrors of Versailles was accompanied by a transformation of style. German architecture and German cities changed visibly and dramatically.

In Berlin and the Rhineland a group of newly rich men – industrialists, bankers, property speculators – built highly ostentatious houses to demonstrate their new position as the makers of the Kaiserreich. The locomotive and engineering magnate Borsig had a Renaissance palace built by Richard Lucae in the Vossstrasse of Berlin. The steel and armaments manufacturer Krupp built – during the depression of the 1870s – a large Palladian mansion surrounded by a landscaped English park with mature trees specially imported. From the Villa Hügel in

Essen it was intentionally impossible to see the chimneys of Krupp's steel mills.

These very grand dwellings set a style for those slightly lower down the social order: for a self-conscious and self-confident commercial and administrative class that had benefited from the economic boom and from the expansion of the civil service. 'Colonies of villas' appeared in Berlin in the Tiergarten and Charlottenburg areas already in the 1860s, and later they moved further out – to Friedenau or Lichterfelde-West in Berlin, or to Wandsbek in Hamburg.

The construction style of the more modest villas as well as of the grandest houses was frequently Bismarckian or Imperial: monumental and historicizing. One of the plans for a large-scale settlement of bourgeois villas was drawn up by Georg Heinrich Friedrich Hitzig, the man who was probably the initiator of the Imperial architecture. He had been trained in Paris at the Ecole des Beaux-Arts, and there was much of Haussmann's Paris in his schemes for large public buildings. The historicist Imperial style was inaugurated by Hitzig's Berlin bourse (1859–63): a giant hall of a building, highly decorated with Renaissance features, and fronted by a double colonnade in doric underneath and corinthian above.[44] Museums, galleries, theatres, universities, town halls and railway stations all went on from here – they all resembled the Berlin bourse. Hitzig designed a pompous central bank building (1869–76) on the Jägerstrasse. Lucae did the ornate Renaissance Technical University, as well as villas for the wealthy. In Nuremberg a large historicist central station (1900–6) by Carl Gustav Ritter von Zenger replaced an original of 1844, which had looked too much like an ordinary burgher's town house. At the high point of this historicizing style, in which elements of renaissance, gothic, baroque and classical were all mixed together, the parliament and the church came in also.

A competition of 1871 to design a new building for the German Reichstag was won by Ludwig Bohnstedt with a plan for colonnades on either side of a gigantic triumphal arch that would serve as the main entrance. It was extremely bombastic, but its exaggerated length failed to give the impression of solidity that emanated from the winning entry in a new competition of 1882. Paul Wallot's design was the basis for the actual building of the Reichstag (1884–94), an exercise which cost some 23 million Marks (or, to put it in comparative terms, almost twice the cost of a battleship in the 1890s). Wallot had defeated a neo-gothic design of Christoph Hehl's – whose sketch bore the motto 'God save the German [i.e. gothic] style', but which looked rather too similar to Barry's Houses of Parliament in Westminster to be a comfortable choice for the new capital of the German Empire.[45] Finally the church: the

National Cathedral – universally held to be the most vulgar and the most fussily over-decorated of all the new Berlin architecture – was created to designs by Julius and Otto Raschdorff between 1894 and 1904. Like the Reichstag, it had a gigantic dome with four corner towers and winged statues looking out from every available parapet. It was supposed to embody grandeur and solidity.

Yet all the Kaiserreich's new opulence was very precarious. The 1870s showed how economic collapse could destroy a vulnerable prosperity. One of the most dramatic collapses was that of the 'railway king' Bethel Strousberg. Strousberg had been born in East Prussia, but lived in London as a journalist and then as an insurance agent, and became a British citizen. In 1855 he returned to Germany determined to grasp the opportunities presented by the economic boom, and began to build railways 'on an English pattern'.[46] His railway empire extended not only over eastern Germany, but deep into Balkan Europe. Much of it was financed by German aristocrats, who were encouraged by Strousberg to feel that they might be left out of the new prosperity. Their participation gave the stamp of social approval and tempted in other, more middle-class, figures. A socially quite heterogeneous group of people seized the opportunities Strousberg presented. It was fundamentally a pyramid scheme, which collapsed as soon as the first difficulties appeared. When they eventually came, in Rumania, many aristocrats lost fortunes. One of Strousberg's principal backers, Prince Putbus, now went with the unfortunate sobriquet Prince *Kaput*bus.

The bankrupt Strousberg was not the only figure who tried to import 'foreign' (English) notions and models as part of Germany's economic learning process. The German banking system – which after the 1870s came to be regarded as a German peculiarity – began as a foreign import as well. The first of the large German investment banks, the Darmstädter Bank, was set up in 1853 with French capital supplied by the Crédit mobilier, and on the model of existing French and Belgian banks.[47] The Deutsche Bank, which became by far the largest of the German universal banks, started business in 1870. Its founders had strong English connections. Georg Siemens, the first Director of the Deutsche Bank, was described by another leading banker in the following way: 'the peculiarity of the commercial strategy that Siemens pursued from the beginning was that he systematically attempted to follow major foreign examples –especially as he found them in England in the bank sector – without attempting to transfer the foreign methods exactly in the German circumstances.'[48] The other major banker in the Deutsche Bank was Ludwig Bamberger, who had left Germany in 1848 as a political *émigré*, and only came back in 1863. He remained convinced of the superiority of English politics and English business practice; so when, for instance, it came to the discussion of a new German central banking system in the Reichstag in 1875, he backed the idea of taking the Banking Act of 1844 (the Peel Act) wholesale from England.

Dramatic success, spectacular failures, and imitation of foreign development: these were the hallmarks of the Bismarckian system. They excited antagonism as well as astonishment from the old-fashioned. In Theodor Fontane's novel *L'Adultera* (published in 1882) a traditionalist conservative, Legationsrat a. D. (retired Diplomatic Counsellor) Duquede, attacks Bismarck himself as the embodiment of the new vulgar and materialist nationalism: 'he has something of the plagiarizing quality, he has simply annexed other people's thoughts, both good and bad, and put them into practice with the help of readily available means.'[49] In this imagined conversation, Bismarck is defended – very characteristically and very symbolically by a baptized Jew with a fresh title granted by the King of Prussia, Kommerzienrat (Commercial Counsellor) van der Straaten. This defence is a powerful demonstration of the newness of Berlin life. Duquede's fictional objections bear a striking resemblance to those voiced by real-life conservatives, such as Leopold von Gerlach who sent these objections in an early letter of warning to Bismarck: 'We have seen . . . [before the French Revolution] the politics of "interest" and so-called patriotism, and where this leads.'[50]

On the one hand, there was the story of the materialism of the new Reich and of conservative scepticism; on the other, a new social polarization. Eclectic architecture and bombastic public display on the one side, and the shoddy rental barracks (*Mietskasernen*) which sprang up in Berlin in the early 1870s on the other: they gave a powerful visual expression to the sharp contrasts and disparities in the new Empire. The spectacular boom of the early 1870s brought a disproportionate increase in the number of those living in poor conditions. In 1867, 50.6 per cent of Berlin's tenement apartments had no or only one heatable room; in 1871 this figure had risen to 55.1 per cent. Between 1867 and 1871 comfortable 'gentlemen's apartments' (*Herrschaftswohnungen*) on the first floor (*bel étage*) increased in number by 13.5 per cent, but there were 31.4 per cent more poor apartments in the fourth floor or above, 34.6 per cent more basement apartments, and an increase of 90 per cent in the number of apartments actually built under the courtyards of tenement blocks.

The promises that economic success would build a nation had been fulfilled in only a limited way: there may have been a unified state, but there was no unified people. Social disparities were more pronounced, and conceptions of what national identity actually meant more widely separated. There was an intrinsic logic to the way in which the advocates of economics for the sake of nation-building now turned their attention to inequalities in the distribution of wealth and income.

The old problem had appeared again – the relationship between national integration and economic development. It was simply posed in a different form. In the decades after 1850, economic growth was very clearly highly dynamic. In 1846, Prussia had mined only 3,200,000 tons of hard coal; in 1871, German coal production was 29,400,000 tons; and in 1913, 191,500,000. In steel, Germany had even overtaken Britain by 1900 (7,372,000 tons as against 5,981,000).[51] She had leading technologies in electrical goods, in dyestuffs manufacture and in the optical trade. Britain now felt vulnerable, and scared by the phenomenon of 'Made in Germany'.[52] On the other hand, growth did not remove poverty, though real wages rose steadily from the 1860s. It certainly did not make for a more equal distribution of wealth and income.

The 24th edition of Roscher's *Grundlagen* appeared in 1906, and contained damning material on the increase in inequality. While, in 1879, 0.5 per cent of the taxpayers owned one-seventh of national wealth, by 1894, 0.75 per cent owned one-fifth.[53] The growth of the very rich even put the previous pre-eminence of the sovereign in the shade. By 1912 the Kaiser was no longer the wealthiest individual in Prussia: he came, according to the calculation of Rudolf Martin, into fifth place behind Frau Bertha Krupp von Bohlen und Halbach (with a capital of 283 million Marks), Fürst Henckel von Donnersmarck in Neudeck (254 million), Generalkonsul Freiherr von Goldschmidt-Rothschild (163 million), and the Duke of Ujest auf Slawentzitz (154 million).[54]

The younger generation of the Historical School believed questions about distribution were crucial for the political stability of the nation. They departed completely from the arguments made by the early Roscher about the undesirability of state interventionism. The new men characterized this as a relic of discredited 'Manchesterite' dogma. They in turn became widely known as 'professorial socialists' (*Katheder-sozialisten*). Adolph Wagner delivered a speech 'On the Social Question' at the height of the commercial speculation following the Franco-Prussian War. He attacked luxury, demanded higher taxes, legislation on conditions of work, and the public provision of adequate housing.[55] The major interest of Wagner and his disciples lay in social policy, in the statistical description of inequality and hardship and in the preparation of a reform programme. They no longer tried to formulate perpetual and inexorable laws of economics.

Among the new generation of economists, Gustav Schmoller was the intellectual leader. He began with the same premisses as his predecessors from the older Historical School. There existed, he believed, a historically identifiable cycle of political and economic growth, maturity, followed by weakness, the development of excessive materialism, and eventually decline.

This became a theory of economic development. In order to promote economic change, an act of political power had to break down traditional obstacles. 'Everywhere the growth of power has given the principal spur to economic development.'[56] Such an act of iconoclasm could only be the work of great statesmen: their task was the destruction of ancient rights, traditions, privileges and institutions and the introduction of rational legislation favourable to economic action. In turn economic change might throw up great heroic leaders: 'Only in such periods are there really great statesmen, who are obeyed by the people.'

Schmoller's formulation of the role of politics in the growth process was much more sophisticated than that expressed by Roscher or Knies. It appeared to be a transplantation into economic theory of one of the components of the Prussian historical view, namely that destiny was shaped by the actions of great men. For Hegel, there were world historical figures. For Clausewitz, there was military genius. Goethe had already spoken of the daimon or driving historical force; and in historical writing Droysen had depicted Alexander the Great as a historical demiurge. Schmoller added economic genius.

After the heroic period of breakthrough, stagnation followed. National degeneration – Schmoller even called it racial degeneration – set in. The state ceased to be effective, and political genius atrophied. Schmoller described this in a formula that much later became (though unacknowledged) a catchphrase from the pen of another critical economic writer:[57] private affluence and public squalor. The growth of poverty, and increasing inequalities, discredited a state which was unable to do anything about these problems. The state lost legitimacy because of its helplessness.

Economists had a responsibility to make statistical measurements to show what was happening; and to raise public consciousness of the social malaise by protesting against the development of pauperization. They should, in short, create an atmosphere favourable to reform.

Economic Politics and the Economic Nation

The state responded to those problems which had excited the demands of the *Kathedersozialisten*. At last Germany produced her own model that the rest of the world might and did imitate – as the first welfare state. The genesis of social welfare policies owed something to contemporary social thought, something to the political and social instability of Germany and something to the relics of the old world. To some conservatives, there appeared to be an almost unbroken transition from a feudal concern for the protection of the lower orders to modern welfare policies. These offered a politically attractive alternative to liberal programmes. In the 1850s Frederick William IV had believed that monarchical protection of the people, successfully applied, might make Germany immune against a new outbreak of revolution. Bismarck had talked with socialist leaders – notably Ferdinand Lassalle – in the 1860s in order to get support from outside the liberal camp and undermine political liberalism. The reforms of the 1880s went alongside a turn to conservatism and the political repression of the socialist party.

The new schemes covered accident (1881), sickness (1884), and old age insurance (1889). By modern standards, they were not generous. Eligibility was strictly defined. Invalids received a pension of one-third of their previous earnings, and old age pensions were set below even this very low level. In part, the schemes were simply a systematization of insurance schemes that had long existed on a local level. Though it was in practice neither as original nor as open-handed as it claimed, Bismarck's social legislation offered workers a basic degree of security. The number of people using the sickness insurance scheme gradually rose. And above all, Bismarck's laws opened the door to a widening of the original provisions, and to further reforms.

Scarcely had the Bismarckian measures been passed than the young Kaiser William II already wanted to go further. He conceived of himself as a popular Kaiser (People's Kaiser, or *Volkskaiser*), who could make reform into a state-building exercise. In November 1888, months after ascending the throne, he promised reform of the conditions of work. In 1890 he set out a programme for reducing hours of work, especially for women and children, for a factory inspectorate and for the construction of special workers' schools, hospitals, churches and savings banks. After 1893, state supervision of the mines was intensified, and miners were given some influence over the formulation of mine ordinances. An expansive foreign policy might fill all Germans with zealous patriotism.

Most analysts have assumed that these strategies of integration failed. The appeal of social imperialism scarcely went beyond the middle classes, and attempts to bring workers into middle-class patriotic associations rarely succeeded. Many workers did not see that they benefited much from the Bismarckian welfare legislation. Opposition grew. The parties which won the biggest increases in support during the Kaiserreich – the Catholic Centre party and the socialist party (SPD) were those hostile to the principles on which the Empire had been built.

However, opposition politics in the Kaiserreich shared many of the characteristics of establishment behaviour. The ethos of the Kaiserreich proved to be highly infectious. If the Wilhelmine elites were cynical, power hungry, and above all materialistic, so too were their opponents. Politics for everyone was concerned in the first place with the distribution of material goods. In this rather limited sense, integration through the economic nation captured German minds.

Though the appeal of German nationalism to immediate self-interest had been evident at least since the 1850s, the political and economic shift of gear of the late 1870s taught a new lesson in materialism. The debate about the protective tariff on cereals and some manufactured goods (most importantly iron and steel) polarized politics around an economic issue. A crucial turning-point was 1878–9: according to the historian Helmut Böhme, this date is so significant that it even marks the second and true foundation of the German Empire.[58] The new tariff legislation came into force in 1880. From then on politics were polarized. On the one side stood a bloc of 'solidarity protectionists' – big business and agriculture, or iron and rye. On the other, politically powerless and vulnerable consumers. Liberals in many rural areas lost support to the protectionist Centre party because their free trade doctrine appeared to be opposed to the interests of rural constituencies. The SPD's propaganda skilfully emphasized on the other hand how much the tariff cost the consumer: how part of the price of each loaf of bread and krug of beer was nothing more than a direct subsidy to the propertied classes.

Was this a peculiarly German phenomenon? It is true that continental Europe as a whole adopted protectionist tariffs at the end of the 1870s or the beginning of the 1880s, and that their introduction was preceded by fierce political debates which involved a large number of people and began to create the phenomenon of modern mass politics. It is also true that the almost universal result was a reduction of politics to calculations about interest – what might be called the 'economicization of politics'. Finally, it is true that all this was castigated by cultural critics throughout Europe as evidence of sickening and decadent materialism. Others commented on how politics had been reduced to interest alone. Anatole France's satire on Third Republic France, *Penguin Island* (*L'Île des Pingouins*) for example made the point that the modern state was built on two central political virtues – respect for riches and disdain for poverty – and that there were only two modern parties – the party that distilled alcohol (from crops) and the party that did not (because it grew vines).

What was so unique about late-nineteenth-century Germany was that the economicization of politics also brought with it the economicization of nationalism. Nationalism translated into a world of material objects. Items of manufacture represented the nation as much as did myths of the past, and national culture revolved around industrial products.

The word *Kultur* has a broader meaning in German than in English. In English, the word includes something of the double meaning of the German term in that it is possible to speak of the culture of trees and plants (agriculture). For Germans, the word refers both to the products of artists and to economic artefacts. In his *Reflections on History*, the Swiss historian Jacob Burckhardt gave a famous definition of culture by exclusion as that which was not religion or state: in other words the essential characteristic of culture was that it was a product of the human imagination and had no claim to any authority. The church and the state had power; in culture there was no single arbiter and no validating instance. Artistic creation was of course a question of initiative and of originality – but so too was economic action. Arts and crafts were originally intimately associated:

> This is an apparent confusion, some of these things having their origin in material, some in spiritual necessities. Yet the connection is actually very close and no separation of the two needs is possible. In the course of any material activity carried on with independent power, and not merely slavishly, a spiritual overplus is generated, be it ever so little.[59]

Bruno Hildebrand described economics as primarily the science of culture (*Culturwissenschaft*). In consequence, it made sense for the transport specialist Max Maria von Weber (incidentally, the son of the composer Carl Maria) to call the railway *das grosse Culturwerkzeug* – 'the great instrument of culture'.[60] He wrote poems as well as technical treatises, but both on the railway. Or equally, the sociologist Max Weber was stating a commonplace in his 1895 Freiburg inaugural lecture when he linked the level of culture to living standards and nationality. The result sounded brutal: 'In West Prussia, economic culture, the relative living standard, and *Germanness* are all identical.'[61] The two Webers demonstrate the way that by the end of the nineteenth century the use of language had shifted even from Burckhardt's time. 'Culture' no longer provided such a sharp contrast in German eyes to state or religion: they had all become national concepts, associated with struggles for power. There was the national state, the national church (which Bismarck tried to uphold in the 1870s in the struggle against Rome, the *Kulturkampf*), and the national economy.

Materialist nationalism was sustained by a popular scientific materialism – best reflected in the writings of Ernst Haeckel. His *Riddle of the Universe* (1899) was hugely successful. By 1908, 240,000 copies of the German edition alone had been printed.[62] Haeckel offered a popularized version of the Darwinian theory of evolution combined with an attack on religious authority. From these premisses, he drew the conclusion that, if only the church were destroyed, 'then, in the twentieth century, human culture, freedom and prosperity will continue their progressive development until they far surpass even the height of the nineteenth century'. A rational ('monist') religion would celebrate the goddesses of truth, beauty, and virtue.[63] Haeckel's view represents, one century later, a crude version of *Sturm und Drang* (he greatly admired Goethe) combined with the materialist determination of the nineteenth century. It may be appropriate to think of him, rather than the Nietzschean preachers of cultural despair, as the popular prophet of the Wilhelmine era. The two most commercially successful expressions of cultural pessimism, Langbehn's *Rembrandt the Educator* and Spengler's *Decline of the West*, both sold only around 100,000 copies in their first eight years.[64]

A consequence of the peculiar definition of national culture in material terms was that the different political and social groupings reinterpreted nationalism in the light of their own perceptions of what constituted their material reality. For East Elbian Junkers, Germany meant Prussia and Prussia meant the large cereal estates east of the River Elbe. For Hamburg merchants, the German nation was the shipping business that took the national flag all over the world. For Rhineland businessmen, Germany lay in coal mines and steel furnaces. Even the labour movement shared what might be termed this 'nationalistic specificity'.

Many of these issues had already been raised in the debate over tariffs between 1876 and 1880. However, the conflict over the economic character of the German state became acute after the beginning of the 1890s, when a new Reich Chancellor, Leo von Caprivi, reduced German protective tariffs for foreign policy reasons to appease the Russians, whose grain exports had been affected by the German measure. Unfortunately, at the same time, and coincidentally to Caprivi's policy, agriculture entered a deep crisis as cereal prices fell and livestock suffered the ravages of epidemic disease. The farmers, however, blamed the state and Caprivi in person for all this misery. They now believed that harmonious economic advance was an impossibility; and that two alternatives, the *Industriestaat* (Industrial State) and the *Agrarstaat* (Agrarian State), stood locked in conflict.

Farmers founded a highly militant pressure group in 1893, the Reich Agrarian League (Reichslandbund). The agrarians knew that they were following a socialist example in economicizing politics, and one or two were sufficiently naive to state this: 'We must shout and shout,' said the Silesian tenant farmer Ruprecht, 'so that our voice reaches the whole people and even the steps of the throne . . . I am suggesting nothing more nor less than that we go along the same path as the social democrats and seriously make a front against the government, so that we demonstrate that we are not willing to let ourself be treated so badly as before and make the government feel our strength.'[65]

The farmers feared that Caprivi was creating a pernicious *Industriestaat* and undermining the true character of the German people, which had deep roots in the old *Agrarstaat*. He himself was a landless Chancellor who owned no broad acres – 'without an acre [of land] or a blade [of corn]'. The Agrarian League leader Elard von Oldenburg-Januschau wrote that Caprivi was 'taking away the sustenance of the German people and indeed – as it later proved – the basis of general prosperity, not to speak of the effect of his measures on the people's strength [*Volkskraft*] and on the inner association of man with the life of nature'. 'A German Empire without healthy agriculture would have to break apart like a man whose spine had been broken.'[66]

The agrarians found in physical strength the idealized expression of national culture: 'disciplined manhood [*Manneszucht*] is the sign of the level of a people's culture'. And this in turn was embodied not in parliament or the press, or even in the monarchy, but in the Prussian army. 'The drum and the crutch, these have been the great bearers of German culture,' was Oldenburg-Januschau's comment.[67]

There was of course a directly political reason for this advocacy of the army as the symbol of the nation. The army still played a vital role in Prussian and German politics. The former Prussian Minister of War von Einem saw 1908 as the crucial year: Chancellor Bernhard von Bülow had attempted to introduce an inheritance tax, which threatened the economic interests of the old elite. The Kaiser had been allowed to discredit himself in the *Daily Telegraph* affair, an unguarded interview with the English newspaper in which the German sovereign made all manner of undiplomatic and improbable claims. The Kaiser's Chief of the Military Cabinet died in bizarre and humiliating circumstances (he was dressed as a ballerina) at an entertainment attended by the Kaiser. Above all, the Kaiser appeared to have deserted the Prussian aristocrats. 'The Emperor, the Chancellor, the Ministers, and the people did not emerge as victors out of the stormy year 1908. Only the German army stood firm and unshakeable.'[68] But even the army was threatened by the inflow of middle-class officers and working-class soldiers.

The middle classes did in fact have a different national identity. If they were militarists, they looked to the sea rather than the land. The Prussian aristocrats and conservatives disliked the navy, and stayed away from it. In consequence, proportionately more of the navy's senior officers came from middle-class backgrounds. The navy also stood as a political symbol of the middle-class liberal movement of mid-century. In 1848, a proposed German navy had been one of the brackets that should bind the nation together. There were also specific economic concerns with naval power. The navy had close links with the powerful steel industry of Rhine-Ruhr. It might protect German commerce overseas. This induced a different language of militarism for the navy. Admiral von Tirpitz, the Imperial Navy Secretary and the man responsible for Germany's dramatic entry in 1897 into a naval arms race with Britain, did not talk about the virile culture of *Manneszucht*. Instead, he explained the naval struggle in industrial metaphors: 'The older and stronger firm [England] inevitably seeks to strangle the new and rising one [Germany] before it is too late.'[69]

Middle-class patriotism also identified much more with German products and manufactures – with the success of German industry. Products had patriotic names – such as Siemens's 'Wotan' light bulb. The trade description 'Made in Germany' became a source of pride. The Frenchman Henri Hauser commented on the self-consciousness of the new middle-class Germany and how 'several of our compatriots, after one or two hurried journeys in Germany, have returned completely hypnotized, as if overwhelmed by that display of wealth and power'. In the magazine *Jugend* in 1912, Paul Rohrbach wrote the following:

> Germany's rise has been favoured by the fact that the political and economic union of Germany coincided with the most wonderful technical progress that humanity had ever seen. And this technique, founded on the methodical knowledge of nature, corresponded exactly in a most brilliant manner with one of the traits of our national temperament – exact and laborious energy.

The Kaiser appealed to this middle-class nationalism. He attended the opening of the German Museum (Deutsches Museum) in Munich in 1906 – a museum dedicated to the exposition of how science should be applied, with major exhibits donated by Germany's large companies. In 1907 in a speech, he announced:

> The powerful, surprising, and almost incomprehensibly rapid progress of our newly united Fatherland in all domains, the astounding development of our trade and commerce, the

magnificent inventions in the domain of science and technics, are a result of the reunion of the German races in one common Fatherland. The more we are able to wrest for ourselves a prominent position in all parts of the world the more should our nation in every class and industry remember that the working of Divine Providence is here manifested. If our Lord God had not entrusted to us great tasks He would not have conferred upon us great capacities.[70]

Middle-class nationalism also had its own political programme. Max Weber's Freiburg lecture of 1895 was one of the clearest statements of the association between national identity and class position. A progressive and politically 'responsible' nationalism, according to Weber, could only be a middle-class nationalism.

The fundamental premisse of the lecture was the primacy of economics in a perpetual struggle for national survival. 'We have to pass on to our successors not peace and happiness, but the perpetual struggle for the survival and the improved breeding of our national type.' But this national type meant a specific class identification, because national policy depended on the material interests of the politicians and the political class which was formulating it. Weber made the striking and highly personal statement: 'I am a member of the bourgeois classes'. If either an economically declining or an economically rising class were to gain political power, national culture would be shaken. There would be an absence of 'political maturity'. This view was set out in the form of a law:

It has always been the attainment of economic power which allowed a class to develop its claim to political leadership. It is dangerous, and in the long run irreconcilable with the interests of a nation, if an economically sinking class holds political authority in its hands. But it is even more dangerous if classes who are developing economic power and with this the claim to political authority are not mature enough to lead the state. Both threaten Germany at this time and hold the keys to the current dangers of our position.[71]

The task for the future was the education of the new classes, and especially of the labour movement, so that they might reach political maturity.

The socialists themselves propagated a populist nationalism in the Wilhelmine epoch. Already in the 1860s Ferdinand Lassalle had strongly supported the creation of what became 1871 Germany, around the Prussian nucleus. His party formed one of the elements in the future socialist party (SPD) (along with a largely South German party much less committed to the Prussian cause). In foreign policy, the new party was pro-German in that it remained constantly hostile to Russia, the seat of European reaction. As Wilhelm Liebknecht put it in 1885, 'Russia is and remains our enemy.'[72] The SPD held to this view right up to 1914. There was also an undercurrent of much more overt nationalism. Some socialist intellectuals argued the case for expansion and empire: Joseph Bloch, the editor of the *Sozialistische Monatshefte*; Karl Leuthner, who wrote there; and Max Schippel, who started a militarist deviation from the mainstream of the party. They argued for Pan-Germany (All-Deutschland), and after 1912 believed a continental war to be inevitable. The *Sozialistische Monatshefte* influenced many of the trade union leaders, and perhaps also the party base; it certainly sold more copies than the more international theoretical organ of the SPD, *Neue Zeit*.

Even the party mainstream was sufficiently worried about the depth of German patriotism to avoid provoking working-class hostility by an over-enthusiastic commitment to international labour solidarity, or by an elaboration of the doctrine of a general strike to prevent 'imperialist war'. More typical than Bloch or Leuthner were Bernstein and Bebel. The revisionist theoretician Eduard Bernstein – who after 1914 opposed the actual German war effort – believed in a positive proletarian nationalism. August Bebel, the great socialist parliamentarian, made no secret of the fact that he believed himself to be a German patriot.[73]

After 1914, the SPD worked closely with the Imperial government. It joined the civic truce (*Burgfrieden*) declared by the Kaiser, not simply out of a blind patriotic devotion, but because the party leaders held that a new militarism and nationalism would go naturally and inevitably with an awakening of democratic sentiment. The mobilization involved in war would lead to an extension of parliamentary government, reform of the restricted property-based franchise in Prussia, and the limitation of the power of the aristocracy. The economic success of wartime mobilization might lay the foundations for a new culture and a new sort of nationalism. One of the SPD leaders noted:

> With this war, a realistic Germany has made her entrance on the world stage. Her economic power and technical expertise is demonstrated in the grandiose performance of her war machine. Her organizational competence beats every record . . . If her world position in the economy and in military affairs is not followed by a spiritual renaissance, we should fear for the future. But I hope the renaissance will follow.[74]

A national state alone could provide the framework for the social reforms envisaged by the SPD – otherwise other outside influences would frustrate ambitions for reform. It was senseless to believe in an effective international solidarity of labour or to rely on English or Russian workers for support. The Baden revisionist Ludwig Frank explained in a letter: 'For the duration, the international idea is superseded by the reality of a national labour movement. Instead of a general strike, we are waging a war for the Prussian franchise.'[75]

For the SPD, politics could only take place within a national community. This made for the *real* sense of nationalism that underlay the party's actions. On the other hand, the SPD held all other types of nationalism to be nothing more than hollow rhetoric and empty phrases. 'Our nationalism', observed Eduard David, 'is not an affair of resounding words, but one of social action and, if necessary, of national actions against the outside world.'[76]

The SPD had in this way become part of a general national consensus: but its vision of what ought to be the national ideal did not correspond to those of other groups with similar beliefs in the national mission. The aristocracy, they thought, were fighting for yesterday's Germany, the middle classes for today's, and they, the socialists, were fighting for the Germany of tomorrow.

In 1914 little lay in the way of a triumphant reassertion of the link between nationality, power, and success. True, there were different views about what constituted that link. But few doubted that there was one. The economic success story found its exponent and its popularizer in Karl Helfferich, who was turn by turn economist, journalist, banker, civil servant and eventually became (after the war) a politician of the German Nationalist Party. His book *Germany's Prosperity* was first published in 1913; by 1915 it had gone through six editions. The old theme came back again: only economic progress allowed military assertiveness and cultural life. 'Only when economic labour brings relief to the great mass of the population, when the provision of the simple means of subsistence no longer takes up all the time of those working manually, can culture become a common good. And the last and highest aim of all cultural progress is that it should become a common good.' Since economics laid the foundation for any feeling of cultural identity, it represented the deep bedrock of nationality: 'the feeling of spiritual, economic and political togetherness fuses the German tribes into the nation.'[77]

Before the First World War it was possible in Germany to give a fully coherent answer to a question that would seem odd from most perspectives – and certainly, in English eyes, completely absurd. What is the purpose of the German nation? The answer was: to provide that economic advance without which the nation could not exist. This answer is a tautology. But the insertion of the economic element into the tautology gave an apparent meaning to the tortured German quest for self-identity.[78] In this way, Rochau's view still held sway: that making a nation was no more and no less than a 'business transaction'.

4

The Incomplete Nation-State: Wotan and Fafner

The German Empire began on 18 January 1871 in the Hall of Mirrors at Versailles. It was doubly incomplete, and there was a double compromise: first, between constitutional state and autocracy; secondly, between the principles of nationalism and dynasticism. This chapter examines cultural and political reactions to this mongrel state form.

Constitutionally, it was a confederation of states dominated by Prussia, whose King William I became the first German Emperor. The permanence of Prussian dominance in the executive power of new Germany was guaranteed by the position of the King-Emperor, and in legislative affairs by a provision which gave the Prussian delegates an effective veto in the upper house of the new German parliament. A lower chamber, the Reichstag, elected on a universal adult manhood suffrage, represented the popular element. Its consent was required for legislation, and thus also for the budget, but it could control neither the Imperial ministers (called Secretaries of State) nor the Chancellor. These remained unconditionally royal appointments.

Slowly Germany acquired the institutional accoutrements of a modern state. Though the Empire's currency and banking system was standardized in 1875, with the creation of a central bank, it took a generation to acquire a coherent and unified legal system. The Civil Law Code (Bürgerliches Gesetzbuch) came into force only in 1900.

Subsequent developments indicated how dangerous this half constitutional and half national ship of state might become once the political load began to shift. The central state's (*Reich*'s) powers to raise revenue and tax were limited: fundamentally the Reich depended on customs revenue. The Reichstag had little by way of Reich policy to control.

Police and education remained the affair of the federal states. The most important area of central state activity was foreign policy, but this was not subject to any kind of constitutional restraint except in so far as the policy involved financial affairs. Briefly, the Reich had a constitution which initially did not directly reach those areas of policy which really mattered.

When foreign policy started to be expensive, it would inevitably move into the centre of constitutional debate, as parliamentary approval of the budget was required; and the additional exposure would make policy subject to more, and more diverse, pressure and awaken greater expectations. If parliament had to be persuaded of the merits of a strategy, such as the fleet expansion of the 1890s, the government was obliged to oversell the strategy and to exaggerate the successes that it might bring.

Secondly, the 1871 Empire stood halfway between a Prussian dynastic and a modern nation-state. This point was expressed symbolically. The eventual flag of Imperial Germany – only introduced twenty years after the foundation of the Empire – merely took over the old Prussian colours (black and white) and added red, rather than adopting the black-red-gold of the populist nationalist movement from the time of the wars of liberation.

There existed yet a further compromise for the new Germany. There were German speakers outside the Empire, chiefly in Austria and Switzerland, and in both countries they debated whether they should try to join the new state. Germany itself included 2.8 million French speakers, mostly in the Saar and in the newly annexed provinces of Alsace and Lorraine (which were thrown together as the so-called Reichsland, and put under direct Imperial control). In the east, there were 2.5 million Poles, and other non-German-speaking minorities included 150,000 Lithuanians, 140,000 Danish speakers, and about the same number each of Wends, Moravians, and Bohemians. About 7 per cent of Germany's population in the 1870s thus did not speak German. This proportion went up: by 1900 there were 3.1 million Poles, and 7½ per cent were officially reckoned as non-German speakers. But this figure contains a considerable distortion, since it under-reckoned the size of the French minority in an effort to demonstrate the success of Germanicization.[1]

However, it was a German Empire and not a multinational one. Throughout its history, the enforcement of German as a language of state became more rigorous. Paragraph 186 of the Reich Constitutional Law (1877) laid down German as the only language spoken in courts. In 1888 German became the sole language of instruction in Schleswig schools; it had held this position in eastern Germany, in the Slav areas, already since 1872. In 1885, Germany expelled Polish-speaking Russian and Austrian citizens, and in 1886 a scheme was introduced to buy up the estates of the Polish nobility in order to 'Germanicize the soil'. Though the latter project met with little success, it was applied again, much more thoroughly, in the 1900s. Meanwhile, as German nationalists noticed with alarm, Polish farmers and land workers pushed forward at the expense of the Germans.[2]

Danish speakers who had chosen in the 1860s to retain a Danish citizenship (the so-called Optanten) also faced the possibility of· expulsion. The French in Alsace-Lorraine in 1871 were given a similar option about citizenship. Subsequently, Imperial control over the province became ever more severe.

The 'Germanness' of nationality, school, and citizenship policies was highly aggressive. For the first twenty-five years of the Bismarckian Empire, this aggression stood in striking contrast to the restraint and moderation of German policy abroad. The Franco-Prussian War and the Peace of Frankfurt which concluded it had made Germany a 'satiated' state in Bismarck's view. It could not safely expand further. In 1875 a war scare orchestrated from Berlin met with a sharp British and French reaction: German politicians now had very little room in which to manoeuvre. Unsurprisingly, from the beginning of the 1880s Bismarck responded to the blocked situation in Europe by looking to the much more available and less clearly demarcated field of extra-European activity. Colonies formed the only possible outlet for national policy; but even the spate of colonial activity in 1884–5 did not last long and was followed by a renewed moderation.

The first twenty-five years might be used to support an argument that Bismarckian *Realpolitik* had placed a stable unit in the middle of Europe which assured continental peace for over a generation. In fact, with hindsight, the international arena of the late nineteenth century appears highly unstable. Bismarck had locked the new German state into an international order at least as volatile as the system whereby Metternich had linked international restoration with the German Confederation. After 1871, Germany formed part of a system made up of five and a half Great Powers: Britain, France, Germany, Austria-Hungary, and Russia, in addition to the disintegrating Ottoman Empire. Austria, Russia and the Ottoman Empire were bona fide multinational empires. The principle of nationality threatened them; but every observer could calculate that if they crumbled, there would be a major territorial rearrangement of central and eastern Europe. Such a revision, which appeared increasingly likely at the turn of the century, might present new opportunities to Germany. Could she not expand her influence to cover the pockets of German-speaking trading settlements spread across south and eastern Europe, reaching as far as the Volga? Could she not extend an economic system to include the gigantic markets – with their newly awakening consumer demands – and the rich raw material sources of the east?

German hopes of exploiting the opportunities offered by the collapse of the post-Crimea and post-1871 settlements depended on the spread of the nationality principle. On the other hand, the application of this theory to the German Empire itself would mean its destruction as well. Germany, unlike France or Britain, had only very partially realized the aims and the dreams of a national state. Her alliances also suffered from this problem. In 1879 Germany concluded a treaty with Austria, and after this became increasingly dependent on the highly heterogeneous Habsburg monarchy as her only reliable partner.

Once the European map began to shake, more political possibilities and likelihoods appeared. The growing diplomatic instability in Europe after the 1880s combined with the development of parliamentary politics in the 1890s and 1900s to generate for many Germans new hopes and expectations – which exceeded the rather limited options actually available to German statesmen.

By the turn of the century, two new sorts of German nationalism had emerged as alternatives to the tradition of economic nationalism and of the economic nation established in mid-century. First, there was the attack from those who believed that economic nationalism was a perversion of the notion of the cultural state (*Kulturstaat*). Secondly, by the beginning of the twentieth century the logic of economic devlopment had carried many to the conclusion that the nation-state no longer formed the appropriate framework in which that development should take place.

Cultural Criticism

The theory that Imperial Germany constituted a betrayal of the German nation depended on a renewed process of redefinition of nationality. The enemies of political liberalism tried to use a loose concept such as 'nation' in arguing that the political system they wished to change had become illegitimate because it was 'unnational'. They thought of the nation in the mystical terms of community and, more and more from the 1870s, of race. Liberal economics had, they held, violated the harmony of this mystical entity.

This theory operated at several levels, which influenced and shaped each other. The anti-materialism and anti-liberalism of iconoclastic but remote intellectuals were bolstered by their similarities to popular beliefs. Anti-liberal aesthetes loved nothing more than to play the game of being popular. Conversely, the rapid growth after the 1870s of a popular critique of modernity owed something to the existence of categories provided by the intellectual elite: it was not simply, as it claimed to be, an autonomous and healthy reaction to cultural degeneration.

Treitschke, Richard Wagner and Friedrich Nietzsche represented an unholy trinity of intellectual anti-liberalism. Treitschke, a formidable and inspirational university lecturer, influenced generations of Berlin students. Wagner tried in the 1870s to develop a mass following, though not in the shape of a political movement or party; but he failed miserably. Nietzsche self-consciously avoided political engagement, but by the turn of the century his work had influenced many would-be disciples to build up a reaction against the old conventions of politics. Nietzsche, of course, has a different intellectual and historical standing to that of Treitschke or even of Wagner. He remains a towering figure, whose insights have profoundly influenced the major streams of twentieth-century thought – from Weberian sociology to structural anthropology to 'post-modernism'. The figure depicted in this chapter is in many ways less the 'real' Nietzsche than Nietzsche as interpreted, and misinterpreted, by Germans at the turn of the century.

Treitschke was committed to the association of nationality, power politics and economic logic – with a dose of anti-semitism added for good measure. In this sense, he did not move far from what might be termed the historical-economic consensus of mid-century. Wagner and Nietzsche on the other hand were profoundly radical in their wish to destroy the foundations of that consensus.

Richard Wagner was born in Leipzig in 1813, a few months before the decisive defeat of Napoleon on the nearby battlefield. After some unsuccessful compositions, a cantankerous period as a conductor in minor German theatres and an immediately catastrophic marriage, he left Germany and went to Paris via Riga. When he returned to Saxony in 1842, he worked on two operas, *Tannhäuser* (first performed in 1845) and *Lohengrin* (written between 1845 and March 1848, and first performed in 1850). They reflect an obvious nationalism, which was much more marked than in any of his later work; and in this, as in their musical style, they resemble the romanticism of Carl Maria von Weber. This was German music about resoundingly German themes, taken in Wagner's case from medieval stories, and laced with an updated patriotism. Something of the more violent and aggressive nationalism of the 1840s appeared in Wagner's works, and particularly in *Lohengrin*. Henry the Fowler in *Lohengrin* summons German armies to prove themselves in battle against the Slavic hordes from the East. *Tannhäuser*'s Landgraf is rather more lyrical but no less committed to German values: *deutsch* he uses as a synonym for healthy and robust.

Nationalism in Wagner's eyes was, however, above all revolutionary and regenerative. Nostalgia and romantic yearning were diversions from a far more dramatic and profound purpose. Already before 1848 Wagner longed for the destruction of the existing order, which had mistreated him, as he believed, so cruelly. In November 1847, he wrote to a Berlin music critic: 'Here we need to break through a dam. The means is: Revolution!'[3] Inevitably, Wagner was swept along by the political current of 1848, and in April 1849 he fought in a dramatic rising in Dresden on the barricades alongside the Russian anarchist Bakunin. When the revolt failed, he fled abroad in fear of his life. For five and a half years, from the completion of *Lohengrin* and the initial outbreak of revolution in March 1848, he virtually abandoned music and instead devoted himself to a political life in which theoretical demands about music, art and popular improvement figured prominently.[4]

Nineteenth-century art, he held, had been debased because of the compromises it had made with the commercial ethic of the age. It no longer embodied popular taste, but aimed at the gratification of decadent sensibilities.[5] In the modern world, man's humanity was no longer realized in his work or his actions. The mechanization of labour produced alienation and an inability to communicate socially. Only a double transformation could put the community back: a political revolution, and a revolution in art so that citizens could see the political process correctly. Artistic activity required communality as much as did political involvement: it meant losing an individual notion of identity and becoming 'I *and* you' – or, as Wagner phrased it, it meant 'the dissolution of egoism in communism'.[6] Only barely a political doctrine, this seems to lead as well to the romantic longing for communion in *Tristan und Isolde* as to *Das Kapital*.

The experience of 1848, of narrow escape and exile, rubbed home the revolutionary lesson. In Switzerland, Wagner formed a close friendship with the revolutionary and democratic poet Georg Herwegh. In 1854, Herwegh introduced Wagner – now musically active once more – to the highly pessimistic writings of Arthur Schopenhauer, which might have been expected to kill in the composer any aspiration for political reform. But in fact Wagner's use of Schopenhauer represents a political distortion of the philosopher's work.

The most Schopenhauerian of Wagner's works was the four-part *Ring* cycle. As he absorbed Schopenhauer, Wagner revised the text again and again. The conclusion, Brünnhilde's self-immolation, becomes not a celebration of love, as it had been in the original version, but a statement of abnegation, of the self-destruction of the will. Until 1872, her final narration included the thought – Wagner himself called it 'sententious' –that 'only love allows happiness in pleasure and sorrow'.[7] Instead Brünnhilde sees in her own death the end of the gods and their order:

> For the end of the gods
> Is now approaching
> So I throw the torch at Walhalla's proud fortress.

This was indeed the appropriate conclusion to the whole cycle. In the second music drama of the cycle, *Die Walküre*, Wotan begins the process of self-renunciation and self-destruction: willing nothingness.

> Let it all fall to pieces,
> all that I built.
> I give up my work.
> Only one thing I want now:
> the end, the end![8]

In the next drama, Wotan allows Siegfried to destroy his spear, the symbol of his power, and from then on remains in his fortress, Walhalla, waiting for 'the end'.

This is self-abnegation. But it is still revolutionary and violent self-abnegation. As well as quiet resignation, there is – much more prominently – also 1848 and Bakunin in the *Ring* cycle. Wagner later thought that the *Ring* was a product of the revolutionary dynamic: 'In spite of all the stupidities, the foundations of German unity were then laid. I believe I myself should never have conceived the *Ring* but for that movement.'[9]

Wagner's Wotan constructed a world which depended on fixed laws, and then he faced the problem of trying to will something in opposition to his previous wish. The system he had created trapped him. He had wanted to become a 'Master' through making contracts, and had ended as a 'slave' to those contracts. A process destroyed itself through its own contradictions, with obvious parallels to the left–Hegelian and marxist diagnoses of the mid-nineteenth-century economy (constrained by iron laws) and political systems: constitutions could provide the means of their own overthrow. The world of economics and politics would end in conflagration or destruction or what the Germans called, untranslatably, 'Kladderadatsch'.

Throughout his life, Wagner continued to admire the destructiveness symbolized to him by Bakunin in Dresden: 'the annihilation of all civilization was the objective on which he had set his heart; to use all political levers at hand as a means to this end was his current preoccupation, and it often served him as a pretext for ironic merriment . . . It was necessary . . . to picture the whole European world, with Petersburg, Paris and London, transformed into a pile of rubble.'[10] In 1871 he applauded the incendiarism of the Paris Commune:

Action is everything to [mankind], in preserving as in destroying. Incidentally, the fact that the Communists really wanted to set fire to the whole of Paris is the one impressive feature; they have always disgusted me with their histrionic style of government, their hypocrisy, their pedantic administration with all its lace trimmings –it is the only way a Frenchman knows; but that their disgust with French culture should bring them to the point of wanting to set fire to it – that really is impressive. As for the Germans, they cannot imagine life without this culture; I realized this when I was planning my 'Artwork of the Future'.[11]

Philistines who clung to a false culture – this was how Wagner saw his fellow countrymen. In 1866, in 'German Art and German Politics', he attacked the middle-class societies and social clubs that proliferated in the mid-century and which seemed to Wagner the essence of philistinism. They were ruled by a commercial ethos, a 'spirit that only cared about external effects and profits'. 'The true heir and realizer of European civilization introduces himself everywhere and also here with a bourse speculation on "Germanness" and "German solidity".' Only the army was exempt from the general sickening air of commercialism: 'Thank God that here at least something is still obeying the laws of rhythm, and that not everything has degenerated into sack coats, cigars, and beards (as Schopenhauer puts it)!'[12]

The events of 1871 and 1873 fanned an already powerful hatred. The stock exchange scandal centred around Strousberg's manipulation of railway stock perfectly incarnated the morals of the new Germany:

It has come to the attention of many wise people that the tremendous successes freshly won by German policy have not in the slightest diverted Germans from a stupid imitation of foreign things, or stimulated the development of a culture peculiar to Germans alone. Our great German statesman [Bismarck] strenuously combats the pretensions of the Roman spirit over faith and morals in church affairs. The continuing claims of the French spirit to dictate taste and morals have not been contained. If a Parisian harlot decides to give her hat a certain extravagant shape, this is enough to make all German women wear the same hat. If a lucky speculator on the bourse wins a million overnight, he commissions an architect – who is already standing ready with the plans – to build a villa in the style usual in Saint Germain.[13]

Despite these attacks, Wagner himself was caught up in the money culture of the 1870s. He wanted to build a new theatre in Bayreuth and make of the theatre and his works, which would be performed there, a national monument to rival the Walhalla or the Liberation Hall. It cost a great deal of money, not all of which could be raised by public subscription. The building of the Bayreuth theatre from 1872 cost 945,000 Marks, and the first festival of 1876 180,000. Wagner went on a hectic concert tour in an attempt to raise all this amount, but in the end needed to borrow and repay over 300,000 Marks from the Bavarian state.[14] Money problems overshadowed the festival. Wagner's old friend Herwegh presented him with a verse account of the commercialization of Wagnerism:

> You must bear all of fortune's slings,
> And learn to see, my friend,
> The one true music of the future rings
> From Krupp's orchestra in the end.[15]

By the end of the 1870s, the difficulties of funding the Bayreuth festival, the lack of support from the central government (which had simply passed Wagner's request for funds on to the Reichstag), combined with the bitterness about the alleged materialism of the Empire, turned Wagner against Bismarck as well. He was 'a bad man . . . What does a Junker of that sort know about Germany?' In 1880 Wagner asked the Great German supporter (and thus anti-Prussian) Constantin Frantz to write a polemical article against Bismarck. 'I have coincided with the most miserable time Germany has ever known, with this beastly agitator at its head.' In this mood he became bitterly prophetic: 'the downfall of a civilization is only a matter of time, like the completion of *Parsifal*'.[16]

Bayreuth and its festivals had failed to revolutionize the German people. Perhaps this meant that the future lay outside Germany altogether. Wagner began to look for a new opportunity for genuinely popular culture that North America might present: 'Like Wotan to Alberich, the Old World can say to America, "Take my heritage!"'. R.[ichard] displays a remarkable knowledge of conditions over there, and he once again expresses his great admiration for the war between the

Northern and the Southern states.'[17] He thought of settling with a colony of faithful Wagnerians in Minnesota.

The search for popular nationalism, and the attack on money and the new Empire, became also a violent doctrine of anti-semitism. In 'Jewry in Music' (1850), Wagner had already associated Jewish emancipation, the denial of nationality, and the power of money. The Jew was a perpetual foreigner: 'the Jew speaks the language of the nation in which he lives from generation to generation, but he always speaks as a foreigner'. This was why Jews could write no national music and thus no genuinely popular opera. But it was impossible to avoid the political and cultural power of Jews as long as there was Jewish emancipation; and Jewish emancipation would be successful for as long as money was the driving force of history.[18]

This pamphlet was in some ways an exception for Wagner in the 1840s. Anti-semitism had a large following in the 1840s among the radical left, who like Wagner associated Jewish emancipation with the commercialization of life. But Wagner's pamphlet represented above all an *ad hominem* attack on one man, Giacomo Meyerbeer, an immensely popular composer working in Paris, who had tried to help the young Wagner. Meyerbeer is never mentioned by name in the pamphlet, but Wagner left little doubt who 'the famous composer of operas' he mentioned again and again might be. The only Jewish composer actually mentioned by name is Mendelssohn, whom Wagner respected and tried – even in this anti-semitic work – to defend.

It was in the 1870s that Wagner's always latent and smouldering anti-semitism flamed up into a consistent doctrine: in response to German unification and to the *Gründerkrise*, as well as to the worries of Bayreuth's finances. The problem was – in Wagner's eyes – that Jews and commerce were now too deeply embedded in the structure of German society for the popular principle to be able to assert itself. Wagner's second wife, Cosima, was herself a hard-bitten anti-semite. Her diaries, however, leave little doubt about the close connections between Wagner's anti-semitic passion and his phobia of commerce: 'Not a very good night for R., but at breakfast he is lively as always, except that the subject he brings up (the regulation of the Greek border, the loan, and the agio) is a very disagreeable one – in everything nowadays, he remarks, all one can say is "Cherchez le banquier".' Reporting Wagner's thoughts she records: 'Everyone is too compromised ever to be able to speak the truth about Israel, because the bankers have now become identified with the idea of property, and everyone's head reels at the thought that he might not be able to turn himself from a poor man into a rich one.'[19]

Wagner then set about applying his revolutionary incendiarism to Jews and commerce. His reflections culminated in the suggestion that all Jews should be burnt alive at a performance of Lessing's *Nathan der Weise* – the greatest literary monument to the German Enlightenment and to Jewish emancipation.[20] Wagner assembled around him in Bayreuth a circle of anti-semites. They centred around his disciple Hans von Wolzogen, who had moved to Bayreuth in 1877 and begun a cult of obsequious devotion to 'the Master'. Their literary organ, the *Bayreuther Blätter* (published from 1878), became the organ for racist theory. Count Gobineau, the French theoretician of race, whose *Essay on the Inequality of Races* Wagner admired, published here. Later Wagner's son-in-law Houston Stewart Chamberlain used Bayreuth as the launching pad for *The Foundations of the Nineteenth Century*, a work of cultural pessimism that took up many of Wagner's themes.[21]

This Bayreuth circle spoke the language of religion and mysticism. It was a 'congregation' of 'disciples' for Wagner, the 'prophet of regeneration' – Nietzsche thought that it stank of incense and gospel. It was a small, exclusive and cantankerous group, and until the 1920s, when Wagner's daughter-in-law Winifred made Bayreuth into the cultural centre of National Socialism, it had little direct political impact. Slightly more significant were the Wagner associations, founded after 1871 in a mixture of missionary zeal and fund-raising calculation. Wolzogen gave a characteristic defence of the Wagner associations (the mixed metaphor is characteristic also) – 'the only ark that promises shelter' from 'the desert of modern materialism, which surrounds us like a flood'. By 1891 there were 8,000 members throughout Germany of the 'General Richard Wagner Association'.[22]

Friedrich Nietzsche was on the edge of Wagner's circle in the early 1870s. His critique of the Kaiserreich was more far-reaching than Wagner's, but it stemmed from exactly the same source. Indeed, Nietzsche's first political manifesto, a bitter polemic published in 1873 against the philosopher of a materialist and Darwinian religion, David Fredrich Strauss, originated in a personal demand of Wagner's. The attack on bourgeois philistinism sounded very close to that emanating from Wagner at the same period, but continued to be a major theme in Nietzsche's writing, even after his break with Wagner. It was a general criticism of modernity – but it was directed explicitly at the peculiar German version of modernity.

According to Nietzsche, the modern German bourgeoisie had no capacity for an independent culture. Everything was imitated – particularly from the French model which Nietzsche and Wagner both disliked so intensely. 1871 and military victory made no difference. Nietzsche echoed Wagner precisely here:

In the present case there can be no question of a victory of German culture, for the simple reason that French culture continues to exist as heretofore, and we are dependent upon it as heretofore . . .

. . . So it is that, compared with past ages, we dwell even today in a carelessly inaccurate copy of French convention: a fact to which all our comings and goings, conversations, clothing and habitations bear witness . . . Take a stroll through a German city – compared with the distinct national qualities displayed in foreign cities, all the conventions here are negative ones, everything here is colourless, worn out, badly copied, negligent, everyone does as he likes, but what he likes is never forceful and well considered but follows the rules laid down first by universal haste, then by the universal rage for ease and comfort.[23]

The result was that in the 1870s national culture ('our lively participation in the construction of the German state', Nietzsche said ironically) meant visits to zoos, conversation in public houses, and a ritual promenade at public exhibitions and galleries. It required nothing more than a watered-down carpet-slipper heroism. 'Art', he quoted the philosopher Eduard von Hartmann as saying, 'is that which perhaps offers entertainment to the Berlin businessman of an evening.' When this wholly artificial culture made historical references, as it often did, the effect was destructive because the historicizing operated gregariously and indiscriminately: 'the Straussian philistine lodges in the works of our great poets and composers like a worm which lives by destroying, admires by consuming, reveres by digesting'.[24]

Nietzsche knew that his antidote to the German poison was hopelessly escapist: Germans should, he believed, be less self-conscious about constructing a new national culture and should instead look back to the Greeks. The Greek superiority lay in their absence of a conscious desire to construct anything: not a society, nor a culture, nor a nation. It just happened.

Later, Nietzsche developed his critique of the Kaiserreich's 'bourgeois philistinism' to encompass Wagner as well. From 1876 relations between Wagner and Nietzsche cooled, though the final break probably occurred as late as 1882. From this moment Nietzsche attacked everything in Wagner, including his anti-semitism. Wagner, nothing more than a Wotan in carpet slippers, was the epitome of the bourgeois and bogus heroism of modern Germany. 'Through Wagner modernity speaks her most ultimate language: it conceals neither its good nor its evil; it has thrown off all shame.' Wagner, like the Kaiserreich, was imitative and derivative: first from the French, then from the Catholic church. 'To everyone familiar with the movement of European culture, this fact however is certain, that French romanticism and Richard Wagner are most intimately related.' And then the final attack – that Wagner had broken down and fallen on his knees before the cross of Christ. 'Is this the German way? . . . What yonder lives is Rome, Rome's faith sung without words.'[25]

Nietzsche's attack on the modern world lacked any systematic political element. No one would now seriously claim that he was the progenitor of totalitarianism, or Hitlerism. His reflections on Greek politics run in a clearly opposite direction. Yet by the 1910s a political interpretation of Nietzsche had become commonplace. For both Thomas Mann and Werner Sombart, for instance, Nietzsche stood for a truly German synthesis of Weimar and Potsdam, culture and military heroism. The emergence of the political interpretation of the philosopher is usually blamed on his completely appalling sister Elisabeth Förster-Nietzsche. She married one of Germany's leading political anti-semites (Bernhard Förster) and set out to turn her brother into a major figure of German life.

This is not a completely satisfying interpretation of the genesis of the Nietzsche myth. On the one hand, no number of wicked or unpleasant sisters could have turned, say, Karl Marx or John Stuart Mill into the spiritual father of Nazism. Nor can it really be said on the other hand that Nietzsche deserved Elisabeth as his evangelist in the same way that Wagner deserved Cosima. The explanation lies in political history. Nietzsche's final madness (January 1889) occurred at a crucial moment for Germany: a time when ideas were, so to speak, thrown into the fairground kaleidoscope of popular politics.

Nietzsche received little attention during his mentally active lifetime. Only after 1890 did he appear as a major influence on Germany, and became aligned with Paul de Lagarde's expansionist nationalism and onslaught on liberalism, as well as with Julius Langbehn, whose bestselling *Rembrandt the Educator* was published anonymously in the year 1890.

Why this success in 1890? Langbehn's book was scarcely so profound as to provoke a major turning in the development of German culture. The thesis that art depended on a proximity to the people and that it was superior to materialist science, the coupling of this thesis with anti-semitism, the appeal for a secret hero to rescue Germany from her present danger – these were not original thoughts. Wagner's prose writings from 1848 to 1850 might just as well have triggered off a similar popular enthusiasm, but in reality they had not done so.

It may have been the end of Bismarck's Chancellorship (1890): the dominating political figure for three decades had suddenly disappeared and left a vacuum at the centre of the Empire. Or the accession of a young Emperor in 1888, who was egocentric, romantic and irresponsible, and whose vanity made the business of day-to-day politics more difficult. But these are not sufficient reasons for the emergence of a popular anti-modernism. The politics of the Caprivi period brought about a fundamental change. It was then that on the one hand the anchoring of conservative politics in economic interests became secure, and on the other hand that the conservatives realized that social change, and 'economic interests', had hurt a number of people who might usefully become their political allies.

Anti-semitism and racial theory provided one of the bridges between the anti-modernism of a Wagner and the grass-roots reaction. Popular anti-semitism and pogroms had long been a feature of both urban and rural life in periods of economic difficulty. Pogroms had not stopped with the Middle Ages. During the French revolutionary wars, the Rhineland brigand Schinderhannes had beaten and robbed Jews and Frenchmen, and won a substantial following among the Rhenish peasantry in consequence. In 1819, after a series of harvest failures had driven up food prices, Jews were attacked. In 1830 mobs converged on the Jews of Hamburg and Frankfurt.[26] Equally, there had been a long-standing tradition of aristocratic disdain for the Jews and for commerce. Bismarck was anti-semitic, but only occasionally and only in this limited sense.

The rise of populist anti-semitism in the late 1870s and 1880s as a consequence of petty bourgeois resentment was a Europe-wide phenomenon. But even the leaders of essentially lower-middle-class or popular movements depended on a respectable 'argument' on which they might hang their emotional feelings of otherness or their desire to manipulate public opinion. They could validate their views by referring to a Treitschke or a Wagner.

The collapse of 1873, the ruin of many people who had speculated in stock and the agrarian depression of the later 1870s left a legacy of bitterness and resentment. Otto Glagau's highly influential articles in the middle-brow periodical *Gartenlaube* (later published as a separate pamphlet) ran under the title 'The Social Question is the Jewish Question'. He began with the stock exchange, and ended by blaming the Jews on the grounds that – as he claimed – 90 per cent of all the *Gründer*, the stock speculators of the early 1870s, were Jews. Pathological individuals recognized a fertile field for anti-semitic appeals, since the subject had been largely left aside by the existing political movements and parties. Typical of this sort of personality are Otto Böckel, a university librarian who collected folk songs and tales, and Hermann

Ahlwardt, a dismissed primary school head teacher. They sought in the first place to mobilize hatred. Max Liebermann von Sonnenberg, who founded the anti-semitic Deutsche Volksverein, did not care about any broader programme or indeed any rationale other than simply a violent dislike. 'First we want to become a political power,' he said, 'then we shall seek the scientific evidence for anti-Semitism.'[27]

Other figures had a more grandiose political vision to which they gradually realized they could only attract support through a use of anti-semitic language: such was the case of Adolf Stöcker, the Lutheran court preacher in Berlin. At first he had tried to bring working-class people into a Christian Social Workers' Party (founded 1878), but found little response until he spoke to a different audience: to the vulnerable lower middle class of Berlin, the small shopkeepers and artisans. As he did this, he made anti-semitism a more and more central part of his programme.

On the one hand anti-semites through conviction; on the other anti-semites through calculation. The result was the development in the 1880s of a multiplicity of small anti-semitic parties: the Antisemitische Deutschsoziale Partei, the Antisemitische Volkspartei, the Deutsche Volksverein, the Deutschsoziale Reformpartei, the Soziale Reichspartei. They presented – usually, but not always, to a rural electorate – a quite traditional picture of the Jew as exploiter. In the early 1890s, during the turmoil of the Caprivi period, Prussian landowners believed that they had been betrayed by the government and that they should turn to a wider farming community for support. As a consequence of these calculations, in an attempt to widen their party's appeal, the German conservatives adopted at a meeting in 1892 in the Tivoli Hall in Berlin a programme with an explicit anti-semitic element: 'We combat the widely obtruding and decomposing Jewish influence on our popular life. We demand a Christian authority for the Christian people and Christian teachers for Christian pupils.'[28] The conservative adoption of anti-semitism, which remained a hallmark of the party throughout its future existence, was probably the most striking example of the use of anti-semitism in political manipulation.

However, anti-semitism was not just a rural phenomenon, espoused by peasants dissatisfied with falling grain and livestock prices and inclined to blame Jewish middlemen and traders for a market that appeared to be working against them. The conservatives would have found it hard to stage at Tivoli such a nakedly cynical political manipulation. They drew comfort from the intellectual popularity and respectability of anti-semitic arguments: among university students, and among teachers. They remembered the claim made by Treitschke in the

Preussische Jahrbücher in 1879–80, as well as his emotive slogan: 'Right into the most educated circles, among men who would reject with disgust any thought of ecclesiastical intolerance or national pride, we can hear, as if from one mouth, "The Jews are our misfortune".'[29]

In this way, the *Gründerkrise* and the Caprivi era left a long-term legacy that outlasted memories of the crisis itself: an alliance between national assertion, intellectual rejection of a materialist order, anti-semitism and popular politics. After the turn of the century, this alliance moulded a new youth movement, which called for a return to the simple natural life. The Wandervögel (literally 'birds of migration') developed from a group of schoolboys from Steglitz who in 1899 went for a long summer walk through Bohemia. They rejected conventional values and the traditional hierarchy and authoritarianism of Wilhelmine Germany in favour of outdoor life and companionship. They poured contempt on dusty academic life and regimented schools and on the beer culture of the tavern. They pledged themselves to abstention from tobacco and alcohol, and to a life of moral purity. Some of the leaders of the movement were highly critical, in the Nietzschean manner, of official patriotism. But at the same time they elevated the old notion of a practical embodiment of a popular community. In this way they offered to conservative politicians a chance to manipulate national symbols and desires for community. The Kaiser saw the opportunities in this new mood. A healthy outdoor phrase went the rounds to describe the feeling of awakening: the nationalists believed that 'they sniffed the air of morning'.

The reasons for the growth of political anti-semitism, and also of the youth movement (which was sometimes but not necessarily or always anti-semitic), in the last decades of the nineteenth century and at the beginning of the twentieth can be understood as follows: an intellectual uncertainty about national identity; an increase in uncertainty when there are powerful fluctuations on housing, farming, money or stock markets; and a definition of national identity against an 'enemy' associated with market operations. The 1870s were the first instance in which this matrix of forces and calculations operated; and they left a longer-term legacy which might be reinforced by subsequent crises.

Greater Germany and Mitteleuropa

Economic reasoning directly produced the other criticism of the Wilhelmine state. What had become a characteristically German way of viewing national identity now was extrapolated into a doctrine about the political shape of the whole world.

The inexorable economic laws of the late nineteenth century, so the argument ran, led away from the nation-state. The search for markets and raw materials meant a continual widening of the economic world. Moreover, economies of scale provided such advantages in the competition for markets that only the biggest units could survive. The world would be carved up into three or four large empires.

A precise analogy existed between nations struggling with each other for power and firms in competition. In the three decades before 1914, cartellization and the formation of large vertical 'concerns' had eliminated many of the medium-sized firms in Germany. Would not the same process occur at the level of international politics?

Germany had, however, suffered the disadvantages of a late start in this race. Her economic growth had begun later than that of Britain or France. Only in the 1880s had she begun to acquire colonies. One of the conclusions resulting from this argument was that colonial imperialism should be pushed farther and harder. Germany also needed to form a larger territorial unit in Europe, and to expand her frontiers in conformity with the dictates of economic geography rather than according to the quirks of linguistic identities. She should form the basis of a new Central Europe (Mitteleuropa). In the west, Germany's frontiers should reach to the Belgian Channel ports; in the east, an informal hegemony would cover the Habsburg and Ottoman empires (or the successors of these empires).

Expansion outside Europe risked conflict with France and Britain. Everyone knew this. Indeed, one explanation of Bismarck's brief colonial venture in the mid-1880s is the cynical one that he wanted to create an obstacle to the rapprochement with Britain that he knew the Crown Prince (Frederick) would wish to pursue once he succeeded to the throne. In this way Bismarck could stymie Frederick politically. On the other hand expansion in Europe risked a clash with Russia.

That these politics – European growth or extra-European empire – were alternatives has been seen very definitely by most subsequent historians, as well as by some clear-sighted contemporary figures. Caprivi was certainly one of these, and believed that since Germany could not afford world policy she should concentrate on building up her European strength. Bismarck had never found a use for a doctrine such as Caprivi's, and in the 1890s among German politicians there were many would-be Bismarcks who could not see why they should either. The political public wanted something grander; as (Naval) Captain von Müller wrote in 1896 in a memorandum to the King's brother: 'Caprivi's policy, now so widely ridiculed, would have been brilliantly vindicated by history if the German people were not coming to accept an entirely different opinion of their ability and duty to expand than that expressed in our naval and colonial development so far.'[30]

After all, economic logic pointed in both directions, at world policy and at a bigger place in Europe; and there existed a long German tradition of following where economic logic dictated. Colonialism overseas and Mitteleuropa in Europe were not necessarily conflicting but might be complementary: organizations such as the Pan-German League propagandized for both. From 1896 the German government also took this position. Germany embarked on *Weltpolitik* – colonial demands, naval construction – without renouncing Mitteleuropa. There was a pleasing deduction that the country in the middle (Mittelland) should want to be both Mitteleuropa and in control of Mittelafrika simultaneously.

The theory of world states was put forward by a group of highly influential historians: Hans Delbrück, Max Lenz, Erich Marcks, Otto Hintze, Hermann Oncken. They presented moral reasons as well as an economic rationale. Colonialism would create a new and better breed of Germans. Thus Hans Delbrück:

> How much it would do to get rid of the old-style petty bourgeois mentality, of the *Spiesser* [self-satisfied and philistine] quality which still clings to Germanness, if a part of our people went as a master race among the wide area populated by the tribes of black Africa and then returned to Germany . . . The health of the much-criticized present generation of our people is revealed by the powerful social drive from bottom to top.[31]

The theory originated, however, in economic rather than social or moral concerns. Gustav Schmoller gave a very clear formulation in 1891:

> Anyone far sighted enough to realise that the history of the twentieth century will be shaped by the competition between the Russian, British, American and perhaps also the Chinese world empires and by their aspirations to make all other, smaller states dependent on them will also see in a central European customs association the nucleus that will save from destruction not only the political independence of these states but also the superior and ancient culture of Europe.[32]

German commercial interests backed the theories of Mitteleuropa and the world states, though business pressure in particular instances was less important than the vague belief among non-businessmen that economic interests required military action. The steel and engineering firm Gebrüder Mannesmann wanted to obtain Moroccan ores, and between 1909 and 1911 contributed to the outbreak of the second Moroccan crisis. But the larger steel firms Krupp and Thyssen had already worked out a deal with French business and wanted to pacify the situation rather than whip up a nationalist storm. The Deutsche Bank financed the Baghdad railway construction, but found it difficult to raise the enormous sums required and needed constant encouragement from the Foreign Office. Both the Deutsche Bank and its rival the Disconto-Gesellschaft tried to block the issuing in Germany of a Bulgarian loan in 1914, though the German government wanted this loan for political reasons.[33]

After 1914, business became much more active. It tried to participate in the drawing-up of a programme for colonies and for Mitteleuropa. The Saar steel industrialist Hermann Röchling in September 1914 drew up a memorandum about the annexation from France of Longwy, Briey, Belfort and part of the Vosges.

These suggestions provided the basis for the extensive set of annexations proposed in Reich Chancellor Theobald von Bethmann Hollweg's September memorandum of 1914: Germany would annex Longwy-Briey and impose a trade treaty that would make France dependent on Germany. Liège and Verviers would be taken from Belgium, and the rump turned into a satellite state. A central European customs association would include France, Belgium, the Netherlands, Denmark, Austria-Hungary, Poland and perhaps Italy, Sweden and Norway as well – all under German leadership. Finally, Germany should carve out a colonial empire in central Africa.[34]

One of the most compelling explanations of how Mitteleuropa should develop was provided in 1915 by Friedrich Naumann, an ex-pastor and a follower of Stöcker's social theory of class harmony who had broken with the court preacher because of the latter's anti-semitism. Nations, and the way in which they had established their legitimacy, belonged to the past. Naumann rejected the cultural components of political identity. That the new world-size units had no political or cultural tradition was irrelevant: 'Central Europe is at the present time a geographical expression which has so far acquired no political or constitutional character. But Austria, too, was once merely a geographical expression, and Prussia was a provincial term denoting only the most eastern portion of the kingdom.'[35] Mitteleuropa could establish itself by becoming a giant collectivist welfare state that would supersede individual *laissez-faire* capitalism. Here, Naumann introduced a notion of stages of development. Just as there existed in history a progression from family to tribe to nation to super-nation, there was a movement from mercantilism to *laissez-faire* market principles to a universal social discipline: 'We were hardly aware that we desired all this in reality: this disciplined work of the second period of capitalism, which may be described as the transition from private capitalism to socialism, if the word socialism is not applied solely to a proletarian vision of great businesses, but is understood, broadly, as an ordering of the nation for the increase of the joint product of each for all.'[36]

In this process, Germany had led the way. The creation of the Empire in 1871 had set in motion a long and historically inevitable process: 'The German Empire, which is generally regarded abroad as a purely military state, is at least equally an economic state, and has been from the very beginning. The two characteristics mutually permeate it and give to the whole its firm stability.' In North Germany, a 'new German type', rational, calculating and ascetic, had emerged. This type was 'incomprehensible to the individualist nations, to whom he appears partly as a relapse into past times of constraint, partly as an artificial product of coercion'. The SPD and its marxist economic theory perfectly embodied for Naumann the rational economic orientation of the modern German: 'This living national machine goes its way whether the individual lives or dies, it is impersonal or super-personal, has its frictions and interruptions, but is as a whole something that has never come to pass exactly in this way before: it is the historically developed German national character.'[37]

In future, economic logic alone would dictate the shape of the nation. 'The Austrians and Hungarians have already had a share in our life for economically they are of our race, even those who speak a different language.' Germany's role would be to teach everyone in the vast area of the future Mitteleuropa a psychological lesson in abstention, collective organization and the Protestant work ethic. 'We must speed up those who are lingering in the old habits of work, so that they approximate to the labour rhythm of the progressive.'

Interest groups – trade unions, craft workers, business pressure groups – would be the fundamental element in political life. Language, the hallmark of the now discredited nationalism of the nineteenth century, played little role. 'The union of the central European states will soften all language disputes and will force them into the background by means of new work, new aims, and new successes shared in common. We hope that no Pole in Prussia and no German in the Banat will in future have unnecessary language difficulties.' Naumann gave a picture of a future utopia in which a Czech official in Prague would greet a German visitor at the Mid-European Economic Commission: all languages were used, 'and besides, what the people who come to us do outside in politics does not concern us, for we represent here nothing but economic ideas. But it seems to me that this itself has a soothing effect politically.'[38]

Naumann, of course, was writing during the First World War; and the wartime economy in Germany, and the increasing political and economic dependence of Austria on Germany, gave a foretaste of the corporatist state socialism he held to be inevitable for the future. The most distinguished exponent of this view, Walther Rathenau, had a hand in organizing this future himself.

Rathenau was the son of the founder of one of Germany's biggest electrical concerns, AEG, and in 1912 succeeded his father as Chairman. In the first year of war, he moved into government, and with the help of a staff largely drawn from AEG created in the War Ministry a War Raw Materials Department.[39] This was a compromise between a market economy which had failed to deal with the problems of wartime supply and a completely bureaucratically centralized administrative system. Private companies owned and run by the firms consuming raw materials directed the supply and allocation, and set priorities.

Rathenau saw in this voluntary collectivism a way out of the dilemmas posed by the relation of economic activity to national identity. Throughout his life, he had been haunted by the wish to identify the meaning of Germanness and by a wish to belong. Partly this longing came from his background: he exemplifies the problems and the wishes of the emancipated Jew in Germany at the beginning of the twentieth century. His parents had been non-observant Jews, and Rathenau described himself as a 'German of the Jewish tribe'.[40]

The issue of nation and the social problem, he believed, had to be solved at the same time. The Bismarckian Empire had been a remarkable achievement, but since then there had been no advance. Rathenau made an interesting commercial analogy:

> Germany was like a businessman to whom someone had paid a lot of money for his business. The fear of losing some of it now prevents him from taking up something new. After living a fairly miserable, rather adventurous but hopeful life up to 1870, he woke up as a well-to-do, satisfied bourgeois . . . German policy has remained defensive since Bismarck's departure. We have not concluded a single effective business deal of our own, and, what is more serious, have not once found a larger, more satisfying aim for our politics.[41]

That aim should be a new egalitarianism. National unity could not tolerate wide disparities in wealth, and a future development would only be possible on the basis of extensive redistribution, a reduction of luxury consumption, and the planned direction of investment. This programme became a vital necessity during the war, because of the enormous sacrifices required of German citizens. 'The trenches', Rathenau wrote in his notes for 1917, 'cannot be paid for with a deterioration of the standard of living.'[42] These views he expounded most systematically in a long essay published in 1917, *On Coming Things*.

The prewar Empire had been at the same time too materialist and insufficiently entrepreneurial or creative. Some of Rathenau's criticisms of 'the arrogance of material life' sound like Nietzsche. The Germans had been excessively imitative: 'In all of the arts and sciences, in personal, social and state life there is scarcely a basic form that comes from our homeland. The forms of building and style, of furniture, pictures, music, novels, drama, of the army, religion, mercantile, commercial and industrial operations, joint stock companies, and constitutions – we let others develop all these models, which still today have foreign names.' Germany had fallen prey to the commercial spirit. Germany was 'living in an intoxication of consumption and enjoyment'. Political life had atrophied because it was dominated by economic interests: 'the parties were only organizations for a particular purpose – to lower or raise certain customs, tax or wage rates, to maintain or destroy certain privileges, to benefit or disadvantage certain groups or persons.'

Germany, the land of the philistine, had become dominated by two symbols of mindless materialism: the beerhouse and the garden gnome. 'Whoever has praised in the tavern the incomparable height of our era of civilization should look on their way home in the shop windows and see that our culture excites strange desires. Whoever sees a lawn spoiled by the stupid forms of clay garden dwarfs or rabbits or toadstools, should recognize in this the emblem of our misdirected economy.'[43]

It was this world that had produced narrow economic nationalism; but the logic of production and development swept in a different direction. 'Rational views' could lead to a supra-national system. 'Great national economic areas will join together in customs unions.' These larger units would allocate investment resources in an appropriate way, and this would be even more urgent in the light of Europe's certain postwar impoverishment. Rathenau as a result felt very happy to work on plans for Mitteleuropa. In December 1913, he had written that the best way to preserve peace and 'reduce the nationalistic hatred of the states' was a Central European customs union. After the outbreak of war, he wanted to include France as well.[44]

Rathenau was a liberal, humane, and internationally minded man, a friend of many artists and writers, who managed to synthesize the two strands of thought examined in this chapter: the cultural critique of materialism, and the desire for bigger and better economic units. Like Naumann, he had welded liberal and social reform and imperialism into a new theory of supra-nationalism.

On the right, figures such as the Pan-German leader Heinrich Class, or the Krupp director Alfred Hugenberg, or Admiral Tirpitz himself (who organized a 'Patriotic Party' in 1917), used similar arguments. There was the same attack on 'English' materialism (most forcefully set out in Werner Sombart's *Heroes and Traders* of 1915); the same cultural pessimism; and the same insistence on the need to expand. Only the conclusion was different: that social reform was part of the 'English disease', and that effective and assertive imperialism made such harmful measures unnecessary.

Both liberal and conservative versions contained enormous ambiguities: they insisted that the German state was too modern and also that it was simultaneously insufficiently modern. But both produced a rejection of affairs as they stood in 1914, and created instead a utopian vision based on the extrapolation of trends believed to be visible in the present. Both constituted a recognition and an affirmation of the incompleteness of the 1871 state.

These contradictory sentiments combined to make the Kaiserreich's policies explosive. The origins of the Great War of 1914 lay back with the aggressive *Weltpolitik* of the 1890s. After 1911, German policy-makers took ever wilder risks in defence of an international position they believed to be weakening all the time. At the same time the external constraints on Germany increased as Britain, France and Russia saw an expansionist power, determined to humiliate Russia, subdue France and supplant England. The calculations behind German policy reflected the simultaneous beliefs that the existing Germany was too small, that she would be crowded out on the international stage unless she took dramatic action, that she was not yet a real nation, and also that a truly popular mobilization, a rallying to the colours, might create a new unity and transcend the material barriers separating the inhabitants of Imperial Germany. A world-weary realist such as Chancellor Theobald von Bethmann Hollweg found the same release in intensifying and bringing to a breaking-point the diplomatic crisis of July 1914 as did the apostles of the Wandervögel and the 'Young Germany' in experiencing it. At once a very complex and intricate diplomatic position and a tortured quest for identity could appear starkly simple. There was a war to complete the incomplete nation. Few summed up this ecstatic exuberance better than did General von Falkenhayn, who in 1914 became Chief of the General Staff: 'Even if it ends in ruin, it was beautiful.'

5

The Weimar Republic: The Economic Nation and the Great Power

Tragically, the illusions and hopes of 1914 shaped the course of German history for long after the military defeat of 1918. This chapter seeks to show how they sealed the fate of the Weimar Republic. On the one hand there were the illusions: that Germany might be a Great Power, shaping the course of world events, or that she might have a large colonial empire. On the other hand, the hopes: for more justice, and for a democratic transformation of society. Inevitably, these conceptions would clash.

After 1918, democracy and nationalism stood as opposites. In popular parlance, 'national' meant right-wing and anti-democratic. Neither nationalists nor democrats could build any consensus about national life. Nationalists believed that democrats were traitors, while the democratic politicians held nationalists to be unrealistic or manipulative hankerers after a past that had vanished.

While the right engaged in obstruction and elevated the concept of the nation at the expense of the Republic, the democratic parties attempted to build a new alternative Germany, but often adopted nationalist stances in usually unsuccessful bids to gain lasting political support. In other words, the nationalist right successfully set much of Weimar Germany's political tone with a call for a return to Great Power politics. That right did not, however, want to compromise itself by taking responsibility for the inevitably weak position of Weimar in international affairs – for a state which could not be a Great Power. All this was a legacy of the lost war.

The gap between nationalist dreams and imaginings and political reality was far greater than it had been in the Kaiserreich. On the one

111

hand, those nationalist yearnings had been excited by the war, which had seemed to promise everything to Germans. Fighting drove up German expectations. On the other hand, all these hopes had been dashed in 1918. Republican reality meant the frustration of the Kaiserreich's aspirations.

Nationalism offered a powerful instrument to those who wished to destroy the Republic. It pointed out everything the Republic could not be: a culturally homogeneous state; a prospering economy; a Great Power in the international arena. More generally, the nationalists asserted that the Republic born out of military defeat could never reflect the true feelings of the German *Volk*. The concerns and interests of the true nation had been cast out. A very similar distinction had been made in nineteenth-century France between the *pays légal* (France's formal institutions) and the *pays réel* (the true France). The people had a 'higher reality' than paper institutions. In 1920s Germany, the right believed that the constitution and the *Volk* were at odds with each other. When the novelist Hans Fallada depicted a peasant protest against the Republic, he showed the demonstrators singing the German national anthem, the 'Deutschlandlied' of Hoffmann von Fallersleben.

Republicans reacted by attempting to create their own national symbolism, a republican one. They did their best to bring Germany back to Great Power status, and at the same time they attempted to generate sufficient prosperity to satisfy the diverse political constituents of the German state. This produced what was to be one of Weimar's most intractable problems: the interpretation of politics and national interest in terms of particular interests. Of course, this too was one of the Kaiserreich's many destructive legacies for the new state.

In the right circumstances, clashing interests could be combined and reconciled. The right circumstances meant above all a reasonable rate of economic growth: at the least the 2.7 per cent achieved by the Kaiserreich.[1] But this the Weimar Republic did not have, and economic upheavals made the reconciliation of interests much harder: the traumatic postwar inflation to 1923; a currency stabilization associated with recession and high unemployment in 1923–4; a new recession in 1925; prosperity until 1929; and then deep depression. On the foundation of the attitudes that had already crystallized before 1914, and that have been examined in Chapter IV, a reaction set in. An aggressively nationalist movement set out a doctrine which claimed to transcend class and material divisions. Weimar seems a perfect illustration of how the 'economic idea of the nation' is destroyed once the economy stumbles.

The Great Power status presented Weimar policy-makers with problems that were just as great. Germany might repeat the experience of 1815 and struggle against an international system which limited Germans' capacity to realize their nationality. The Congress of Vienna had left Germany divided and politically fragmented. The system created in 1919 at Versailles was intended to put constraints on German action. Ever since the appearance in 1919 of the British economist John Maynard Keynes's *Economic Consequences of the Peace*, there has been a debate as to whether the Versailles treaty was too harsh or too mild. Since the failure of Weimar, many analysts have reached the common-sense conclusion that the peace treaty contributed to the collapse of democracy. Versailles, they argue, should either have been so severe as to cripple Germany for ever and destroy any capacity to be an aggressor, or so lenient as to make Germany feel a confident and happy member of a democratic society of nations. Given the political situation in France and Belgium, and also the extent to which in Germany a radical nationalism dissatisfied even with Germany's frontiers of 1914 outlasted the First World War, the second of these options was always unreal. The first option, however, is not the only solution that might have preserved a stable order in Europe of the 1920s and 1930s. Versailles actually stabilized politics because it was a harsh treaty – though not excessively harsh – that could be dismantled step by step if the defeated Germany showed a political will to cooperate. It provided a focus for German grievances. In order to satisfy, or attempt to appease, the nationalist right, Weimar regimes confronted the international order, and tried to chip away at it.

Governments faced a dilemma: the limited sovereignty they possessed under the Versailles system offered them a convenient explanation of economic failures. Germany was suffering because of the Allies. If, however, governments wanted to show that they had command over the situation (and most governments like to give this impression), it became less easy to argue that everything bad in Germany resulted from the government's lack of real authority.

An additional problem was that the difficulties of economic stagnation and foreign political weakness confronted Weimar with especial force because this was a political system vulnerable and highly responsive to pressures. Pressure groups from business, agrarian leagues and labour unions all saw it as their mission to alter government policy by sponsoring Reichstag deputies, paying money to political parties, lobbying, and controlling appointments in the ministries. Lobbyists had already played a prominent role under the Empire; and as the autocracy yielded to a republic, the possibilities for their activities grew.

The Republic was a highly developed constitutional state, with a near-perfect proportional representation system whereby the number of parliamentary seats reflected not only the share but also the quantity of votes. Its President was chosen by the whole electorate, and a second chamber composed of representatives from the federal states (*Länder*) completed the legislative picture. The central state was rather stronger in relation to the *Länder* than the Kaiserreich had been. It had more extensive powers of taxation, and in theory it controlled the army (the Prussian army disappeared). But above all, the function of the central state lay – as was the case with the Kaiserreich – in the problematic task of representing Germany to the outside.

Did Weimar eventually fail because it was too constitutional and thus because it articulated too perfectly the conflicting aspirations of its citizens? Did the institutional regulation of too much conflict lay Weimar open to the charge that it could never adequately represent 'the nation'? Or did Weimar fail because it stood at variance with a traditional type of political culture that so gripped the still influential Wilhelmine elites that they found that they could not work within the system of compromises required by Weimar's constitution and by the practical politics of Weimar? Or because of the hostile foreign political environment? Or simply because of the chance event of the unexpectedly severe economic crisis at the beginning of the 1930s? All these arguments have been put forward by contemporary commentators and by subsequent historians either as single explanations of Weimar's collapse, or in clusters.

Improvised Democracy[2]

The creation of democracy and the collapse of the Empire occurred with great rapidity in 1918–19. The transformation was set in motion by the grim military figures of Field Marshal Paul von Hindenburg and General Erich Ludendorff, who since 1916 had dominated the Imperial government. They presided over a military defeat which came so suddenly as to take many Germans by surprise. The balance of advantage had tilted against Germany and her allies from the moment in 1917 when the military leadership insisted on an unconditional submarine warfare and thus in April brought the United States into the war; but the folly of the German action did not appear immediately to everyone. German armies still fought well. Indeed, as the Russian Revolution and the collapse of the Russian armies affected fighting on the Eastern Front, the German troops moved forward and imposed in March 1918 a brutally annexationist peace at Brest Litovsk. Though the peace treaty included a provision that no indemnities should be paid, in August a supplementary treaty obliged Russia to pay a sum of six billion Marks in gold and goods.

In the east, Germany had clearly won a war and been able to impose a Carthaginian peace.

On 21 March 1918, German armies went on an offensive in the west as well; though by July the series of German attacks had petered out, and on 18 July an Allied advance started with the counter-offensive at Villers-Cotterêts. By August, the German armies had clearly suffered their first major defeat on the Western Front, and in September Ludendorff called for an armistice and for constitutional reform. By 9 November, Hindenburg had come to the conclusion that the Kaiser should abdicate, though he tried to keep himself out of delivering this brutally disloyal message to his sovereign.

Until August 1918, almost no one had contemplated the possibility of defeat: in most German imaginations, the worst that could happen would be a continuance of the long stalemate and then a negotiated peace without annexations or indemnities. The war had been financed in the optimistic belief that high rates of taxation would not really be necessary. Instead the government borrowed on the assumption that its loans could be repaid by giant indemnities imposed on the hostile powers. Karl Helfferich, Secretary of the Treasury and then of the Interior, talked about the 'lead weights of the milliards' which Germany would hang round the necks of her enemies. When it came to the issue of Germany's paying for the war, Brest Litovsk, with its cession by Russia of over a million square kilometres, and the auxiliary treaty of August, had made an appropriate beginning.

Military events raised the question of constitutional change within Germany. As the war stagnated and as food supplies in Germany collapsed, political measures were required to rebuild national consensus. In April 1917, the Kaiser's Easter message held out the possibility of altering the restrictive three-class franchise in Prussian elections. In July 1917 the Reichstag took the initiative in foreign policy for the first time in its history. The centre and left passed a resolution calling for peace without annexations. What looked at first like an assertion of parliamentary authority in the face of the claims of the military power in fact represented the product of a complicated and machiavellian struggle. The peace resolution had been preceded by negotiations between the military and key figures from the Reichstag parties – in particular Matthias Erzberger (Centre) and Gustav Stresemann (National Liberal). The resolution began in the Reichstag with a speech by Erzberger examining the difficulty of Germany's military position and the consequences of the collapse of her allies in the Balkans. Everyone assumed, rightly, that Erzberger's information came from the army. Ludendorff saw in the dissatisfaction of the Reichstag an opportunity to discredit and dismiss Chancellor Bethmann Hollweg and to replace him with a puppet in the hands of the soldiers.

At the same time as the military leadership flirted with parliament, it began to work on the use of democracy for the seduction of the people. In September 1917, Admiral Tirpitz founded the Patriotic party (Vaterlandspartei) as a more populist and less interest-specific conservative movement. Ludendorff hoped that the new party would get support from a country fired by war propaganda and galvanized by the news of the appalling war casualties. It would set a counterweight to the liberal and socialist parties, and it would support annexationist demands. At least in its membership figures, it succeeded quite dramatically: by July 1918 it had one and a quarter million members – more than the SPD had ever had.[3]

Then came the panic of 1918, when Ludendorff realized that only a constitutional state could make a peace on the basis put forward by President Wilson. The Kaiser named Prince Max of Baden as Chancellor with the goal of democratizing Germany at breakneck speed. By 9 November the Kaiser had abdicated, and Max named as his successor as Chancellor (though this was formally unconstitutional, the circumstances were after all exceptional) the socialist leader Friedrich Ebert. The navy mutinied in protest against what many sailors believed were orders to put to sea for a final suicide attack on the Western powers, and in the major German cities workers' councils began to operate.

The right and the military found it impossible to come to terms with the rapidity of change: they developed their own theory as to why the Empire had fallen. The collapse of 1918 had come not through military defeat, or military inferiority, or the commencement of Atlantic submarine warfare, but from domestic unrest. Labour unrest and major strike waves in April 1917, January 1918 and November 1918, demoralizing letters about conditions at home sent to the trenches, and widespread undernourishment and starvation, had radicalized Germans and in the end also affected the army's morale. It was much easier for German conservatives to believe that the society they lived in was fundamentally rotten than that their army had been at fault. Above all they used the legend of the *Dolchstoss*, or stab in the back, to show that *they* had not lost the war. An internal enemy had been responsible for Germany's defeat.

The *Dolchstoss* theory may even have been first enunciated by Ebert rather than by the nationalist right. Welcoming troops back to Berlin on 11 December, and attempting to raise their spirits so that they could be relied upon to fight radicals on the left, he said: 'I salute you, who return unvanquished from the field of battle.' One year after the end of the war the legend was fully in place, prompted by the meeting of a Commission of Inquiry into responsibility for the origins, continuance and brutality of the war. The old guard put on a show of bluff force. Karl Helfferich ignored the questions put to him by the commission, and instead formulated some of his own: 'Who is the cause of our ruin? I will tell you, it is Erzberger, whose name will forever be linked with the misery and shame of Germany.' He blamed the signatories of Versailles, who had betrayed the army leadership (Erzberger had been at Versailles, though his name does not appear under the peace treaty). Field Marshall von Hindenburg also appeared, and in his statement to the commission used publically for the first time the word *Dolchstoss* as a description of the revolution and the collapse of 1918.[4]

Dolchstoss became the slogan of the German right and of the reaction against Weimar politics. Hitler made much of the concept: it provides the central event in his narration of *Mein Kampf* ('My Struggle'). He describes how he received the news of revolution and defeat in a military hospital while being treated for poison gas injuries:

Would not the graves of all the hundreds of thousands open, the graves of those who with faith in the Fatherland had marched forth never to return? Would they not open and send the silent mud- and blood-covered heroes back as spirits of vengeance to the homeland which had cheated them with such mockery of the highest sacrifice which a man can make to his people in this world? Had they died for this, the soldiers of August and September 1914?[5]

At this moment, he says, he decided to enter politics.

Sovereignty and National Integrity

The Republic was created in a major social and political crisis, but also in an atmosphere of great foreign political uncertainty. During the winter of 1918–19, it was not clear what sort of institution would replace the defunct Kaiserreich – and whether a new system would be born of revolution, or imposed by the Allies. Two parallel governments in Germany were created in November 1918: on the one hand, Ebert's Council of People's Commissars (*Rat der Volksbeauftragten*), which eventually in January 1919 called elections for a National Assembly; and on the other, a Congress of Councils that looked at first like an imitation of the Russian Soviets. Ebert's regime was by no means stable. In January 1919 a communist uprising in Berlin failed and was bloodily suppressed. The two leading communists, Karl Liebknecht and Rosa

117

Luxemburg, were murdered. At the same time the elections to the National Assembly yielded a large majority for the three clearly republican and democratic parties: the SPD, the Democratic party (DDP) and the Catholic Centre. They had been the parties of opposition under the Kaiserreich. A final uncertainty was that no one at this time knew what sort of peace treaty would be concluded. From 18 January, the day before the Assembly elections, the Allied powers met for the peace conference of Paris, preparing the terms that would be presented to Germany at Versailles.

These three more or less simultaneous events – the Spartacist rising, the National Assembly elections and the Paris conference – made any outcome seem possible, at least for a while. Every value and assumption about the German situation was thrown into turmoil. For an example of the way in which a conservative German nationalist reacted to the rapidly changing world, the diaries of the novelist Thomas Mann are very revealing. He lived in Munich in 1919, through the rule of a short-lived soviet republic and through its bloody suppression. For him, the Allied threat was more important than the communist one: 'Rejection of the peace terms by Germany! Revolt against these bourgeois windbags. Let us have a national uprising now that we have been worn to shreds by the lying claptrap of that gang – and in the form of communism for all I care; a new August 1 1914! I can see myself running into the street and shouting, "Down with lying western democracy! Hurrah for Germany and Russia! Hurrah for communism!" '[6] Mann's hostility to the Western Allies is clear in these words – as is the feeling that their intervention in German affairs represented a fundamental wrong. The most essential attribute in this view of nationhood was sovereignty: Germans should be able to run their own lives.

The nation had always been seen in the light of visions of how a better society might be ordered. After all, a nation involved the binding together of different classes in a shared, and just, social organism. A political collapse such as 1918 (or 1806) represented an ideal opportunity to achieve such a reordering and to realize simultaneously the goals of nationality and justice.

But Germans had very differing perceptions of how a new society should be ordered. One of the problems that any regime would face stemmed from the resentments, and even more from the hopes, that had been building up during the war. Political consensus during the war had been built by a mortgage on the future. The misery of the hunger winters of 1916–17 and 1917–18 that had followed as a result of the Allied blockade as well as from an inadequate administration of food supplies had been compensated by a belief that a glimmer of light was shining over the German horizon. The future would be better. When the SPD supported the war effort and voted for credits for the Imperial government, and when it worked with business and army authorities in administering the labour direction provided for by the Auxiliary Patriotic Service Law of 1916, it believed that it was making immediate sacrifices in order to win eventual reforms.[7] Some of these aspirations were indeed realized in the course of 1918–19: the ending of the exclusive three-class Prussian franchise, the imposition of the eight-hour day, the achievement of freedom to conclude labour contracts. Other demands of the labour movement were not met: for a greater degree of shop-floor control, or for the nationalization of key businesses.

Labour was not alone in cultivating hopes about a new dispensation for the postwar period: farmers thought that they had been sacrificed to patriotic necessities during wartime, but should recover their position once peace broke out.[8] Peacetime businesses required a return to profitability. Rentiers fully expected their war loans to the government to be repaid. In general, the legislation passed in 1919 by the National Assembly combined offers of reform (often considerably watered-down versions of the original aspirations) with the promise of a speedy return to normalcy.

The Republic's initial stabilization occurred on the basis not only of a pact between the army and the SPD but also of a tactical alliance of labour unions and business interests: the so-called Stinnes-Legien Agreement of November 1918. Social peace required industry to accept union representation, factory councils to negotiate wages, labour contracts, an eight-hour working day and a Central Committee to allow contacts between labour and business. The Weimar constitution imposed factory councils to regulate working conditions. In return businessmen received not just support for an alternative to what they feared as Bolshevik chaos; they also had the assistance of labour representatives in putting through increases in the prices of controlled goods – especially coal. As business paid higher wages, and labour agreed to raised prices, a spiral started that fuelled Germany's damaging postwar inflation.

In fact some or all of the hopes of Germans for a better, higher-paid or more profitable postwar future were bound to be disappointed. Inflation could only bring temporary or illusory gains. In the first place, the economic realities of the postwar years frustrated optimistic aspirations. The German hopes could have been realized only if there had been an economic miracle. Instead, the war had left Germany impoverished. German agriculture had been starved of fertilizer and feed during the war, and shackled by official price controls. It would be years before the fertility levels of 1913 could be restored. While there was overcapacity in some industries (steel and also – obviously – armaments manufacture), there were bottlenecks in the civilian trades that had been shut down for the duration of the war. Financial institutions were weakened by the legacy of reckless wartime finance. These initial conditions constituted a straitjacket for Weimar.

In addition to this situation – which would have been grim even with no Treaty of Versailles – there were the 'economic consequences of the peace'. The loss of parts of Silesia (and uncertainty about the future of other parts), of Alsace-Lorraine, the Saar and parts of Schleswig contributed to the problem of shortages. For instance, Germany lost an estimated 75 per cent of her iron ore deposits. The most desperate economic problem of the immediate postwar period was the unavailability of fuel and power: a consequence of the collapse of the coal supply. Again, this was only in part due to losses of coalfields (26 per cent of prewar coal deposits). Forced deliveries also played a role, though Germany actually delivered substantially less than the amounts provided for in the Treaty. None of these reasons, however, entirely explained the dramatic fall in output from the mines still remaining in Germany: before the war, the giant Ruhr field had produced 9½ million tons a month, and in October 1918 still 8½ million; in February 1919 the figure had fallen to 5½ million.[9] This loss resulted primarily from a dramatic decline in labour morale and productivity.

The story of the proposals for socializing key sectors of the economy – one of the demands of 1918 – provides a fine illustration of the way in which the actual circumstances of the postwar economy limited Germany's freedom of action, of how new ideas about a just order collapsed and of how politicians confronted the difficulty of explaining this restriction to themselves and to the public.

In 1919 and 1920, two socialization commissions met to settle the key issue of Germany's future economic constitution. The first commission recommended the control of the coal and potash industries by Reich Councils on which consumers, employers and workers would be represented. A law of March 1919 allowed for nationalization with compensation, but did not specify which if any industries should actually be nationalized. Socialization was in fact eventually rejected partly on efficiency grounds: it was feared that the dislocation occasioned by the transfer to state ownership would lead to a productivity fall at a time when Germany could ill afford this. Germany did not have sufficient competent administrators to handle a big nationalization programme.

However, bourgeois experts and even many socialists – including the Economics Minister, Rudolf Wissell – put forward a second argument, concerned with reparations and with the limits these placed on the German room for manoeuvre. A large state-owned sector would make it easy for the Allies to threaten expropriation with the aim of extracting surpluses from the German economy.[10] There is in fact little evidence that the Allies thought along these lines, but the argument was crucial in Germany. The external framework of Weimar's founding, it was claimed, limited the domestic actions of its politicians. Germany could blame her failures on pressure from the Western powers.

At the same time, Germany fought desperately to maintain the ideas of sovereignty and national integrity. Much more significant for the political psychology of the early postwar years than the debate about socialization and reparations was the broad issue of Germany's acceptance of the peace treaty. The conflict over acceptance left a deep scar on Weimar.

When the terms were presented to the German delegation on 7 May 1919, the territorial clauses and Article 231 (the War Guilt clause) produced an immediate shock. Under the Treaty, Allied troops were to occupy the left bank of the Rhine for fifteen years. The greatly reduced German army was excluded from the left bank and from a demilitarized zone fifty kilometres deep on the right bank. Parts of Schleswig and Silesia were ceded. Poland's access to the sea required Germany to lose a 'corridor', and East Prussia was consequently cut off from the rest of Germany. The limits on sovereignty through military occupation and the national humiliation of Article 231 constituted the Carthaginian peace that the Allies intended to force Germany's government to accept.

At first, the SPD could not agree on a stance toward the Treaty. The party newspaper *Vorwärts* and the SPD Chancellor Philipp Scheidemann urged rejection. 'Which hand', Scheidemann said, 'would not wither if it laid these chains on itself and on us.'[11] Eventually, after the Allied ultimatum of 16 June, the party reluctantly agreed to signature as the only means of avoiding an Allied occupation and the threat of a dismembered Germany. The Catholic Centre party decided on rejection in straw votes, but eventually most of the party swung round behind the realistic course of acceptance. The smallest of the Weimar coalition partners, the DDP, refused to vote for the Treaty and left the cabinet. To some extent this move reflected a tactical calculation about electoral politics: the DDP feared that the large number of middle-class voters who had supported it in the January elections – partly because all the other middle-class parties had collapsed – would slip back to reviving conservative and national-liberal parties.

There was, however, more behind the DDP's action than just tactics and the knowledge that the DDP vote did not really matter, since the peace treaty would pass anyway. Hugo Preuss, a leading Democrat and the author of Weimar's constitution, believed Versailles to be an insupportable mortgage on Weimar: Weimar would forever bear the stigma of national humiliation. Friedrich Naumann argued in the same way, and another Democrat, Konrad Haussmann, even went as far as to say that a possible Allied occupation would not have such damaging effects as the shame of accepting the peace treaty.[12]

The issues of 1919 were concerned with German sovereignty. Signing the peace treaty constituted the price of keeping Germany as a single sovereign state. But in accepting responsibility for Versailles, the SPD found itself defending a constitutional, political and economic system that inevitably led to the betrayal of the hopes cherished by most of its supporters. The question that the DDP's argument raised – one that still remains an acute issue – is whether it would not have been better if the Allies had taken responsibility for the postwar situation in Germany and not crippled the new regime with such a heavy burden, both in national questions and in social issues (as happened, with considerable success for the future political stability of Germany, between 1945 and 1949).

The Symbolism of Sovereignty and Nationhood

Though Weimar's leaders repeatedly insisted on Germany's national integrity and national sovereignty, they were able to do little to create a national and republican iconography. And what they did do frequently turned out to be counterproductive. On republican coins and emblems, for instance, the old Imperial eagle was stripped of his crown and his coat of arms. The Republic's enemies said that this 'bankrupt vulture' (*Pleitegeier*) epitomized the new spiritual and material improverishment of Germany.

Weimar had rejected the old, but found it difficult to create a new political style. Though Germany had a republican form of government, the central state was still called the Empire (Reich), with a Reich Chancellor, Reich government, Reichstag (parliament), Reich postal service and so forth. Germany adopted the black, red and gold flag of the War of Liberation and 1848, but it turned out to be highly controversial: many organizations continued to use the colours of Imperial Germany, black, white and red. One government fell because of a dispute as to whether the merchant navy should be allowed to use the old colours.

The political right used violence against the republic, its symbols and its leaders. In 1920 a military coup (the Kapp putsch) drove the government out of Berlin. In 1922 the radical right tried to assassinate

Philipp Scheidemann (SPD) and in 1921 Matthias Erzberger was killed. In 1922 Walther Rathenau too became a martyr for republican politics. In Schleswig-Holstein in 1927–8 peasants responded to tax demands and to the state's bailiffs with bombs. Later in the depression, eastern farmers assembled for violent stone-throwing demonstrations against Chancellor Heinrich Brüning.

In the face of this constant threat, Weimar could have built up a positive image only if republican leaders had been willing to risk civil-war-style propaganda. They might have presented the Republic's existence as the embodiment of political and moral values under attack from other values. Republicans, however, continued to believe in an ideal that should be harmonious and free of conflict. Succeeding regimes clung to the idea of a united nation even when they faced a polarized and bitterly divided people. They attempted to avoid political confrontation and the assertion of high principle.

The tension between highly polarized politics and republican attempts to avoid polarization is evident in the handling of funerals. State funerals are often the monumental apogee of the self-presentation of modern republican states. Weimar's obsequies were always controversial and frequently led to outbursts of violence. Two of Weimar's great leaders died at the hands of the right. On 26 August 1921 Erzberger was shot dead by nationalist terrorists as a warning to the German signatories of the peace treaty. The newspapers of the right – such as the *Berliner Lokalanzeiger*, owned by Alfred Hugenberg – carried on this attack even after Erzberger's death. The last rites took place away from Berlin, in Oppenau, and were organized by the Catholic labour movement. Canon Weber gave a strictly non-political funeral oration.[13] It was the left in Berlin that demonstrated on behalf of Weimar's republican regime.

Less than a year after Erzberger's assassination Rathenau, the Republic's Foreign Minister, was killed while being driven down the Königsallee in Berlin-Grunewald on 22 June 1922. Rathenau's funeral was a major public event and began in the Reichstag building. It became a highly political occasion at which different views of Germany clashed with each other. Once more the right continued its campaign even after its victim's death. The *Deutsches Tageblatt* made the preposterous allegation that Rathenau had not been shot for political reasons, but because of affairs with women. In an angry debate in the Reichstag, Chancellor Joseph Wirth accused Helfferich and the German Nationalist party (DNVP) of inciting the assassination and concluded: 'The enemy stands on the right.' Right-wing deputies boycotted the funeral ceremony in the Reichstag. Indeed, the right refused to distance itself from the campaign of defamation against Rathenau: all that the DNVP leader Oskar Hergt would say was that he and his party opposed physical violence in politics.

Afterwards there was a political demonstration: an estimated 200,000 proclaimed their support for the Republic in a gathering in the Berlin Lustgarten. There were similar events all over Germany, sometimes ending in violence. In Darmstadt, for instance, a crowd forcibly removed the right-wing liberal Eduard Dingeldey from his house, where he had hidden in a laundry cupboard, and paraded him in front of a gallows from which hung a lifesize puppet of Rathenau's enemy Helfferich. Finally, Dingeldey was beaten up.[14]

When in 1929 Gustav Stresemann died, another large official funeral was held in the Reichstag: again – though his death had not been violent – the right was angry and offensive. The wing of the DNVP led by the radical right-wing politician Alfred Hugenberg refused to attend the Reichstag commemoration.[15]

These had been the occasions on which the centre and left had an opportunity to use the sentiments of civil war; but they were exceptional. In general, Weimar politicians wanted to stay within that consensus that they found it impossible to achieve in practice.

The closest that a Weimar political funeral came to being a genuinely national occasion was in 1925. Weimar's first President, Friedrich Ebert, died at a time when the political right had begun to accept compromises with the Republic, after part of the DNVP had voted to accept the reparations plan, and when the radical and racist (*völkisch*) right had lost a great deal of support. But it is also striking how Ebert's funeral avoided the republican and instead embraced Imperial traditions. Ebert had after all been the leader of the largest opposition party in the Kaiserreich. That oppositional element eluded his eulogists in 1925. Reich Chancellor Luther emphasized Ebert's desire to 'awaken the force of unity among the German people, irrespective of party direction': 'at the right time, he proclaimed again the song of all Germans, "Deutschland, Deutschland über alles" '. The socialist deputy and President (i.e. Speaker) of the Reichstag remembered in his speech above all 'the circumstances under which Friedrich Ebert was called by Reich Chancellor Max of Baden into the Imperial government'. Earlier, the leader of the DNVP, Schulte, had said that Ebert had 'in difficult circumstances taken the decision which at last, after many failures, had opened the road to recovery'.[16] In other words, if Ebert had been a national hero, it had to be as a hero of the right.

One of the most effective celebrations of national unity occurred when in March 1930 the last French troops left the Rhineland; though the celebrations made much of the theme of liberation, they referred little to Stresemann's foreign policy – which after all had made the evacuation possible. The Rhineland celebrations illustrated something both peculiar and at the same time very characteristic of Weimar: that the Republic could only make itself popular by echoing the right, struggling against the international political system and removing the limits and obstacles imposed upon Germany.

Foreign Political Constraints and Opportunities

In fact Weimar lived for so long not by creating a new society, and not by inventing a powerfully effective symbolism, but because of its struggle against the international order. The same debate over foreign policy and the choices open to German policy which had been fought over in 1918–19 recurred once more in 1923–4. It was conducted in very similar terms. Again there existed a catastrophic domestic situation: first inflation and then, from the summer of 1922, hyperinflation led to profound social and political disruption. Farmers complained about price controls. Savers who had bought government paper, often during the war and for patriotic reasons, faced ruin. Radical political movements increased their support. In the case of the Bavarian National Socialists and the Saxon Communists, they posed a military threat to the Republic. In Saxony a substantial Red Army ('the proletarian hundreds') had been recruited. In Bavaria, the Nazis laid plans to march on Berlin and stage a coup (Mussolini had just given an example with his march on Rome). And again there existed a foreign menace. Once more the territorial integrity of Germany stood at risk. The French occupation of the Ruhr (from January 1923) led to a danger of a separatist Rhenish state; a French plan to create a Rhineland currency independent from Berlin was a first step along this path.

Both the left-centre and the right had theories which depended on making adjustments in domestic issues as a response to the international environment. For Reich President Ebert, the stabilization of the currency and the end of the inflation required an inflow of foreign loans. But Germany could not expect to get these without first making certain essential changes: the imposition of effective central (Reich) taxes for the first time, and a reduction in the size of Germany's swollen civil service. These measures would be highly unpopular domestically – but they could be explained by reference to the foreign political situation. In other words, the supposed pressure on the part of the Western powers gave to the German government a certain leverage to deal with urgent domestic problems. Such problems resulted from the war and would have existed even had there been no reparations, no Versailles and no potential foreign creditors.

Big business and the German right had a different reform programme for which again they wanted to use the Allied presence and threat. They bitterly resented many of the elements of the social compromise that they had been forced to accept in 1918–19 as a substitute for the much more sweeping changes demanded by the revolutionary movement.[17] The eight-hour day, price control through the Reich Coal Council, factory councils, wage contracts – these represented an uncomfortable limitation on entrepreneurial action, to which business was not accustomed and which it tried to remove. One way opened up during the discussions of 1922–3 on how the hyperinflation could be ended. A stabilization package would, all parties felt, set in a definitive way the framework within which the future politics of industrial relations could move. Could not the Allies be induced to demand – as part of their price for collaboration in German stabilization – an end to the experiment in German welfarism? The steel magnate Hugo Stinnes presented the argument in this way: foreigners should be made to see that what he called the 'socialist economy' was damaging Germany's ability to export in order to pay reparations. They would then react with outrage and insist on the dismantling of the eight-hour day and of the factory councils. Then they, rather than the German right or German business, which was still rather weak and lacked the self-confidence to impose a big domestic political package, would take the blame for ending a promising social experiment.

The settlement of 1923–4 was something of a compromise between the plans of Ebert and the wishes of heavy industry. The inflation ended with a stabilization based on high taxes – which severely hit industry and agriculture – and by cutting back public-sector employment. Exceptions were permitted to the legislation on hours of work, but in return employees gained an arbitration system for industrial disputes that initially appeared to be highly favourable to labour.

At the same time, the international agreements – recommended by the Dawes Experts' Committee and then accepted by the London conference – instead of controlling Weimar's politicians, still left Germany a considerable amount of autonomy or sovereignty. Weimar politics were pulled back and forth between the consciousness of foreign political limitations and the desire to assert independence and reclaim Great Power status. The Dawes settlement made a step in the latter direction.

Instead of the strictly controlled central bank that had first been proposed (with a note-issue department outside Germany, so that Germany could not stage another inflation), the new Reichsbank was subject to only very loose control from a General Council half composed of foreign representatives. The task of the newly appointed Agent-General for Reparations was restricted to making the transfer payments from Marks into foreign currencies. It was a post destined in advance to impotence. He did not have – as did the Commissioners appointed by the League of Nations to supervise the Austrian and Polish stabilizations –the right to control the budget and to block expenditure.[18] In the light of the later history of the 1920s, these limitations proved to be highly significant.

They mattered, as well, in terms of the Republic's relations with the political right and with the army. It would have been difficult to slip past an effective foreign budget-controller the politically explosive secret rearming of Germany and military cooperation with the USSR. The limitations on foreign control also allowed a financial policy that created social stability through the running of budget deficits. Parker Gilbert, the Agent-General, stood by, disapproving but impotent, as German governments – at central, state and local levels – spent more. Total government spending as a proportion of GNP rose from 25.0 per cent in 1925 (compare 1913 with 14.8 per cent) to 33.5 per cent in 1930.[19] To a substantial – and critical – extent this could not be funded by new sources of revenue, and the German government covered the gap by borrowing.

The stabilization compromise of the later 1920s worked by allowing influential pressure groups to put their demands to the government. For a few heady years, it appeared that all the aspirations of all Germany's groups and interests might be met at once. Business asked for subsidies – particularly where it could say that it was operating in border areas or zones of strategic significance. After 1926, world food prices started to decline, and Germany's farmers organized militant and effective lobbies. As a consequence, the government went far beyond its original concession to agriculture, the reintroduction in 1925 of the Bülow tariff of 1902. Tariff levels went up again and again. In addition, debt relief for the impoverished eastern areas of Germany (*Osthilfe*) went to an area defined with increasing generosity: by 1933 it covered the whole of Germany. Civil servants were placated with a big pay increase in 1927 (the basic rate went up 33 per cent). Personal and corporation tax rates fell. The Reich Labour Ministry was able to claim that its actions had helped to raise the general level of wages in Germany (and this was a claim that is vindicated by available wage statistics, particularly with regard to 1927 and 1928 in the aftermath of the civil service increase).

Weimar was operating like a caricature of the economic politics of the

Kaiserreich, in which each group had a vision of national interest which it identified wholly with its own exclusive concerns. The only way of reconciling the different interests was to buy them off; but this solution could last only as long as Weimar's short-lived prosperity held out.

By competing in such an adversarial way, the pressure groups made long-term economic prosperity – as distinct from a short-term stabilization – less likely. First, in the mid-1920s, union-backed wage claims and government-arbitrated pay awards constituted a source of weakness.[20] After 1928, many employers, particularly in the heavy industries of Rhine-Ruhr, believed that the most urgent task was to reduce wage pressure rather than to build long-term markets; and they took into account that this objective would require major political and constitutional changes. This meant a more authoritarian system, though not a Nazi-controlled state (except in the vision of a relatively small number of businessmen).

Moreover, the resolution of conflict that Germany tried to achieve in the 1920s – through subsidies, tax cuts and pay rises – cost the state a great deal of money and thus increased the likelihood of economic disturbance. There emerged what might be called a fiscal crisis of the state. By 1929 Germany's ability to borrow on both domestic and foreign capital markets had been critically impaired. The major attempt to fund the Reich deficit domestically in 1929 turned into an embarrassing failure. Abroad, Germany's position worsened and the prominent Wall Street banker J. P. Morgan started to refer to the Germans as 'second rate people' because of their poor credit standing.[21] This financial weakening, which had already occurred *before* the world depression set in, made Germany especially vulnerable to the effects of economic depression because it limited the scope for fiscal expansionary policies when these might have been most needed, at the bottom of the slump.

The economic collapse at the end of the 1920s was the immediate cause of the failure of Weimar's experiment in democracy. Weimar governments were faced with more or less insoluble dilemmas; the economic crisis cut their tax revenue. As unemployment rose steadily from 1928 to reach over six million in 1932, the state needed to spend larger sums on relief (even though it tightened conditions of eligibility and reduced benefit rates). Finally, because of conditions on the international capital markets, it could not borrow abroad. In these circumstances, almost any decision on the part of the government – to cut expenditure or to raise taxes – inevitably encountered fierce opposition.

Political parties realized that opposition to government policies was likely to win more votes, and that on the other hand participation in government led to a loss of support. It is not difficult to see that this produced an impasse for any democratic party in its relations with government.

The drift away from government had begun under the Great Coalition government presided over by the SPD Chancellor Hermann Müller. This coalition included right-wing liberals (DVP) and the SPD, as well as representatives of the Centre and the DDP. Its task was to wrestle with the beginnings of the Great Depression. The DVP pressed for cutbacks in unemployment benefits, while the SPD and especially the left and the labour unions resisted any compromise on this issue. A reduction in benefits would be a betrayal of their supporters. An even more striking example is the small Bavarian People's Party, which left the government because Bavarians would be hit by a proposed increase in beer tax.

Under the Chancellorship of Heinrich Brüning, the failure of government to win parliamentary support became openly evident. Brüning could never command a majority in the Reichstag, though he remained in office for two years. Neither could his two short-lived successors, Franz von Papen and General Kurt von Schleicher. All these politicians could rule only by emergency decree.

The DVP had never been fully convinced by democratic politics, and it moved into semi-opposition during Brüning's Chancellorship. The SPD, which had suffered in the elections of 1930 because it had been the key supporter of Brüning's predecessor, Hermann Müller, believed that it was necessary to distance itself in public from Brüning's deflationary politics; otherwise it would alienate its predominantly working-class support. So parties which had earlier calculated that they should win votes in order to obtain political influence now reversed their reasoning and held that they should lose political influence in order to win votes.

The Democratic party, DDP, and the Catholic Centre, Brüning's own party, were driven in a no less damaging direction by the force of events. They saw participation in government as an act of noble self-sacrifice, a deliberate, reasoned strategy of doing what was needed in spite of the hostility of the electorate. True patriotism, their theory went, required at least a temporary defiance of democracy. They deemed large parts of the German electorate unfit for democracy. Brüning, for instance, was sympathetic to a permanent reduction of the democratic part of Weimar's constitution, and wanted in the long run a restoration of monarchy.

At the extreme ends of the political spectrum, the Nazis (NSDAP) and the Communist party were uncooperative and intransigent. They increased their vote on the basis of a reputation for radicalism and for hostility to 'the system'. Faced with such a threat from the wings of the parliamentary system, neither reaction of the parties in between – that of a limited rejection of government (SPD and DVP), or that of partial rejection of democracy (Centre and DDP) – was illogical. Indeed, the Weimar constitution had foreseen that there might be a need for exceptional measures that would not find parliamentary consent. Article 48 of the constitution allowed the President (after 1925 Paul von Hindenburg) to rule through emergency decrees. This provision had been the basis for the inevitably unpopular measures which in 1923–4 had successfully halted the great Mark inflation: budget-balancing by means of expenditure reductions (which required the laying-off of civil servants and other public employees), and dramatic tax increases which hurt farmers, businessmen and income- earners in general. In addition, Article 48 provided for military measures to guarantee security.

In 1930–2 Chancellor Brüning used emergency decrees for a similar purpose: he tried to reduce expenditure by cutting back social security payments, reducing civil service pay, eliminating jobs and pruning capital spending severely. Article 48 was again used to enforce civil order: to ban the appearance in uniform of paramilitary groups – a measure directed chiefly against the Nazi Storm-troopers, but also against the Communist Red Front Fighters' League.

Government and the Nation

During the depression, the government also tried to use nationalist language to justify the unpopular measures which it felt obliged to pursue. The depression had been caused, many Germans contended, not by conditions in Germany or as a consequence of German policy, but by the collapse of the international economy and the adoption of protectionist tariff legislation by many of Germany's important customers. The 1930 American Smoot-Hawley tariff generally took a great deal of the blame for the European depression. But Germany suffered especially because she was obliged by the peace treaty and by the reparations plans to pay substantial sums, which could only be managed if she were to export freely. Reparations, Germans believed, ensured that Germany was the worst-hit of the continental economies. This argument contained some elements of truth. It was certainly correct that an economy traditionally dependent on exports would run into trouble in the world of the later 1920s.

Many German observers concluded that any policy response to the depression would have to deal with international conditions. Somebody else – not the Germans – would have to act first. Any solution would have to grasp the thorns of the international politics of reparations. Britain should be urged to force France to see common sense. The Americans should be obliged to cancel their war loans to Britain and France.

Since it was important for any German government at least to be seen to be doing something about the depression, the diplomacy of reparations revision played a major part in domestic politics. On 6 June 1931, when Brüning announced a new austerity decree which cut spending, reduced unemployment insurance benefits and established new taxes, he combined it with an appeal to the Allies to end reparations: 'the limits of the privations we have imposed on our people have been reached.'[22] It is unlikely, of course, that ending reparations alone would end either the world depression or the German slump; but the subject provided quite a handy political lightning conductor. Brüning could be seen to be doing something to ease the German burden.

As in the socialization debate over ten years earlier, in one sense the reality or otherwise of foreign limitations hardly mattered. The 'foreign' arguments presented simply a more digestible way of explaining the narrowness of Germany's room for manoeuvre than a more rigorous and penetrating analysis would have done. The problems of the German coal business in 1919, or of German banks in 1931, were complicated and intractable. Partly for this reason, the memoirs of both Brüning and Hans Luther, the central-bank president at the time, rely heavily on an account of German motives which showed Germany struggling to remove her foreign burden.[23]

Reparations revision served a wider function besides simply showing that the government was doing something. The politics of revision held German party politics within certain limits. Since 1924, reparations had, paradoxically, placed a political muzzle on the German right. When in 1924 the Dawes plan had been accepted, it represented a significant improvement to the previous schedule of reparation payments. The London ultimatum of May 1921 had required an annual sum of around 3 billion Gold Marks;[24] the Dawes plan by contrast specified 1,000 million Marks, rising over five years to 2,500 million. In addition, accepting the Dawes plan meant a promise that foreign private capital would stream into Germany. The result posed a considerable dilemma for the German right: should they accept the Dawes plan, and the repugnant principle of reparation for the sake of the economic benefits it would carry (which would assist in particular the economic interests they represented)? The DNVP split when it realized its vote was crucial (some parts of the Dawes plan required constitutional changes – which needed a two-thirds majority in the Reichstag). The divided Reichstag vote of the DNVP on 29 August 1924 was the first step that the DNVP took towards accepting responsibility as a governmental party (it later moved into centre–right coalitions).

The second major occasion when the foreign political pressure exerted by the reparations burden stabilized German politics was in 1929–30. The political complexion of the Müller government was incoherent: the cabinet contained diametrically opposed views on how economic management should be conducted. What held this coalition together for so long was the wearying process of negotiating an improvement of the Dawes plan – in other words, in agreeing the Young plan. Young would bring a reduction in payments, and hence the possibility of a general round of tax cuts benefiting all the various interest groups represented in the government. Accepting a definitive reparations schedule in addition constituted an important part of Foreign Minister Stresemann's strategy for negotiating a premature withdrawal of Allied troops from the whole of the Rhineland. France naturally viewed this prospect with alarm, and needed reassurance about German intentions; and this is what the reparations commitment would accomplish. It would also persuade Britain to coax France into acquiescence. Only by paying reparations, then, would Germany be able to think about a return to real sovereignty.

Thankfully, it took a long time to deal with an issue as complex and as internationally emotional and traumatic as the end of occupation, reparations and war debts. First there was the meeting of the Experts' Committee in Paris, then the first Hague conference to discuss the recommendations, then a second conference at The Hague. Finally the Reichstag had to vote on and accept the plan (11 March). Two weeks later (27 March) the Müller cabinet collapsed.[25]

The argument that reparations stabilized democracy may seem strange in the light of the right's ferociously fought campaign of 1929 against the Young plan. The Nazi party scored its first notable poll successes in 1929. It was the joint DNVP and Nazi sponsored plebiscite against the Young plan that took the Nazis back into the centre of the political scene, the party's support having collapsed after Hitler's prison sentence of 1924 and subsequent rancorous internal party disputes. Their proposal for a popular legislative initiative demanded that the German authors of the reparations plan be punished as traitors. The Nazis revived the rhetoric of opposition to Versailles, and invented strange stories to support their attack. They claimed, for instance, that the Allies really required not the export of goods but the export of people in an attempt to depopulate Germany. The Nazi economic expert

Fritz Reinhardt, in a brochure entitled 'The Young Plan and the Export of Humans', stated that 62 million Germans would be reduced to between 20 and 25 millions.[26]

But in reality the Young plan plebiscite of December 1929 dealt a blow to the right. It had drawn surprisingly little support. Though the total vote against the Young plan was over 5 million, only in the north and east of Germany did the electoral turnout rise above 10 per cent.

Nevertheless, after 1930 the radical-right campaign against reparations continued. In the September 1930 elections, the NSDAP called Brüning the 'Young Chancellor', the unemployed 'Young victims', and the employed 'Young slaves'. How much this campaign contributed to the rise in the Nazi vote in 1930 cannot be stated with any accuracy. Rural unrest and particular grievances did, however, play a great role in bringing votes for the Nazis. In 1932 Hindenburg stood for a second term of office as Reich President, and Adolf Hitler opposed him. The Nazis tried to show that by signing the Young legislation Hindenburg himself had stabbed the German people in the back. 'Think of the 13th of March' the Nazi slogan went – this was the day in 1930 on which Hindenburg had signed the Young plan.[27] However, Hitler did not win this election; and in general, though reparations played a vital role in politics between 1930 and 1932, there are many other reasons why the Nazis gained votes.

Thus reparations had a two-way effect on Weimar politics. The radical right and the Communist party took reparations as a powerful anti-republican argument. For the political centre, however, they continued to have an integrating effect: they helped to keep parties in government and withstand the powerful political pressures to get out.

The same logic as had sustained Müller's Great Coalition cabinet for so long helped to keep Brüning in power for some time after March 1930. Brüning staked his political future on a gamble to secure for Germany a final relief from the burden of paying reparations. Only he, he suggested, might gain the confidence of the Western powers necessary to accomplish this task. This calculation indeed restrained the DVP's attacks on the government, and also provoked divisions within the DNVP. The more moderate and anti-Hugenberg DNVP leaders felt uncomfortable about the militancy of Hugenberg's nationalist rhetoric.

Brüning's reparations offensive eventually produced the successful result of a *de facto* cancellation at the Lausanne conference (June–July 1932). At Lausanne, there was still a quantity of German reparations bonds outstanding, but actual payments were dependent on the current valuation of the commercially issued Dawes and Young Loan bonds, the quotations of which showed little sign of recovering from their very low depression levels. Lausanne, however, came too late to save Brüning.

He had already been dismissed by President von Hindenburg, and he believed that he had lost power only 'a hundred metres from the goal': the goal of ending reparations and ending the German depression.

Once there were no longer any obstacles in the way of a highly favourable reparations settlement, once the French had been brought to agree to Lausanne, the right could put its demands with some insistence and much more uncompromisingly. The kind of calculation that the DNVP had made in 1924, or the DVP in 1929, or the anti-Hugenberg Nationalists in 1930–1, was no longer important or interesting. The right could take a much tougher line on rearmament and on the Geneva negotiations. In domestic politics it could be more confrontational. The tacit support or toleration policy (*Tolerierungspolitik*) of the SPD was no longer required on foreign policy issues, and the need to make bargains with socialists thus no longer existed. In the light of the story of the events of 1924 to 1932, is it too much to say that reparations were the (relatively cheap) price for keeping Weimar democracy alive? Reparations ended in July 1932, and the Weimar Republic itself collapsed six months later.

Weimar as a Failed Great Power

There appears to be a common pattern in each of the crises of Weimar's foreign and reparations policy. They were crises about the making of national policy and the existence of national choices. Weimar's politicians lived in a world shaped by the hopes and expectations generated during the political transformation of 1918–19, which had produced a powerful and costly push for social reform: limitation of the hours of work, the institution of wage contracts and of state arbitration of labour conflicts. At the same time they lived in a world shaped by the Allies' hopes and expectations of 1918–19: in particular the French insistence that the Germans should pay a major part of the costs of the war; and the American demand for the repayment of the inter-Allied war debt. And finally, they were in a world whose real economic performance was so weak that expectations were likely to be disappointed. Swallowing disappointment would come to be a major requirement both in Weimar and in world politics. Unfortunately most people and most nations are very bad at doing that.

Weimar could solve many domestic and distributional questions only by pointing to its limited sovereignty. When the political centre and right wanted to argue against socialization in 1919, they pointed out that it meant a danger in reparations policy. When Stinnes wanted to abolish the eight-hour day, he thought that the Allies could insist on it. When Brüning needed to keep the budget balanced, he explained that it was really because of reparations.

Limiting German sovereignty was thus of central importance to the stability of Weimar's political system. If there was no foreigner to blame, domestic conflicts ran the risk of becoming insoluble. It is also for this reason that there is a connection between the great German foreign political success at Lausanne and the unstable and rapidly deteriorating situation at the end of 1932 and the beginning of 1933.

The dilemma of Weimar politics could be put as follows: it was important to have someone to blame – preferably a foreigner. It was also important to assert Germany's Great Power status – and that meant not allowing foreigners to intervene. In that case, how could foreigners be blamed? The idea of the great nation, together with the history of nineteenth-century economic strength, made it difficult to live with the realities of vanished prosperity and the traumas of a nation that was no longer great. There was a great risk that the collected political venom of Germans would turn on internal targets – and particularly on the Jews. 1919 and 1924 were partial triumphs for the sovereignty and Great Power principles; but it was not until the end of reparations in 1932 that the foreign shackles vanished altogether, and with them disappeared the limiting and stabilizing factor in German politics. A Hitler government before this date could have done little damage because of the limitations, imposed from abroad, on its room for manoeuvre. At any time after this date, however, any government – and particularly a Nazi one – could prove immensely powerful and ferociously destructive.

The Brown Nation

It is notoriously difficult to apply categories of historical description to National Socialism. Recounting the results is much easier: the outbreak of war, mass murder and military defeat. With the military defeat of 1945 came the destruction of the political manifestation of German nationhood and the discrediting of German nationalism. From 1933 to 1945, the nation and National Socialism had come to be identified with each other.

National Socialism could easily establish an association with many political, cultural and intellectual ideas and movements because of its theoretical vagueness and diversity. The nation is only one of many concepts that during the Third Reich acquired a deep brown stain, one which proved difficult to wash out after 1945. After the end of the Second World War the use of National Socialism as a term of political abuse indicates how diversely its political language had resonated. In the postwar world, National Socialism could be and has been used by association to discredit conservatism, nationalism, anti-communism, liberalism, private business, economic planning, socialism and ecology movements. The theme of this chapter is how National Socialism established its association with the nation: how it laid its eggs in the German national nest and passed its progeny off as a different creature.

Part of the difficulty in describing the character of National Socialism is an analytical one: it was a constantly changing and evolving movement. Though it claimed to have a hard core of doctrine, no one quite knew what this might be. Nazism had all the properties of a pseudo-religion: a cult, ritual, incantations, priests and a giant congregation. Like many false religions, National Socialism preserved an air of mystery about its innermost secrets in order to conceal an inner emptiness. The knowingness of the priests and the partial ignorance of the congregation were both carefully calculated.

National Socialism also changed its outward face continually and visibly. In the years after the party was founded in Munich in 1919, it altered its political programme, and the geographical and social composition of its support. For instance, the most obvious constant element in Nazi ideology, anti-semitism, played a prominent part in the party's activities in the early 1920s and in Hitler's writings – notably in *Mein Kampf* (1925). In the early 1930s, at the time of the party's greatest electoral successes, the Nazis paraded their anti-semitism much less openly: they hid it when addressing respectable middle-class and business audiences, and they deployed it chiefly in those places where they might reckon on a political audience – especially in the countryside – with a long history of anti-semitism.

In 1920, the party's 25-point programme contained many socialistic elements: it promised the expropriation of big landowners, the national-ization of trusts, the breaking of 'the thraldom of interest'. After the mid-1920s Hitler also tried to capture a respectable business vote. In Munich he turned himself into a socially respectable figure who could hold his own with members of old Munich families, such as the piano manufacturer Bechstein, the publisher Bruckmann, or the art-dealing house of Hanfstängl. When he spoke in 1926 to Hamburg businessmen at the conservative Nationalklub von 1919, he wore a tail coat. He repeated this bourgeois performance in a sombre suit in January 1932 in front of Rhineland businessmen in Düsseldorf, and in January 1933 when he appeared as the new Reich Chancellor in a tail coat. Elsewhere, the social nature of Nazism varied considerably. Joseph Goebbels, the Gauleiter of Berlin, who came from a more well-to-do background than Hitler's, cultivated a much more proletarian style. In other areas, such as Schleswig-Holstein. the party assumed the air of a traditional peasant movement.

The main basis of the Nazis' support shifted from the early 1920s. Then it had lain in Catholic Bavaria, where the party had been founded and where it had developed as one of the most radical of a large number of anti-socialist 'citizens' self-defence forces' that had emerged in the aftermath of the war and the revolution. Before 1928, most of the party's supporters were in towns; but in 1928, National Socialism was still a very minor movement on the outer fringes of German politics. Its integration of small racist parties from northern Germany did not lead to a substantial strengthening of the movement: on the contrary its vote collapsed after 1924. After 1928 the significant gains in votes were unthinkable without the systematic development of a rural following, especially in northern Germany. Falling livestock prices, high interest rates and large tax bills provoked a wave of peasant unrest from 1927. In 1929 and 1930 the Nazis moved in and systematically exploited farmer discontent. During the depression period, Germany's north and east provided a higher share of the Nazi vote than did Bavaria.

The shifting character of Nazi support reflects a change in ideology: a change made consciously and with a pragmatic vote-seeking calculation. The chameleon strategy of presenting different faces in different areas followed from the decision to gain power not by a violent coup (as Hitler had tried to do in 1923) but by electoral means.[1] The rural vote, for instance, was an obvious source of ballot fodder because of the economic problems which crippled Germany's countryside.

In the few years before 1933 the Nazi vote increased dramatically. In 1928, the party had had an insignificant 2.6 per cent of the vote in the Reichstag elections; but in September 1930 its vote rose to 18.3 per cent, and in July 1932 to 37.4 per cent. The consequence of the Nazi strategy was that no one could tell what exactly Hitler and his party would do if ever they achieved power. What sort of anti-semitic programme, if any, would they actually enact? Would the NSDAP nationalize big industry and the banks, and embark on a full-fledged policy of state socialism? Would it spend money in order to get Germany out of the depression? As far as possible Hitler avoided any clear commitment on any of these issues. In May 1932 one of the most influential Nazi leaders, Gregor Strasser, made a speech promising to spend 10 billion RM on work-creation on roads, drainage, settlement projects and agricultural improvements. This was a populist programme designed to beat the economic slump. But Hitler quickly changed his mind on counter-cyclical economic strategies. The Nazis rapidly stepped back from the Strasser proposal as their enemies accused them of being irresponsible and of advocating a repetition of the traumatic post-World War I inflation.

Hitler as a mature politician distrusted specific political programmes and promises. Nazi spokesmen tried to target peasants, or small traders, or workers, or the respectable middle classes, locally. Where they were not appealing to particular local interests, they cultivated something much vaguer. Speeches resounded with highly generalized claims and statements: 'Germany must rise again or Germany must collapse'; 'Germany must be healthy'; 'Germany must root out the bacilli'. This technique might be described as the cultivation of an attitude or feeling or sentiment: it concerned national self-assertion, and expressed itself in opposition to the peace treaty, to reparations and to the Weimar governments which had plodded along hoping to achieve a gradual revision. A central element in this assertion was played by the idea of a national community, defined against an external enemy, but also against internal, 'non-German', elements. Anti-semitism of course meant that the Nazis found it easy to choose who this internal enemy should be.

With this went a view of culture. Art had a role in the making of the community and in the defining of enemies. Cultural modernism, already before the war, but especially in the Weimar period, had not been 'close to the people' in the manner of the old-style art. The previous proximity had been destroyed and replaced by a relentless quest for originality that had led to an unintelligible abstraction with no emotional appeal: bolshevized art (*Kunstbolschewismus*). Bolshevized art meant a cultivation of idiosyncrasy at the expense of community and belonging. It had not attacked the people's enemies. The destruction of values had accompanied social fragmentation. Only conscious cultural politics could recreate a people's community of feeling: *Volksgemeinschaft*. The task of art in constructing this order was not, as the modernists believed, to criticize, but to express the deeply felt emotional needs of the people. Art had to create values, not destroy them.

Finally, there was a Nazi 'feeling' about economics. Without economic prosperity there could be no *Volksgemeinschaft*. The problem posed by previous economic growth arose from the creation of inequalities that had made it harder to attain a genuine community. Growth, if it should be accompanied by a more generally and equitably distributed improvement of lifestyles, could build a people. And, in turn, only a people that saw itself as a community could avoid dissipating its energies in the sectional strife so characteristic of 1920s politics, where small farmers had been set against large estate owners; farmers against traders; retailers against wholesalers; workers against retailers; workers against farmers; big businessmen against small producers.

Nazism did not of course derive from every tradition that had ever existed in the German past. Few historians would now be prepared to argue that a dictatorship founded on a mass party represented the only and inevitable outcome of previous German development. Germany had long histories of democratic, federalist and liberal belief and action. The south and west had had reforming liberal bureaucratic governments in the eighteenth century and liberal politics in the middle of the nineteenth. In the Rhineland and Bavaria, traditions of political Catholicism made centralization by Protestant Prussia appear as a threat.

On the other hand, National Socialism did present a powerful synthesis of many of the ways Germans had characteristically thought about Germany since the early nineteenth century: as a Great Power on the world stage; as a social grouping defined by shared cultural traditions; as the guarantor of greater economic success and prosperity. If Nazism did not exist as the only possible response to the German past, it nevertheless grew out of a wish to reformulate national traditions and identities in a period when economic aspirations attached to the national unit had so clearly been disappointed.

Foreign Policy

The strong nation lay at the centre of Nazi propaganda and of the Nazi appeal. Before 1933, the Nazis made the most of the charge of national betrayal levelled at Weimar's leaders and taken from the political arsenal of the old right in the 1920s. After 1931, and particularly after the Lausanne reparations conference had in 1932 liquidated a major financial and moral legacy of the war, the old right moved closer to National Socialism. The risks of an aggressive foreign policy had been reduced. Conservatives felt that a more adventurist policy would now be tolerated by the Western powers, and that it might reap great gains for Germany. Dramatic foreign programmes helped to bring the old and the new right together. Nationalism played a role in bridging the differences between the highly varied groups that supported Hitler and the Nazis in the early 1930s.

Nazi nationalism had a clearly manipulative function: to create a more widespread base of support for the Nazi programme. The Nazis also mounted a continual campaign against those they regarded as having too narrow and sectarian a view of political activity. There was, they said, no purpose in workers thinking that they could improve their position at the expense of small traders and farmers by imposing strict price controls, or farmers demanding wage cuts from labour. The nation had to see itself as a community, and foreign policy would help it to do just this. Recovery and renewal could only come about through a collective effort: an act of national assertion.

After 1933, defiant nationalism always helped to remove or defuse opposition to the regime – whether opposition from the general population or from Germany's conservative elites. During the summer of 1935, secret police reports painted an increasingly worrying picture of public opinion. Workers believed that their wages had been held down, and that they had not received their due share of the benefits of economic recovery. Farmers would have liked better prices. Rentiers and savers feared that there might be a new inflation. In March 1936, however, Hitler scored his first major foreign policy success. German troops moved into the demilitarized Rhineland without encountering any opposition from France. The language of national recovery opened up into a new reality. After this striking demonstration that the order imposed at Versailles had been superseded because of Germany's new strength, the domestic opposition crumbled.

This encouraged the Nazis to take a more radical stance in domestic policy as well. In the early years of the Third Reich, there had been an uneasy compromise between conservatives and Nazi ideologues. During the first year after the Nazi 'seizure of power', in 1933–4, everything remained uncertain. Local units of the party took individual initiatives against the old bureaucracy and against businesses. They beat up employees, they hoisted swastika flags and proclaimed the need for a 'second revolution'. A boycott of Jewish shops endangered Germany's foreign trade and foreign policy. The uncertainty ended with the bloodbath of 30 June 1934, when Hitler personally supervised the arrest of the Storm-troopers' leaders. Many of the SA leaders were killed. However, this lawlessness temporarily put an end to the lawlessness practised by the socially radical elements in the Nazi party. On the whole the old order in business, in the army and in the civil service felt agreeably relieved.

After 1936, the conservatives became less happy. Tensions mounted in the business world as industry and commerce suffered under the economic controls imposed by Hermann Göring's Four-Year Plan. Part of the army leadership feared a military expansion that was taking place so quickly that the officer corps had been inundated with committed ideological Nazis. Other soldiers believed that the pace was too fast, and that Germany faced the risk of a war for which she would not be prepared. By the summer of 1938, a substantial conservative opposition existed around men such as Carl Goerdeler, the former Mayor of Leipzig and the Third Reich's Price Commissioner, General Witzleben and General Ludwig Beck. But the coherence of this opposition was destroyed at a stroke by Hitler's foreign coup of September 1938: the Munich agreement, at which France, Britain and Italy awarded Germany the Sudetenland at the expense of Czechoslovakia and with no use of military force and no loss of life. Hitler was able to celebrate himself as the greatest of the world's peacemakers.

Hitler's conception of foreign policy had been worked out in the 1920s and recorded in *Mein Kampf*, and in the unpublished so-called 'Second Book' written in 1928. It derived from a theory of geopolitics as preached in Munich by Karl Haushofer, a friend of Rudolf Hess, from ideas about Mitteleuropa circulating since before the First World War, and from Hitler's own experience of the war itself. In other words, it contained enough ideas drawn from the old world of German nationalism to be clearly continuous with a well-established German tradition. This facilitated the compromise between Hitler and the old German elites: it allowed, for instance, the Foreign Office to continue with relatively limited personnel changes until the late 1930s.

Though both *Mein Kampf* and the 'Second Book' are violently anti-semitic, Hitler's foreign policy views did not come primarily from the specifically Nazi racial view. His arguments depended on a pseudo-scientific theory of 'living space' (*Lebensraum*). An imbalance between population and resources meant that without expansion states would become increasingly impoverished. By nature, all populations and all countries pressed against each other for more 'living space'. European states – and especially those without a colonial empire – faced a disadvantage compared to North America.

There was something of this vision in prewar theories of Mitteleuropa, and it remained a popular interpretation in the 1920s. Hans Grimm's novel *Volk ohne Raum* ('People without Space'), published in 1926, had reached a print run of almost 600,000 copies by the Second World War. Grimm set out quite explicitly to show that there was no longer enough soil in Germany, and that the 'German needed room and sun and inner freedom in order to become good and beautiful'. During the depression, conservative thinkers argued that the high level of unemployment had resulted from excessive industrialization, and that only a return to the soil ('settlement') of large numbers of urban workers could solve the economic problem and the social ill. Often there was the additional implication that this could not occur within the limits of Germany's current frontiers.

Hitler's version of the theory was scarcely different from that of the advocates of conservative revival:

> Regardless of how Italy, or let's say Germany, carry out the
> internal colonization of their soil, regardless of how they increase
> the productivity of their soil further through scientific and
> methodical activity, there always remains the disproportion of the
> number of their population to the soil as measured against the
> relation of the population of the American Union to the soil of the
> Union. And if a further increase of the population were possible for
> Italy or Germany through the utmost industry, then this would be
> possible in the American union up to a multiple of theirs.[2]

Thus no fundamental improvement could be achieved through greater industry and ingenuity. In addition, nations required a more active sort of existence. Trading and producing alone could not satisfy man's fundamental and biological drives. 'The danger to a people of economic activity in an exclusive sense lies in the fact that it succumbs only too easily to the belief that it can ultimately shape its destiny through economics.'[3] Hitler concluded that if Europe was to escape decline and impoverishment, she needed more territory. This could be acquired in the east, at the expense of Russia, or overseas.

Hitler's aims were to be accomplished in stages. First Germany should build up a power position in Central Europe. Then she could devote herself to becoming a world power with a navy. Unlike Germany between 1914 and 1918, the future Nazi state should not go about pressing all these demands simultaneously. Germany should form an alliance with Italy and Britain in order to defeat France and to break out of the Versailles system. Then she could turn against Russia.

The continental position came first. However, there was a problem for Nazi ideology: in making this calculation, essentially a pragmatic one, any theory of racial or *völkisch* nationalism flew out of the window. Hitler's thinking resembled prewar ideas about world empires far more than it did a consistently nationalist programme.

This is particularly evident with respect to the issue of the South Tyrol, and more generally in dealing with the German *irredenta*. The South Tyrol had been a part of the Habsburg Empire, but had been awarded – despite its linguistically predominantly German population – to Italy at the peace conference. The rights of the South Tyrolese, and the obvious breach of Woodrow Wilson's principle of national self-determination, were favourite themes of the German Nationalist Party (DNVP) and of the non-Nazi racist (*völkisch*) movement in the Weimar Republic. Hitler on the other hand believed that championing the cause of the South Tyrolese represented nothing more than an exercise in futility.

Other Germans outside Germany existed in Hitler's eyes only for the sake of aiding the German state's policy of expansion. In particular they could be of use in Germany's campaign against the political order of Versailles. Their agitation should be turned on and off at will, as it suited Germany's political situation. One of the widely acknowledged problems following from the 1919 peace treaties was the real or alleged mistreatment of national minorities. It was a problem because it seemed to compromise the theory of Wilsonian self-determination; and it could be used as a valuable tool by the have-nots to embarrass those powers that upheld the *status quo*.

Hitler and the German Foreign Office worked out a way of using this challenge: the demands of Germany for the Sudetenland in 1938 were preceded by a carefully organized agitation from the Sudeten German leader Konrad Henlein. In 1939, Germans in Poland and in Danzig were orchestrated in the same way in order to prepare for the dismantling of Poland. On the other hand, earlier in the decade, when Germany had been seeking security on her eastern frontier and thus an accord with Poland, the Danzig problem was put on one side, and the local Nazis behaved themselves – on instructions from Munich and Berlin.

Little in this concept changed between the enunciation of Hitler's programme in the 1920s and the beginning of its realization as war broke out in 1939. Tactical considerations required a pact with Poland (1934). The idea of an *entente* with Italy and Britain remained fundamental. In 1936, Germany moved closer to Italy. Hitler tried to woo Britain in order to take her out of the coalition of hostile powers. In 1938–9, he may even have believed that he had succeeded. Neville Chamberlain, the British Prime Minister, gave in at Munich. A fawning Germanophile, Nevile Henderson, served as British ambassador to Berlin and conveyed apparently sympathetic messages from Whitehall. 'I honestly endeavoured', he wrote in his memoirs, 'where I could do so without sacrificing the principles or the interests of my country, both to understand the German external viewpoint and to see what was good in its social experiment, without being blind to what was bad.'[4]

The *détente* constituted a necessary backdrop to the building-up of Germany's military resources. Within the foreign-policy-making machine, little disagreement existed about the overall goals of German policy. The argument concerned *how* they should be pursued; and in particular what degree of belligerence should be employed. The army feared that it was unprepared to fight a major war. Many of the leading Foreign Ministry officials, including the Secretary of State, Ernst von Weizsäcker, opposed war passionately on ethical as well as pragmatic grounds. Weizsäcker even went so far as to inform foreign states about German aims and to instruct them how to act in order to limit Hitler's designs. The ambiguity of policy covered both peaceful and military expansion; and it remained so ambiguous that Weizsäcker, who fought ferociously to avoid war but thought Germany should expand peacefully, never before September 1939 questioned Hitler's ability to provide leadership on foreign policy issues.[5]

As Germany took up a peaceful expansionist programme intended to dismantle Versailles, she also rearmed for an aggressive conflict. By 1936, Germany began to prepare to fight a defensive war within the next four years, and to be ready for an offensive war in eight. Since 1935, there had been universal conscription. The Four-Year Plan announced in 1936 laid the economic basis for the long wars Hitler believed would be fought in the second half of the twentieth century.[6]

The theme of *Lebensraum* appeared over and over again. Germans had failed in the First World War because of problems with their food supply – but now they had the opportunity to become a world people. They had an advantage, Hitler told army officers in early 1939, in that they were greater in number than the French or the British. 'World peoples' of 60 or 70 millions still built empires: but in Mitteleuropa there were 86 million Germans. They could expand, Hitler said in 1941. 'Europe reaches as far as does the Nordic-Germanic spirit. The time of Bolshevism in European Russia was nothing but a twenty-year preparation for German rule.' Only this would provide the economic security of a stable food base. 'We will become . . . the most autarkic state that there has been.'[7]

The war against the USSR in 1941 became the true war of National Socialism. At the same time, it drew together old-style German nationalism and the specifically National Socialist and racist elements in Hitler's programme. For the first time, Hitler did not need to sacrifice racial nationalism for the sake of pragmatic political calculations; 1941 was an ideological war against Bolshevism – that attracted the old German order. It was the geopolitician's war for *Lebensraum*. Germany would ensure her place as a 'world state', and that of Germans as a true 'world people'. And simultaneously it was a racial war against the Slavs – that pleased the Nazi party's racial thinkers.

Political Culture

Just as Nazi foreign policy contained many features that appealed to the old establishment as constituting little more than a bold continuation of previous German longings, so the Nazi view of culture included traditional elements. On the surface it was anti-modern, and served the political cause of mobilizing sentiment in defence of a reconstituted old order. Hitler believed himself to be a political artist, who would mould a new political system. But artistry meant something peculiar to Hitler: the representation of popular taste. Nazism claimed to be the true expression of the people's will. Here, as with foreign policy, he developed and then went beyond traditional conservative prescriptions.

At first, Hitler had wanted to be just an artist. In 1907 and 1908, as a young man, he had applied for admission to the Austrian Academy, but had been rejected because his drawing was 'unsatisfactory' – presumably because his style was too conventional and traditionalist. For a time he lived in Vienna by selling paintings and making up advertising sketches; at the same time he consoled himself by preparing monumental architectural plans for the rebuilding of whole cities. His existence in Vienna was impoverished and rather sordid, but Hitler had a simple explanation of why it was sordid. Modernism had eroded the aesthetic vision of life.

He became persuaded by the popularized cultural pessimism of turn-of-the-century Germany and Austria – and especially Vienna. As modern cities grew, he believed, cultural life died. Dirty and crowded slum areas had destroyed a traditional landscape and produced a desperate and rootless individualism. The essence of culture, which lay in the creation of community, had been killed off: 'In the nineteenth century our cities began more and more to lose the character of cultural sites and to descend to the level of mere human settlements.' An inverse correlation existed between the size of a community and its propensity to produce genuine culture: 'When Munich numbered sixty thousand souls, it was already on its way to becoming one of the first German art centres; today nearly every factory town has reached this number, if not many times surpassed it, yet some cannot lay claim to the slightest real values.'[8]

Many aspects of this doctrine corresponded perfectly with a widespread conservative response to modernist culture. The Weimar Republic had, the cultural conservatives complained, made modernism its official ideology. The commanding heights of German culture had fallen: the impressionist Max Liebermann, the leader of the Berlin Secession, had in 1920 been appointed President of the Berlin Academy of Arts. Reich President Ebert attended the sixtieth birthday celebrations of the socially critical writer Gerhart Hauptmann. In the theatre, Leopold Jessner imposed Expressionist performances on the staid audiences of the former Royal Schauspielhaus. Populist writers such as Grimm or the *völkisch* ex-pastor Gustav Frenssen, or the propagandist of the 'conservative revolution' Edgar Jung, saw in all this sickness and decay. Jessner, brutally attacked by the right, resigned in 1930.

There was, however, more to the Nazi view of art than a simple pandering to the sentiments of a culturally outraged middle class. As the leader of a political movement, Hitler regarded art as central to his politics. In the 1920s and 1930s he prepared architectural sketches for buildings, monuments and cities. Many aspects of the Nazi fascination with art reflected little more than a romantic nostalgia for a vanished past. But Nazi art also had a conscious manipulative function: the artist, Hitler and his movement believed, had a unique power to exercise his will and to bend that of other people. Art meant building a community by the imposition of an artistic vision; and art, mass suggestion and political propaganda became part of a general enterprise.

Throughout his life, Hitler was fascinated by architecture as the most manipulative of arts. Architectural forms shaped the way large numbers of people encountered and responded to each other. Those constructions which paid most attention to problems of human movement in a public space he consistently found the most interesting and important. For instance, he always admired Charles Garnier's Paris Opéra because of the way that the giant staircase integrated a socially diverse theatre public. The Paris theatre represented for Garnier (and for Hitler) a microcosm of political society. Hitler's own plans aimed at the managing of the interaction of very large populations. He wanted to rebuild and redesign whole cities which would be designated 'Führer cities': Berlin, Munich, Nuremberg, Hamburg, Linz. The whole city would be organized into gigantic symmetries with grandiose ornamentation. Hitler spoke of imitating the tallest American skyscrapers, and of covering Germany with a dense network of motor highways (*Autobahnen*) in order to demonstrate the power of a nation of eighty million people. These plans were largely unrealized simply because of the monumental sizes envisaged. Berlin, for instance, was to have a central dome modelled on St Peter's, with a diameter of 825 feet. It was so big that the architect anticipated a problem of clouds forming inside the dome.

The Nuremberg stadium for party rallies was to be the physical focus for the unity of the nation-community. According to the plans for this construction – again never realized – the stadium was to hold twice as many people as the Circus Maximus in Rome. It would cost 200–250 million Marks to build – twice the cost of a major battleship. Size and expense alone gave meaning to the project, Hitler explained. 'Why always the biggest? I do this to restore to each individual German his self-respect. In a hundred areas I want to say to the individual: We are not inferior: on the contrary, we are the complete equals of every other nation.'[9]

In 1937, in a speech to the party conference, he said that great buildings 'contribute more than ever to the political unification and strengthening of our people; in German society they will become an element in the feeling of proud togetherness'. Reverting to this theme when addressing army officers in 1939, he claimed: 'a great cultural people [*Kulturvolk*] is unthinkable without documents of its culture. There is no better way to educate a people to self-consciousness than grandiose communal tasks which show each individual that such a people is at least equal to all other nations.' Monumental constructions would bridge the social rift that had torn modern society apart and heal the division between proletarians and bourgeois. A united nation should replace the class-divided nation.[10]

Joseph Goebbels, the Nazi 'Minister of Propaganda and Popular Enlightenment', established himself as the master of a cynical and manipulative mass suggestion. Like Hitler, he put a front of slightly jaded romanticism on this. A mystical romantic vision would hold the people together. In 1934, at the Nuremberg rally, Goebbels said:

> May the bright flame of our enthusiasm never be extinguished. It alone gives light and warmth to the creative art of modern political propaganda. It arose from the very heart of the people in order to derive more strength and power. It may be a good thing to possess power that rests on arms. But it is better and more gratifying to win and hold the heart of the people.[11]

Goebbels added something more subtly appealing than the Hitlerian obsession with bigness. He tried to import the most convincing and modern American advertising techniques. Ideal propaganda consisted of a mixture of obvious political material and a camouflaged popular entertainment which would simply make people feel better about themselves, and in consequence about their community, their nation and their race. It was better to mask explicit political suggestions under the guise of, say, erotic literature:

> Even entertainment can be politically of special value, because the moment a person is conscious of propaganda, propaganda becomes ineffective. However, as soon as propaganda as a tendency, as a characteristic, as an attitude, remains in the background and becomes apparent through human beings, then propaganda becomes effective in every respect.[12]

Popular sports had the same effect: they involved individuals in the community and in the crowd without any ostensible political association. People absorbed new values without being conscious that these had been manipulated into a political framework. After a football match between Germany and Norway, for instance, Goebbels wrote: 'The public is raving. A fight such as there has never been before. The game as mass suggestion.'[13]

These advertising techniques could be applied in pursuing the general goals of Nazism. Nazism depended on a doctrine of the assertion of the will. In the end wars could only be won by propaganda which inspired that will. Hitler believed that the home front in the First World War had collapsed because the Imperial government had not known how to mobilize opinion. Goebbels thought that psychological manipulation could replace military strength. Suggestion could be a substitute for reality. A machine for dispersing political leaflets over enemy territory thus became in his eyes a 'machine for winning the war'. Few would deny that morale matters in war, but morale on its own is hardly sufficient to ensure victories. The Nazi doctrine of the will as the essential ingredient of national unity became during the war more and more a way of avoiding or denying reality. It compensated for the failures of the grand schemes for social integration through material improvement.

Technical Advance

At the root of Hitler's vision of the economy, as of his foreign political blueprints, lay a brutally materialistic concept of human motivation. Cultural values could only mask a basic and perpetual struggle:

> Regardless of how high the cultural importance of a people may be, the struggle for daily bread stands at the forefront of all vital necessities. To be sure, brilliant leaders can hold great goals before a people's eyes, so that it can be further diverted from material things in order to serve higher spiritual ideals. In general the merely material interest will rise in exact proportion as ideal spiritual outlooks are in the process of disappearing . . . Sooner or later . . . physical collapse brings spiritual collapse in its train. Then all ideals also come to an end.[14]

Here a dilemma existed. Economic growth, which alone could provide a way out of misery and chaos, had also divided society into classes and destroyed the united nation.

Mein Kampf included a standard conservative criticism of industrialization and class conflict. Hitler gave an idealized presentation of pre-modern rustic life: 'In the country there could be no social question, since master and hired hand did the same work and above all ate out of the same bowls. But this . . . changed. The separation of worker and employer now seems complete in all fields of life.'[15] Industrialization had made workers into slaves and had destroyed their health through inappropriately long hours. This had led to the dissolution of the old communities and the waging of class war by one part of the people against the other. National communities had crumbled, and the enemy of the nation had won. Class war, Hitler deduced, had been invented by Jews, who alone benefited from the falling apart of old communities and nations.

Hitler reached a peculiar conclusion, one far more radical than the back-to-the-land remedies of traditionalists: the cure for the maladies of industrialization lay in yet more intensive industrialization. Only a high level of technical advance could take society out of its impasse. Like artistic activity, technical progress came from the application of will. Historical latecomers, such as Germany, had a particular chance. 'It depends on the will. One can't leave things to take their own course. Countries which are rich and have everything don't need discoveries any more. What for? Discoveries are uncomfortable. People want to go along in the old way. These rich peoples, England, France, and America, only want to sleep.'[16] In Germany, Hitler admired not well-established manufacturers, but those creative 'genuine entrepreneurs', such as the automobile producer Ferdinand Porsche, who had designed new machines.

New inventions would allow a new wealth to be widely distributed: 'There was [in the past] the stupid thought that living standards could not be raised further . . . Progress consists in making life more beautiful for people!'[17] The state should take charge of redistribution. Nazi economics developed along highly *étatiste* and collectivist lines. In announcing the Four-Year Plan for the German economy in 1936, Hitler said quite bluntly that if the private economy failed, the state would act instead. Business had to subordinate itself to the political conceptions of the regime. This is in fact what was meant by the idea of National Socialism. Hitler believed that 'socialism is the expression of the twentieth century, while nationalism was that of the nineteenth. In National Socialism the Führer has reconciled the nineteenth and twentieth centuries. We think and act collectively.'[18]

This was in Hitler's eyes a revolutionary concept: it required the destruction of an old social order for the sake of the re-creation of genuine national community. A greater degree of national integration through economic harmony also required a new leading class. Looking back at the 1920s, Hitler explained that he 'developed such a contempt for the bourgeoisie [*Bürgertum*]'. By the middle of the twentieth century, Hitler believed, the historical role of the bourgeoisie had been played out.[19] Goebbels became the most systematic exponent of this view. He believed the Nazi movement was engaged in a struggle against an old world of decadent aristocratic values. In Germany he hated the upper-class politicians of the right, the men who had played such a major role in 1932 and 1933 in bringing the Nazis to power: the Papens or the Meissners (Meissner was Hindenburg's Secretary of State). Outside Germany, France and Britain had old-style politicians, who would – the Nazi leadership believed – surrender as easily as the old order in Germany had done in 1933. Only when all the class states throughout the world had disappeared could there exist any genuinely national state.[20] National Socialism believed that it was accomplishing the immanent logic of the historical process. Technical progress would bring the destruction of the bourgeois and the emancipation of the nation.

Thinking the Unthinkable

These three areas of Nazi 'feeling' – foreign political self-assertion, cultural conservatism and economic progressivism – formed part of a general wish to belong to a secure framework which might make sense of a hostile world. None of them stood at variance with the mainstream of German nationalist thinking as it had developed from the outset of the nineteenth century. Its sentiments are not really appropriately described either as a backward-looking 'reaction against modernity' or as a forward-leaning 'embracing of modernity'. To be sure, cultural conservatism appears as reactionary, but Hitler liked his cultural conservatism to be technically progressive. This mix of backward and forward theories had been characteristic of almost all theories of nationality which wanted to build the new and preserve the old simultaneously.

National Socialism's historical peculiarity lay in the way these sentiments expressed themselves and not in the feelings themselves. Cultural conservatism, for instance, had been widespread enough; but it existed as a general world-weary pessimism, not as a detailed programme for action. Nazism offered a concrete realization of dreams that had previously seemed unreal: the magic of Albert Speer's 'cathedral of light' at the party rally of 1936; the pride in aeronautic performance and in military achievement. Nazi foreign policy too involved this realization of the unreal. Logically it contained little that had not been in the plans of Imperial Germany before 1914; but it took the premisses of prewar diplomacy and set about making them into political accomplishments and political facts. It demonstrated how limited the practical application of grand ideas had been before the advent of the Third Reich. It showed how Germany under her new leadership could always embark on yet more exciting foreign political adventures.

National Socialist 'racial policy' followed the same lines of concretizing previously expressed aspirations. It developed an assortment of old prejudices and resentments, and feelings about the niceties of social distinctions, and set out to apply these in a brutally and murderously systematic way in the real world. At the end of the nineteenth century, popular anti-semitism had been a reaction to economic crisis. A political anti-semitism then had linked a cultural rejection of the values of contemporary society with populist reactions to business difficulties. National Socialism drew on this tradition and, in the wake of an economic collapse, formulated an old response in a newly systematized way.

In 1933 the 'Law on the Professional Civil Service' excluded Jews from the state bureaucracy. The economic persecution of Jews started with the 1933 boycott of Jewish shops. Simultaneously, the reordering of professional interest organizations shut out Jews and thus marginalized them economically. In 1935 in Nuremberg during the party congress, the Reichstag passed a law defining citizenship, disenfranchising those 'not of German blood' and prohibiting marriage and sexual relations between Germans and Jews as 'race defilement'.

Doubtless the 1933 Civil Service Law and the Nuremberg laws corresponded to many ancient feelings about the character of the state and about the undesirability of Jewish–Gentile matches. In the nineteenth century, there had been a notion of the 'Christian state': it had been extolled by Bismarck in a speech in the United Prussian Parliament of 1847. Bismarck had then claimed that the state's mission lay in the implementation of Christian belief, and that he personally would lose all joy and honour if he should be required to obey a Jewish civil servant. However, in the middle of the nineteenth century, theories of the Christian state used religious criteria. Converted Jews encountered few problems in entering the state's service: the most prominent conservative philosopher, Friedrich Julius Stahl, came from exactly this background. After the 1870s, anti-semitism was recast in terms of racial theories, which claimed to provide scientific and biologically exact accounts of human development. This racial anti-semitism reached well beyond the small, explicitly anti-semitic parties: the conservative party and the Centre took up its slogans without fully or publically setting out the theory behind the phrases. There developed a commonplace but only half-articulated web of prejudice. In the 1920s there were frequent references to the 'Jewish question': a rather vague notion which evoked the association of materialism, cultural modernism, social fragmentation, financial and economic manipulation. University students in medicine and law complained that they could not find employment because too many Jewish doctors and lawyers were practising. The depression and particularly the banking crisis of 1931 led to a generalized distrust of the financial world – which in the popular mind was (the Nazis insisted) usually associated with Jews.

An example of the malign pervasiveness of this global identification of a 'Jewish outlook' is provided in a striking and surprising way by Thomas Mann, who wrote the following words in his diary in 1933 after he had fled Germany and made an open breach with the Nazi regime:

The Jews . . . It is no calamity after all that . . . the domination of the legal system by Jews has been ended. Secret, disquieting, persistent musings. Come what may, much will remain that in a higher sense is repellent, base and un-German. But I am beginning to suspect that in spite of everything this process is one of those that have two sides to them.'[21]

The Nuremberg laws were worked out and supported by non-Nazis as well as by members of the National Socialist party. But the rigour of their implementation is characteristic of the Nazi mentality. The Nazis at Nuremberg had determined by law matters that had previously been left in a vague and undefined area of social convention. Nineteenth-century conservatives or twentieth-century snobs would not have imagined the precise legislating of a social code. Someone like Thomas Mann felt nothing but disgust at the actual form of Nazi legislation.

By an automatic logic this legislation set off a process of formulating half-expressed but half-latent prejudices and resentments as legal and administrative measures. Previously latent feelings appeared first in words, then in political programmes, then in legislation and then in action. The Nuremberg laws laid the basis first for the casual harassment of Jews, and then for the massive nationally organized pogrom of November 1938, for the expropriation in that year of Jewish business property and the prohibition of Jewish medical or legal practice. Finally they prepared the way for deportations and mass killings.

This logic encouraged the unrestrained expression of more and more prejudices. Men and women who thought they had been bold in breaking taboos to speak about, and act upon, one set of beliefs, found that they should go further, say more and do more.

Hitler led the way in this progressive breaking of conventions. *Mein Kampf* is an example of how in practice this progressive radicalization and loss of inhibition operated. The logical consequence of anti-semitism and *étatisme* meant that the state should take action to remove all Jews from Germany. After the outbreak of war in 1939, Hitler applied this logic. He incorporated a large part of Poland into Germany, and then explained that the old and new areas of the Reich should be cleared of Poles and Jews. As German armies overran Poland, they began a relatively systematic attack on Poland's intelligentsia, with the goal of making the Poles into a slave- or sub-people. The same logic appeared in the 'Commissar Order' of 6 June 1941, which directed the killing of the Soviet elite: 'the originators of barbaric Asiatic methods of warfare are the political commissars. Accordingly measures must be taken against them *immediately* and with full severity.'[22] The systematic mass killings of Jews, gypsies, Jehovah's Witnesses and homosexuals began with the invasion of Russia in 1941. Simultaneously, two Nazi dreams became real: the destruction of the Jews and the conquest of Bolshevik Russia. In the summer of 1941, German soldiers and SS supervised the construction of annihilation camps in eastern Europe. In the autumn, the SS experimented with poison gas in Auschwitz. Mass executions began at Chelmno near Lodz in December 1941. At the Wannsee conference of January 1942, Heinrich Himmler's deputy Heydrich explained the process of the 'Final Solution of the Jewish Question'. Jews from all of Europe were to be transported to the eastern death camps. Gas chambers in Majdanek and Treblinka began operating in the first half of 1942. In 1943 and 1944 Auschwitz-Birkenau became the principal killing-place for the Jews of Europe.

These killings went on until shortly before Soviet armies reached the camps. Even then, in forced evacuation marches, tens of thousands of prisoners were intentionally marched to death. In all, almost six million Jews had been killed.

These killing actions did not form part of a publicly proclaimed doctrine of nationality. The National Socialist leadership shrouded the holocaust in circumlocutions, euphemisms and evasions. Within Nazi ideology, however, the secrecy of the holocaust served a quite definite purpose. It was supposed to be a secret that *many people* knew to be a secret. Its function derived from the world of terrorist practice. The killings were to represent a shared guilt: the executors bound themselves together by a brotherhood of crime. A tie of this order might become so powerful that nothing external could destroy it. In a fragmented society, and in the absence of natural national cohesion, very powerful unifying bonds were required. This was the most horrifying example of how a synthetic national identity was to be created.

The attempted destruction of European Jewry represents the most extreme form of thinking the unthinkable. The crime against the Jews chose its target because of the historical legacy of anti-semitism and because of Hitler's own experiences and obsessions. It was also consciously a crime. This crime was entirely novel. National integration along National Socialist lines required not just anti-semitism but also an act of criminality: without complicity, there could be no absolute surrender for the sake of the national (and National Socialist) cause.

The identification of conspiracy and crime with the nation produced a legacy that has outlasted 1945 and the defeat of National Socialism. Did not the crime discredit any nation that required so evil a means of artificial integration? That is why many Germans searched hard for the 'good Germany' that opposed National Socialism and found its strength and unity in opposition. This was the 'other Germany' (*das andere Deutschland*).

Das andere Deutschland, wo liegt es?

The Third Reich had never won the consent of all Germans. There was a wide range of opposition activity. At one end was active resistance: of the army officers who launched the bomb plot of 20 July 1944, or of individuals, such as the cabinet-maker Georg Elser who placed a bomb in the hall where Hitler spoke on 8 November 1939. The military conspiracy had involved a large number of people, and after its failure around five thousand Germans were executed. Other opponents of the regime distributed pamphlets against the regime: such as the resistance group in Munich called the 'White Rose' and organized by students at Munich University. The labour movement and the left was heavily involved in resistance: until 1939, the SPD headquarters in Prague orchestrated an illegal and underground movement in Germany, which held clandestine meetings and produced illegal literature. A secret Communist Party structure remained in Germany and produced pamphlets as well as engaging in active measures against the Nazi government: sabotage, and the collection of intelligence material. The Communists and the SPD could frequently even work together in accordance with the Comintern's belated adoption of a Popular Front strategy against fascism. At the other end of the spectrum of opposition, there were isolated acts of defiance or illegality which lacked any political motive: black-marketeering, or shirking work, or forming youth bands.

What made Germans resist Nazism? National thinking, of course, played an important role for the conservative opposition to Hitler, which included such figures as Generals Witzleben and Beck, or Hjalmar Schacht, who had been Economics Minister from 1934 to 1937. The formulation of a coherent and politically successful non-Nazi foreign policy played a central part in their demonstration that Hitler had betrayed the German cause. As well as drawing up plans, the conservative opposition tried to realize its vision through an extensive range of foreign contacts. Karl Goerdeler, the former Mayor of Leipzig, kept in touch with Britain before and after September 1939. The diplomat Ulrich von Hassell, who had been Ambassador in Rome from 1932 to 1938, met British agents in Switzerland, and Josef Müller used the peculiar status of the Vatican as a sounding-board for the anti-Hitler plans of the German Abwehr (Counter-Intelligence). These men wanted to preserve Germany as a Great Power, with the frontiers of 1918 as well as perhaps the gains of the Munich settlement. Germany could then be a satiated power and not disturb the European peace. Such a conception of a Great Germany on an anti-Hitler basis might have seemed to conservative and aristocratic circles a plausible solution in 1939 and 1940. It required, however, the acquiescence of other states, or in essence a continuation of the British appeasement policy of the 1930s. The replacement of Chamberlain by Churchill reduced the chances of its success. After 1942 it became less and less probable as the war spread beyond a merely European conflict and as the German position deteriorated.[23]

As it became apparent that the Allies could not accept a Great Germany, even without Hitler, resistance hopes of producing a nationally attractive foreign policy option collapsed. The opposition could no longer claim to offer an obviously preferable foreign policy option in which Germans would preserve the gains of 1930s diplomacy without paying the Nazi price of fighting a war. The conservative resistance faced a dilemma: both while Hitler was winning the war and when he was losing it, he took away the basis for their foreign policy arguments. They had to wrestle with Hitler's powerfully attractive public image.

One of the most successful accomplishments of Nazi propaganda lay in the creation of an image of Hitler, as distinct from the National Socialist party, as the embodiment of conservative patriotism. Hitler never allowed himself to be associated with the actions of party zealots in removing crucifixes from churches and schools. Catholics and Protestants prayed with some sincerity for 'Führer and Fatherland'. Hitler presented himself before 1939 as Europe's statesman of peace. 1936 and the reoccupation of the Rhineland meant so much because not a drop of blood was spilt. In September 1938 Hitler peacefully solved a tense international crisis at a series of summit meetings – Berchtesgaden, Bad Godesberg, Munich – that eventually produced a complete victory for Germany's demands. The exiled SPD received reports such as this: the Rhineland crisis of 1936 had 'impressed all, who are otherwise less than enthusiastic about him . . . Everyone felt that there was an element of justification in Hitler's demands. The spirit of Versailles is hated by all Germans. Hitler has now torn up this cursed treaty and thrown it at the feet of the French.'[24] In 1940 after the fall of Poland and France, Hitler became the great statesman-soldier whose painless victories had restored Germany's international pre-eminence.

After the defeats of 1942–3 in Russia, and after major bombing raids on Germany from 1943, popular enthusiasm for the heroic Hitler myth began to wane. But a new source of patriotic legitimation took its place. Germany was now fighting a costly and desperate war of survival with Bolshevism. A failure would lead to the annihilation of the German people. Goebbels used this theme with great dramatic effect in his call to fight a 'total war' in the 1943 Berlin Sportpalast speech. Both the pre-1941 image of Hitler as the conservative and far-sighted statesman, and the post-1942 presentation of the German army as Europe's shield against Bolshevik barbarism, made it politically exceptionally hard to explain resistance from a *national* point of view.

In addition, presenting an alternative to Hitler would involve active resistance and possibly civil war. Justifying this on national grounds posed a logical question and an ethical dilemma. Since active resistance meant treason, it could scarcely be justified by drawing on the values of the state itself, or by talking about the nation. Only ethical and religious considerations provided an alternative.

Socialist resistance looked to a humanitarian ethical tradition that was independent of the state. Despite penetration by police spies, and continual arrests, communist and socialist groups circulated illegal literature, kept contacts with exiled organizations and even prepared for risings against the dictatorship. A communist spy ring ('the red orchestra') provided the USSR with valuable information. Some socialist politicians – notably Gustav Dahrendorf, Ernst von Harnack, Wilhelm Leuschner, Adolf Reichwein, Carlo Mierendorff and Julius Leber – had contacts with the military resistance. In the last days of the war, there was a full-scale, and brutally suppressed, workers' rising in the Bavarian mining town of Penzberg.[25]

Religious opposition played a key role in popular politics, as well as in convincing many men and women to make the commitment and sacrifice of active conspiracy. It was when the Nazi party attempted to interfere with religious practice that it suffered its most embarrassing public setbacks. In Oldenburg in 1937, the party had tried to remove crucifixes from school walls and had been forced to retreat. In 1941 in Bavaria massive rural protests against a similar campaign produced another Nazi retreat, and, allegedly, a personal rebuke for Gauleiter Wagner from Hitler. There are even a few cases where church opposition halted the regime's inhumanity – or, more accurately, obliged it to take steps to conceal its actions better. In Württemberg, popular resistance obliged the SS to close an extermination centre at Grafeneck. Cardinal Faulhaber of Munich and Bishop Graf Galen of Münster spoke openly against the 'euthanasia' of the mentally ill. The Protestant pastors Martin Niemöller and Dietrich Bonhoeffer set up an alternative church organization to resist Nazi attempts to use the Protestant church for its propaganda. Almost a third of Germany's pastors supported Niemöller's organization, though it was weakened by his arrest in 1937. Bonhoeffer too was arrested, and then hanged only a month before the end of the European war.

Religious and ethical feeling played a crucial role for the military and conservative resistance around Karl Goerdeler, but also with the much more liberal Kreisau circle centred around Helmuth James Graf von Moltke. For Moltke, only belief could stop modern barbarism: 'An unbelieving mass will sell itself to any politician, but a class of believers will not.' In a memorandum for the British government of April 1942, Moltke wrote:

> The forces in Germany striving for the latter possibility [the establishment of a civilized German government] are inspired by the ideas and the circles of the Christian opposition which has crystallized in years of struggle against national socialism. Militant Christianity in its widest sense is the only unbroken core of resistance within the Nazi state, and it has now formed powerful contacts with groups hitherto indifferent to Church and Religion. The key to their common efforts is a desperate attempt to rescue the substance of personal human integrity, equally threatened by Nazism and anarchic Bolshevism.[26]

The German nation as a guiding principle for would-be German resisters presented far more problems than an ethical ideal such as communism or socialism, or religious faith.

The Kreisau circle believed that the war showed that the epoch of nationalism was over. Moltke and his allies saw a postwar Europe composed of small units joined in a federal structure. It was a vision very similar to Naumann's Mitteleuropa, but now stripped of nationalist language altogether. In a memorandum of 1941, Moltke developed the idea of a 'pan-European state divided up into smaller, non-sovereign state structures'. The old conflict of France and Germany could only be ended by the abolition of these states. Resistance thinking developed some of the themes that after 1945 appeared in the quest for European integration.

Only a supranational unit could pursue those aspects of national life which had been of value. The report of the third conference of the Kreisau group formulated this proposition as follows: 'The free and peaceful development of national culture is incompatible with the retention of absolute sovereignty by each individual state. Peace demands the creation of an order that spans the separate states.' Already in 1939 Adam von Trott zu Solz had written: 'Europe is something far deeper and more living than an ethnic or aesthetic dream image, and her spirit will emerge all the more clearly for her crushing self-surrender.' Any relics of the nation-state might present an insuperable obstacle to European stability. 'The group', Moltke wrote in 1943, 'believes that an indisputable military defeat and occupation of Germany is absolutely essential both for moral and political reasons.'[27]

If the resisters looked to a past, it was a very distant past, and a Prussian rather than a German one. Since the early nineteenth century, most of them now believed, German history had been disastrous; the course of this history now required to be unravelled. Hans von Schlange-Schöningen explained: 'We must build up the new state, not so that the infernal cycle of German history repeats itself, but so that we *begin a new* history. It is not true that the era of dictatorship is beginning; it has ended.'[28]

The national conservatives and much of the army opposition had formerly held expansionist ideas about Germany's frontiers: many of these men felt happy with the annexationist plans for Mitteleuropa of the First World War (as distinct from Naumann's more liberal and more federalist order). But they also clearly believed and stated that Germany should not fight for such goals, and after 1942 many of them were prepared to accept some of the Kreisau ideas.

In 1945, the end of the war brought the end of Germany – from two sharply opposed viewpoints. The nationalism of the right had always had an apocalyptic element. Germany would be a world power or she would cease to exist. Hans Grimm, for instance, had written in January 1932: 'We know that the Empire of all Germans, that had become possible in the years 1914–18, will either be created by the national movement or will vanish in its most magnificent potential.' Hitler fully shared this bleak either/or view. Already in 1933 the philosopher Count Hermann Keyserling observed the destructive nature of Hitler's faith:

He embodies a fundamental trait of the German nation, which has always been in love with death and to whom the tribulation of the Nibelungs is a constantly recurrent basic experience. Germans only feel integrally German when this situation is given; they admire and they desire purposeless death in the shape of self-sacrifice. And they sense that through Hitler they are once more being led towards grandiose destruction, a tribulation of the Nibelungs. That is what fascinates them about him. He is fulfilling their deepest longing. The French or the British want victory; Germans always only want to die.[29]

Hitler himself gave up the Germans and their Germany, and set out to destroy the country whose leader he considered himself to be. In late 1944, Hitler began to revive the story of the *Dolchstoss* from the First World War. The 'home front' once more had betrayed the men in the field. All the themes of November 1918 returned. In August 1944, he told the Nazi area commanders (Gauleiters): 'If the German people was to be conquered in the struggle, then it had been too weak to face the test

159

of history, and was fit only for destruction.' On 26 December 1944 Hitler explained to the German generals: 'The German Reich is now fighting an ideological war for its very existence. The winning of this war will, once and for all, stabilize this great power, which quantitatively and qualitatively is already in existence. The loss of this war will destroy the German people and break it up.' In the early spring of 1945, Hitler still believed, hopelessly, in a military and political miracle. By 2 April he had changed his mind. The German people had betrayed him: 'The ignominies and the treachery we experienced in 1918 will be as nothing in comparison with what we may now expect. It is beyond comprehension that, after twelve years of National Socialism, such a thing could happen. My imagination boggles at the idea of a Germany, henceforth deprived of her elite which led her to the very pinnacles of heroism, wallowing for years and years in the mire.'[30]

On the other hand, most of the opposition, which clearly had a greater stock of moral legitimacy, also took the view that nationalism of the nineteenth-century type belonged firmly to the past, and not to the future, which they saw in European terms.

7

Potsdam:
Goodbye to Berlin

After the unconditional surrender of 8 May 1945, Germany no longer existed as a political entity. In legal terms, sovereignty passed to the United Nations (the name for the wartime coalition from January 1942): in practice to the four occupying powers, the USA, the USSR, Britain and France, operating through the military commanders in the Allied Control Council. The German capitulation included the phrase: 'This act of military surrender is without prejudice to, and will be superseded by, any general instrument of surrender imposed by or on behalf of the United Nations and applicable to Germany and the German armed forces as a whole.' This prospect of a general peace treaty still plays a role in arguments over what has become 'the German question'.

Some Germans made it clear from the outset that they did not see 1945 as the end of the nation. The Foreign Minister in the last Nazi government, that formed by Admiral Dönitz, still announced in a radio speech on 7 May: 'We wish to devote the future of our nation to the return of the inmost and best forces of German nature, which have given to the world imperishable works and values. We view with pride the heroic struggle of our people, and we shall combine with our pride in that struggle the will to contribute, as a member of Western culture, honest, peaceful labour – a contribution which expresses the best traditions of our nation.'[1]

This was, of course, as the speaker made clear, the nationalism of the right in a barely disguised form. It could scarcely be popular in the circumstances of 1945. The Third Reich and its ideology of the total state had in fact collapsed totally. The 'Werewolves' feared by the Allies never appeared; after the Second World War, no German Freikorps

161

operated. The change in political thinking was as dramatic. Like the Kreisau circle, democrats usually tried to escape from nationalism altogether. Alfred Weber, Max Weber's brother, in an influential book with the significant title *Goodbye to Past History*, said that only cultural nations (*Kulturnationen*) should be resurrected. Rival sovereign states would have to yield to international syndicates for political and economic government.[2]

The actual shape of the new Germany depended exclusively, however, on what the Allied leaders believed, and not on what Germans might think about the future of their country. Since January 1943, when the doctrine was formulated at the Casablanca conference, the Allies had been fighting for unconditional surrender. Between November 1943 and the end of the European war, the Soviet Union set the pace for Allied decision-making. Stalin thought of the brutal losses inflicted on his country by the German armies and of how Germans had betrayed his trust when they attacked the Soviet Union on 22 June 1941. At the summit meeting in Teheran in November 1943, he stated bluntly that Churchill's and Roosevelt's plans for preventing a resurgence of German nationalism were too feeble. He explained that Germans had always been subservient to an authoritarian state. He told how Leipzig workers in 1907 had failed to attend a demonstration because they could not find a railway official to cancel their train tickets. Roosevelt had proposed to extinguish the word 'Reich' from the German language, but this did not go far enough. Germany needed to be split up into several states.[3]

Roosevelt was moved by the force of Stalin's remarks. He came up with a plan to create seven small German states, of which five could be self-administering. Churchill remained more sceptical and believed that the destruction of the historic state of Prussia, which he saw as the fountain of German militarism, would be sufficient to ensure peace in Europe. Decreeing the end of Prussia as an administrative unit in fact became one of the major Allied concerns on the conclusion of the European war. Teheran, however, produced no determinate conclusion on the German question.

A systematic handling of Germany's future was left to a European Advisory Committee (EAC) which in 1944 drew up a scheme for the division of Germany into zones of occupation. But there were also initiatives completely outside the setting of the EAC, such as the plan of the US Treasury Secretary Henry Morgenthau for an agrarian, de-industrialized and divided Germany. Roosevelt, perhaps influenced by Stalin's powerful performance at Teheran, took up this scheme, and at the second Quebec conference (September 1944) Churchill also added his initials. According to Morgenthau's papers, Roosevelt said: 'We have got to be tough with Germany and I mean the German people not just the Nazis. We either have to castrate the German people or you have got to treat them in such a manner so they can't just go on reproducing people who want to continue the way they have in the past.'[4]

At the Crimean conference (Yalta, February 1945), the goal of a substantial deindustrialization of Germany remained: 'We are determined to . . . eliminate or control all German industry that could be used for military production.' The division of Germany (and of Berlin, which was treated separately) between the powers into zones whose military governors would exercise a *de facto* sovereignty caused little controversy, though the USSR resisted until the last moment a French participation in the occupation of Germany. Eventually, the French zones were carved from the territory originally in the zones of the other two Western powers. However, France, which had not been represented at Yalta, was also excluded from the next conference, held after the end of the war at Potsdam.

After Yalta, the emphasis of the Allies' German policy shifted significantly. The business of discrediting the Nazi regime had been partly accomplished by the military defeat and could be concluded by judicial proceedings (at Nuremberg against the major war criminals). Economic problems came to the fore at the expense of the earlier political and security concerns. A weakened, deindustrialized Germany posed an insoluble problem not just to Germans, but to all Europeans. Europe had been devastated by the war, and the Allied leaders believed that German resources should play an important part in the reconstruction of their countries. Britain and France wanted German coal, and the USSR had a broadly conceived reparations programme. But this required some economic activity in Germany, and raised the issue of how the administration was to work. A divided Germany did not look like an economically viable proposition. Coal and steel came mostly from the British zone, which lacked food (without which the miners could not work). The south (in the American zone) and middle Germany (Soviet) had food but lacked fuel. For practical reasons, the Allies began to consider one Germany – a notion which had been unthinkable at Teheran.

Potsdam dealt with the internal organization of Germany, and with her boundaries. A final frontier was set in the west of Germany, but not in the east. The line of the Oder and the western Neisse rivers was to be the provisional German–Polish frontier, but 'the final delimitation of the western frontier of Poland should await the peace settlement'.[5] Peace settlement or no, most of the German-speakers of Poland were either expelled or fled from their homes. In addition, the Saar was placed under French administration. Germany was to supply reparations. The final declaration of Potsdam spoke of some measure of central direction of German affairs: 'For the time being no central German government shall be established. Notwithstanding this, certain essential central German administrative departments, headed by State Secretaries, shall be established, particularly in the fields of finance, transport, communications, foreign trade and industry.'

In practice, disputes among the Allies obstructed the creation of the central agencies. France suspected the resurgence of a new German nationalism. The French leader Charles de Gaulle believed the creation of the agencies posed a question of 'life or death' for his country. The USSR demanded reparations on a scale that the Americans and British held to be socially and economically damaging, and politically unsustainable. In 1946 the US administration began to share the French fear of a united Germany, since it now thought that a single German unit might be manipulated by the Soviets. In public, the decisive turning-point was the speech made in Stuttgart by Secretary of State James Byrnes (September 1946), in which he seemed to appeal for the merging of all four zones. Two key statements ran as follows: 'We do not want Germany to become the satellite of any power.' 'If complete unification cannot be secured, we shall do everything in our power to secure maximum possible unification.'[6] The first statement expressed American fears of Soviet intentions; the second developed the notion that a preliminary merging of the Western zones might not be out of the question.

In December 1946 the USA and Britain combined their zones into an economic unit, Bizonia. At this time the Cold War flared up – first civil war in Greece and Turkey, then manipulated elections in Poland. And then international attention focused on Germany, which from 1947 became the centre of the Allies' security conflicts.

The USA now came to reinterpret retrospectively the ideological struggles of the Second World War. After December 1941, many Americans believed they were fighting, in alliance with the Soviet Union, against a racially based ultra-nationalism in Japan and Germany. After 1947, the war took – in a new hindsight – the form of a crusade for liberty and democracy against a totalitarian dictatorship: in other words, American motives acquired a distinctively anti-Soviet accent. The implication of such an interpretation was that the Western powers should not accept in Germany a new and dangerous alliance of communist totalitarianism with old-style nationalism articulated as zeal for a united Germany. Washington and London prepared to accept the Parisian line that only German partition could guarantee the stability of the international order, and drew the consequences of this interpretation.

8

The GDR:
Socialism in One Nation

After 1949, two states called themselves German. Their creation and early life derived from international political conditions rather than from any peculiarly German circumstances. Germany was the focus of the Cold War in Europe. The external constraint took a particularly dramatic form in the case of the German Democratic Republic (GDR). This did not, however, mean that the GDR did not wrestle with problems traditionally faced by states within the geographic area of Germany: the building-up of legitimacy, on a national basis, on the foundation of a strong economy and on an interpretation of historical precedent. The GDR identified itself with the characteristically nineteenth-century visions of an 'economic nation' (which existed to promote a strong economy and a unified society) and with a cultural nation.

Of all the adaptations of foreign models made by Germans in their quest for institutional identity, that of the GDR, founded in the Soviet zone of occupation in 1949, is the most obvious and direct. In 1945 and 1946, however, at least it appeared that political activity developed without much intervention from the outside. After 1947, East German politics underwent an unremitting process of Sovietization and Stalinization. The ruling party of the GDR came to play the same role in government as the CPSU in the USSR. The SED (Socialist Unity Party) had been created in April 1946 in the Soviet zone out of the fusion of the prewar SPD and a Communist party (KPD) whose key leaders had spent the 1930s and the war in the Soviet Union. Communists who had remained underground in Nazi Germany, or who had been imprisoned in Hitler's camps, found it hard to work in the post-1945

KPD. In 1946 the Soviet authorities applied considerable pressure on leading SPD politicians to agree to the fusion: those who refused were imprisoned and persecuted. An estimated 130,000 political prisoners, many of them socialists, were kept in NKVD-run concentration camps.

At first the SED saw itself as a German party fighting a battle together with all the other 'anti-fascist' movements: Christians and even conservatives as well as socialists. This alliance had emerged out of the struggles of the 1930s to create a popular front against Nazism. In 1945, this popular front had been victorious in the eastern sector only because of the help of the Red Army; but it did not intend to impose any kind of Soviet system on Germany. On the contrary, the SED's political programme featured 'a separate German road to socialism' from that travelled by Russia. Anton Ackermann, the most explicit advocate of such German socialism, pointed out that, unlike Russia in 1917, Germany had an advanced industrial economy. It would be relatively simple to restore prewar capacity to productive use. Germany would not need the same type of stringent political control as the USSR had applied in the 1930s. While the Russian working class had been small during the period of the Bolshevik revolution, Germany had a large proletariat. As a result of all these considerations, the harshness of the Soviet experience of the 1920s and 1930s could and should be avoided. Germany's more advanced position 'will mitigate the domestic political struggles, reduce the burden of sacrifice, and hasten the evolution of a socialist democracy'.[1] This meant that the KPD argued for a very modest economic reform programme: confiscation of the large estates (which had been an SPD suggestion in Weimar), but otherwise the creation of a society based on recognition of the principle of private property.

At a local level, in line with the overall strategy of an anti-fascist front, the KPD and then the SED shared power with other parties – a Christian democratic movement (CDU), and liberals (LDPD). Later these were joined by a peasant party (VdgB) as well as in 1948 by an organization aimed specifically at integrating former Nazis into the new order (NDPD). But the KPD always ensured that its functionaries took key positions – for instance as deputy mayors with a 'bourgeois' politician as Lord Mayor, or in the police force, or as 'people's judges'.

By 1947, the SED had moved much nearer to the Soviet model. In April the Soviet political adviser of the military occupation criticized Ackermann's conception of a separate German path. The SED joined in the general Moscow-led denunciation of Titoist or national deviations. The other parties now recognized the SED's 'dominant position'. Those leaders who wanted to keep an independent line (such as Ernst Lemmer or Jakob Kaiser in the CDU) lost their positions in December 1947. By the time the German Democratic Republic was established in 1949, in direct response to the creation of the Federal Republic in the Western zones, no doubt existed as to the subordination of the non-socialist movements and the 'leading role of the party'.

This theoretically multi-party, but, in practice, one-party system operated in Poland and Czechoslovakia as well. In the GDR, as in these states, it survived past the 1950s as the vestige of an attempt made between 1945 and 1946 at multi-party rule.

In the economy, the GDR adopted a Soviet-style planning system: first through a Ministry of Planning, which was soon renamed (in 1948) as the State Planning Commission. This drew up five- and seven-year plans in the Soviet manner, and sent orders downwards from highly centralized offices. Almost no flexibility existed. Administrative regulations and directives travelled in one direction, from the Commission to the enterprises. By the early 1960s growth rates collapsed, and the planning mechanism showed severe strain; but even in attempting to reform, the GDR drew on Soviet experience. Guided by the economist Yevsai Libermann, the USSR had experimented with decentralization and the introduction of incentives – a freer determination of prices, and profits – under the Khrushchev regime. In the GDR Libermann's economics became the NÖS (New Economic System). Predictably, when Khrushchev fell, the GDR also revised the NÖS by returning to a more centralizing system.

In the early years, much of German heavy industry operated in directly controlled 'Soviet joint stock companies'. All banks had been taken over by the state. Collectivization of agriculture having represented a central part of the Soviet achievement of the 1930s, the SED's party congress set collectivization as a priority in 1952 within a framework of the 'construction of socialism' on explicitly Soviet lines. It was actually applied in the GDR only later, in 1959–60. Between 1949 and 1955, the GDR took over a Soviet-style school system. Special workers' and peasants' faculties within the universities worked to create a 'new intelligentsia'.

In Germany, the personal cult of Stalin reached depths of obsequiousness. The first new street to be rebuilt in Berlin after the war, on the site of the old Frankfurter Allee, was the Stalinallee; architecturally, the wedding cake architecture intentionally came straight from Russia. Walter Ulbricht, the First Secretary of the SED, a man who had spent the 1930s in Russia, presented Stalin as the 'greatest scientist of the present', whose work would 'influence the course of world events for centuries', and called for 'the appropriation of Soviet science and its creative use in daily work'.[2] The Stalinist purges of the 1950s had their counterpart in the GDR. One hundred and fifty thousand members were expelled from the party. The Politbureau, the party executive, and the ministries were all purged – especially of those 'old communists' such as Alexander Abusch and Albert Norden who had not been in the USSR but had spent the Hitler period in the West. Unlike in Hungary or Czechoslovakia, however, no show trials were held and none of Ulbricht's former collaborators received death sentences.

In one aspect there was a striking difference between the politics of the GDR and the USSR: the stability of political leadership in the GDR. The GDR had no death of Stalin, and no deposition of Khrushchev. Instead one man, Ulbricht, remained at the helm until 1971, with a carefully cultivated personality cult of his own. It is true that Ulbricht had almost fallen in 1953 and 1956 as part of the Soviet shift to de-Stalinization. In 1953, German rivals – Wilhelm Zaisser and Rudolf Herrnstadt – waited in the wings, prompted by part of the Soviet leadership and especially by Lavrenti Beria, to step into Ulbricht's place. Strangely, Ulbricht survived the death of Stalin because of the East German workers' rising of 17 June 1953. This began with a protest march by building workers in the Stalinallee against an economic reform proposal which included higher production norms. The reform represented part of a 'New Course' designed by Ulbricht to meet the changing political requirements of the post-Stalin era. The demonstrations rapidly became a GDR-wide protest against the political leadership and the party's position. Soviet troops and tanks ended the revolt, but also ended the careers of Zaisser and Herrnstadt. The repercussions extended east. In the USSR, Beria's fall may have been a consequence of East Germany's problems. At such a volatile moment as this, however, Moscow believed that replacing Ulbricht would pose too great a risk.

Since Ulbricht had modelled himself so closely on Stalin and the cult associated with Stalinism, the great de-Stalinization that began at the Twentieth Party Congress put him at risk once more. He succeeded in formulating a quick response: 'Stalin cannot be counted among the classical authors of marxism.' The rest of Ulbricht's performance constituted an exercise in damage limitation. There could be, he explained, no question in the GDR of de-Stalinization: 'since there is no Stalinism, nothing can be de-Stalinized.'[3] If this verbal performance had not been sufficiently original to save Ulbricht, the Hungarian rising (23 October) was decisive. Once again the replacement of the figure who guaranteed German stability posed an unacceptable risk.

In the 1950s the GDR suffered from a continual exodus of population to the West. While the frontier with West Germany had been sealed, Berlin as a four-power city offered a relatively easy gateway. By 1961, over three millions had left the GDR, and the intensified pace of mass flight contributed significantly to the sudden falling-off of growth at the beginning of the 1960s. In August 1961, Ulbricht dealt with the erosion by putting a wall around West Berlin. The construction of the Wall changed political conditions in the GDR. Since flight had become nearly impossible, the government could intensify its political control without risking depopulation.

Ulbricht managed to adjust to the Khrushchev period quite well, largely because there were no Soviet foreign policy initiatives that posed the question that most concerned the GDR: relations with the other German state. Khrushchev's policy consisted of a series of wild flurries. Leonid Brezhnev's slower and more systematic *détente* presented a much more serious problem because it raised the German–German issue in a way unacceptable to the GDR's leadership. The whole of Germany, in Brezhnev's eyes, might be a suitable test-tube in which laboratory experiments in East–West relations could be conducted relatively harmlessly. The USSR required East Germany to move to better relations with the Federal Republic, as a demonstration in miniature of how *détente* might work on a wider scale. Such a move towards accepting the existence of the Western state challenged Ulbricht's claim to have built a state superior to the FRG. It also raised practical issues about improving access between East and West for ordinary people: a subject on which Ulbricht felt unhappy, since mobility would undermine the closed society he had systematically built up in the East after 1961. As a result, Ulbricht did his best to drag East German feet; and the Soviet leadership made its irritation public. In consequence, in 1971 Ulbricht retired on 'health grounds'.

His successor, Erich Honecker, had long been the SED's heir apparent, and he dealt with the inner-German *détente* of the early 1970s much more promptly and successfully. In the mid-1980s he found the *glasnost* era of Kremlin leadership highly uncomfortable. In particular, the cultural and literary relaxation in Gorbachev's Russia was unwelcome to the SED. The SED's policy explained that reforms and changes which might be urgently needed in the USSR might at the same time be inappropriate for a more highly urbanized and economically advanced state. The GDR, Honecker believed, no longer required foreign models; and at last a German road to socialism existed.[4]

In practice, there were tight limits to German autonomy. It remained true that internal party struggles in the USSR translated into GDR politics. A striking example was the fall of the East Berlin party leader, Konrad Naumann. Naumann belonged to a younger generation (he was born in 1928) and saw himself as a likely successor to Honecker (who was born in 1912), and engaged in rivalry with a much greyer bureaucratic figure, Egon Krenz. The Soviet struggle after Chernenko's death found an East German imitation. When Mikhail Gorbachev removed Grigory Romanov as the head of the Leningrad party, Naumann in Berlin went too – amid the same revelations of high living, drunkenness, mistresses and political corruption.[5]

There was a clear problem in modelling any political system on the USSR, where fundamental upheavals and reversals of policy occur irregularly and unpredictably, but always spectacularly. Soviet political tides can flow very suddenly and quickly. The GDR risked being left high and dry with the last, inappropriate, model. Ulbricht survived this periodic political and intellectual shipwreck by chance. Honecker's attempts in 1987 and 1988 to distance himself from Soviet reforms began to raise the question of whether he had not also finally run aground.

These problems were common to other East European states, but the leeway for changes and independent initiatives, or for what in the 1950s was called 'national communism', was greater there. The GDR had a peculiar difficulty which lay in the constant nervousness of its leaders that Moscow might be willing to surrender its interests for the sake of a global accommodation with the West.

In 1947 and 1948 the USSR remained, rather surprisingly, more attached – at least on the surface – to the four-power administration of Germany than any of the Western allies. It was, for instance, willing to make concessions over the issue of who would control the printing presses in a four-power currency reform for Germany – the issue over which the relations of the wartime Allies finally collapsed, and which immediately prompted the eastern blockade of Berlin (1948–9). During the London Foreign Minister's Conference (December 1947) the following extraordinary conversation occurred in the flat of the British Foreign Secretary, Ernest Bevin. Soviet Foreign Minister Vyacheslav Molotov was asked what he really wanted:

Molotov: I want a unified Germany.
Bevin: Why do you want that? Do you really believe that a unified Germany would go communist? They might pretend to. They would say all the right things and repeat all the correct formulas. But in their hearts they would be longing for the day when they could revenge their defeat at Stalingrad. You know that as well as I do.
Molotov: Yes, I know that. But I want a unified Germany.[6]

On 10 March 1952, the USSR handed the three Western powers a note offering a unified Germany within the boundaries of Potsdam, with free political party life and free elections. The only restriction on the new state was that it was not permitted to enter into military alliances, and especially into one directed against any of the wartime Allies. At Geneva in 1955, all four powers agreed that they had a responsibility in German issues and that reunification should take place by means of 'free elections'. However, Khrushchev quickly explained that, without a fundamental revision of the European security system, prospects for any speedy reunification remained slim.

Whether the Soviet offers of 1952 and 1955 were genuine or not is an issue that has attracted great political and historical controversy. Without access to the Soviet archives, it was impossible to solve this mystery definitively. Particularly in West Germany, the story of the lost opportunity for unity became a tool against Konrad Adenauer's Chancellorship. Doubtless the calculation that it would played a part in Soviet thinking. It is easy to see the 1952 proposal as a means of discrediting Adenauer and his pro-Western strategy, of wrecking his treaties with the Western powers and of blocking West Germany's entry into any European Defence Community. The most important witness as to the sincerity of Stalin's offer, an Italian politician called Pietro Nenni, claimed that Stalin and the Politbureau were 'really willing to make sacrifices to obtain unification. They would have sacrificed the East German communists so as to bring about a Germany ruled by a government friendly to the West but containing a strong leftist opposition as in Italy today.'[7] Whether Nenni could really know what Stalin believed may be doubted; it is more likely that Beria and Georgi Malenkov saw the attractions of this proposal. In any case, the note had an immediate application as an instrument against German participation in a European Defence Community, of which the Soviets had a quite natural suspicion.

Whatever the calculations and the politics of the Moscow move, Stalin's note gave the GDR leadership a shock. They may well have seen how easily they could be abandoned; and without the USSR, their position had little support. Intimidating Ulbricht in order to keep him in line may even have been as important to Stalin as frightening Adenauer. The 1955 Geneva proposal is easier to interpret. It too was rather more than simply the meaningless verbiage characteristically produced by high-level diplomatic meetings, for it constituted a new bid to humiliate Adenauer and frustrate West German participation in NATO.

In the shadow of the USSR, with the continual possibility of a reordering of the German and European map, and with a highly attractive Federal Republic next door, the GDR found it hard to establish an identity of its own. Article 1, Paragraph 9 of the original (1949) constitution explained that there existed only one German nationality. This view also appeared in the national anthem (as it did for West Germany):

> Resurrected from the ruins,
> Turned towards the future,
> Let us serve you for the best,
> Germany, united Fatherland.
> The old needs will vanish
> If we act in unity
> For we must accomplish
> That more beautiful than ever we see
> A sun shining over Germany.[8]

After the construction of the Berlin Wall in 1961 sealed off the last remaining contacts between the GDR and the West, and split the 'united Fatherland', the problem of identity was solved in a negative way – by the international isolation of the GDR. This state now existed only because it was recognized by the USSR and by the countries of the Warsaw Pact.

In the 1970s, the Basic Treaty with the Federal Republic (1972) ended the diplomatic isolation, and the GDR entered the United Nations. The movement of people became easier: large numbers of West Germans and West Berliners could cross the border, and East Germans could pass the other way on 'urgent family business'. Western television reached most East German homes. All this produced renewed questioning about how the GDR differed from the rest of what had once been Germany.

Honecker explained that the GDR required a delimitation (*Abgrenzung*) from the West. In one of his earliest appearances as the new leader of the SED, at the June 1971 party conference, he declared: 'Between the GDR and the FRG, two states independent of one another and with opposed social orders, a process of delimitation emerges by necessary laws [of history].' In 1972 he called the FRG a 'foreign country' – something which Ulbricht had never been willing to do.

East Germany's position needed to be reformulated, and a new doctrine of nationality evolved. From 1972 the East German regime tried to avoid using the word 'Deutschland', which it now associated with the discredited old order of Imperial Germany; it substituted instead the initials DDR (GDR). Becher's words for the national anthem (with the reference to 'Germany, united Fatherland') disappeared from East German public life, and the music alone was played.

The definition of the GDR as a class nation representing the interests of workers and peasants became part of the constitution on 7 October 1974. This way of thinking about the nation and nationality, as a reflection of group-specific economic interests, had a history going back to the days of the great tariff conflicts before the First World War. It had appeared in Ulbricht's speeches and declarations as a means of attacking the legitimacy of the West German state. The two halves of Germany were separated 'only [by] imperialism and militarism and not [by] the Wall'. Since militarism and imperialism had been condemned by the inexorable laws of history, there could only be one genuinely progressive nation. 'Here where the GDR is, is the foundation of peace, here the people decide. [This] is Germany.'[9]

A nation could be defined by materialist and objective conditions and did not depend on ethnic similarities or on whomever, by chance of geography, was its neighbour.[10] Only the FRG's ideologists had any stake in intellectual obfuscation and in masking the 'class and social content of the national question'.[11] Each of these two opposed nations had an independent culture which determined the scope of its national life. Socialist culture had a 'national mission':

> What does the humanistic-socialist culture and style of life that we aim at have in common with the denial of humanist traditions and the anti-human excesses of the late capitalistic unculture and the Americanized style of life practised in West Germany? And even where is the identity between the stammering of words, notes and colours which for some artists in capitalist countries is the expression of a lack of spiritual orientation, and our own longing for mastery and for the high accomplishment of socialist forms?[12]

Albert Norden, who had been a member of the KPD since 1920, deduced that the two German nations were separate, and not just the states: 'There are not two states of a single nation, but instead two nations in states of different social orders.'[13] Honecker argued for the division of the German nation into two along the axis of progress/reaction. In a New Year's address for 1979, he explained: 'The GDR is the German state of social progress, the heir to everything progressive and humanist in the history of the German people.'[14]

The claim of the historical necessity for eventual reunification did not need to be completely given up. In 1981, for instance, Honecker explained: 'If the working people begin the socialist transformation of the Federal Republic, then the question of the reunification of both German states would be put in a completely new way. How we would then decide is not open to any doubt.'[15]

173

The concept of progress that lay at the centre of the GDR's definition of nation meant social reform: cheap transportation; cheap housing (though this helped to produce an acute housing shortage that is only now beginning to be solved); cheap basic foodstuffs; the absence of unemployment, and a high degree of labour security. The most direct expression of progress could be found in national accounting statistics: between 1951 and 1955, net material product *per capita* rose at an annual rate of 13 per cent (a Western figure gives the much lower rate of 5.2 per cent, though even this still represents a spectacular progress). For 1956–60 the official figures give an annual rate of 7.1 per cent. Immediately before the construction of the Wall, there was a crisis. In the early 1960s the economy faltered: the need to respond played a great part in the calculation about adopting the more decentralized and less bureaucratic NÖS. Nevertheless, the rate of growth of net material product fell to 3.4 per cent over the period 1961–5.[16]

In the 1960s the 'scientific-technical revolution' became the slogan for advance. Ulbricht and Norden explained the NÖS as a national act. Ulbricht declared in 1963: 'in the interest of the whole nation [i.e. East *and* West] we are determined to prove the superiority of our socialist order economically over the capitalist system in West Germany.' Or later: 'As a solid component of the socialist world system our GDR furnishes the proof of the superiority of socialism under the conditions of a highly industrialized country and the successful establishment of a technical revolution.' Norden laid out the economic base for socialist thought: 'Our whole people must learn to think in economic terms and they must learn to understand that everything depends on our own work; a better life just as much as the protection of our republic and the securing of the peace. The stronger we are economically, the more hopeless will be the Bonn imperialists' war plans.'[17]

In the 1970s Honecker turned to consumer goods in an effort to demonstrate the superiority of the GDR's social order. The opening to the West after 1972 raised that question of comparability that had been stifled in the decade after the building of the Wall. Consumer prosperity, he told the Eighth Party Congress of 1971, 'means further political and economic stability in the GDR'. Attention would be directed to improving the supply of automobiles and washing-machines. The West German experience of the 1950s – that consumerism could generate political stabilization – was being rerun in the East twenty years on. In 1984 Honecker was still writing: 'The economy forms the central field for our social policy. Without strong economic growth, we can satisfy neither the material and cultural needs of men or strengthen the socialist state and its defences.'[18] But after 1980, the GDR economy stagnated.

From the 1950s, the cult of economic growth had replaced anti-fascism as the dominant myth of the GDR's legitimacy. In each decade it was reformulated as the achievements of the past decade seemed questionable. When central planning crumbled, the slogan became 'scientific-technical revolution'; in the 1970s enhanced consumer prosperity came in as a new motto.

In the 1980s another state-supporting myth became important: the myth of history. Like the CPSU, the SED's marxism had always been a historical doctrine, concerned with 'progressive emancipation' and with 'evolution'. It could encompass a national history as part of the overall historical process. Honecker in the 1970s carefully selected the best strands of German history to weave into the GDR's tapestry: the progressive legacy of Beethoven, the social struggle in the early sixteenth century of peasants and of Thomas Müntzer against the authoritarian Reformation of the princes and of Martin Luther. The GDR, according to an official statement in 1984, was 'the heir and the continuator of all that is good, progressive, humane and democratic in history, because it is itself the embodiment of progress, democracy and humanity'.[19]

In the 1980s the GDR came to accept rather more of its history. After the fifth centenary of Martin Luther's birth (1983), the conservative Luther figured more prominently than the radical Thomas Müntzer. For part of 1983, the Luther anniversary attracted more attention than the centenary of Marx's death. Clausewitz, the military thinker of the Prussian reform era, was restored to honour with the help of sympathetic quotations from Friedrich Engels. Even Frederick the Great and Bismarck attracted sympathetic attention and major biographical treatments. The rebuilt old Dresden opera house and the Goethe house in Weimar were also celebrated. The centre of East Berlin was rebuilt for the 750th anniversary of the city with remarkable historical accuracy. 'Our Republic has become the Fatherland, the home of all its citizens,' one of East Germany's leading historians, Willibald Gutsche, wrote reassuringly in 1984.[20]

This historical interest stood in sharp contrast to the radical iconoclasm of the early years of the Republic, when the regime in 1950 demolished the old Imperial Palace on an island in the Spree river, though it had hardly been damaged in the war, or when Christian Rauch's statue of Frederick the Great was first hung over with drapes and then removed (also in 1950). Indeed, the Rauch statue was returned to Unter den Linden in December 1980 at the time of the Polish Solidarity crisis – and so Frederick again sat on his horse in the centre of Berlin, facing Silesia.

175

This historical re-evaluation attracted a substantial amount of attention in the West, much of it rather exaggerated. There was really no evidence, for instance, that the GDR leadership believed that the statue of Frederick the Great pointing towards Silesia really constituted a serious warning to Poland. The nationalism deployed in television shows about Luther or Clausewitz or 'der alte Fritz' was hardly very vigorous or assertive, or very dangerous. It was, for instance, much less obviously threatening than the gigantic military or military-style parades that had traditionally been part of East German public life.

The new nationalism was certainly, however, part of a conscious decision to display more interest in the past. It also served a political function, though a rather modest one.

The boom in East German history was little more than an attempt on the part of the regime to chip away at a society that had become more and more withdrawn and privatized. It was harder for any government to have a substantial hold over the population. The GDR turned into a 'Nischengesellschaft', a society of nooks and crannies (or, as the joke goes, a society of crooks in government and nannies who look after the rest of the population), kept in line by an ubiquitous secret police. Family and friendship contacts, and 'good relations' with others (shopkeepers with access to scarce goods), functioned quite independently of the ties sponsored by the state or the Party or the officially established mass institutions: trade unions, women's leagues and so forth. The sort of history that the GDR leadership now wished to present was more likely to appeal to a polite and slightly bored, certainly not politically emotional, Sunday-afternoon crowd of GDR citizens than to whip up the masses into a frenzy of nationalist hysteria.

The old methods of creating national consensus and legitimacy in the GDR behind an anti-fascist or a progressive marxist line had failed. Throughout Eastern Europe, marxist-leninist ideology collapsed. The SED had to work with a highly sentimental picture of the German past and present, rather than with a story of continual economic advance. For the GDR, history stopped being a scientific principle and became a souvenir shop instead. It is plausible to think that a political structure can be saved by economic performance; but it is ridiculous to look for salvation in a mixture of nostalgia and kitsch.

9

West Germany:
The Nation is Fed Up

It was the creation of the Federal Republic of Germany in 1949 that led to the Soviet-directed foundation of the GDR. The conditions surrounding the birth of these two states were similar. Both initially had broken economies. Both owed their existence to the tensions of world politics, and in particular to the collapse of relations between the wartime Allies. The Allies left their mark on the areas of Germany they respectively occupied. The GDR adopted many features from Soviet politics and economies. The Western powers had an important voice in setting the Federal Republic's constitutional, political and economic order. However, here the resemblances stop. Many of West Germany's most characteristic features emerged also as a German reaction against pressure from outside.

Like the Weimar Republic, West Germany initially developed as a constrained state: with the exception that the limits on the Federal Republic were far more restrictive. As in the case of Weimar, the constraints strengthened rather than weakened the new state. Unlike Weimar, however, the Federal Republic evolved into a secure political structure. Its eventual success should not make us overlook the paradox of the positive contribution made by the difficult circumstances of Bonn's birth. The highly stable West German parliamentary system emerged out of a deep hostility to Allied impositions.

When the external limits on Weimar and on Bonn began to be removed, hard questions about identity immediately posed themselves for Germans. Fortunately the dissolution of the post-1945 order has occurred very gradually, and not with the breathtaking speed with which, in the early 1930s, the system of Versailles crumbled. The gradual nature of post-Second-World-War change in the 1980s allowed a gradual adaptation by West Germany to the new world environment. Only in 1989 did the pace of change accelerate dramatically.

Birthmarks always stay. Two of the most central aspects of the early period remained as burning political issues: first, the division of Germany in 1948–9, which left the Federal Republic as a 'rump state' that nevertheless – under the terms of its Basic Law – represented all Germans. The preamble to the Basic Law (23 May 1949) included the following qualification of West Germany's statehood: the parliamentary council (a kind of constituent assembly) in drawing up the Law 'also acted on behalf of those Germans who had been excluded from participating'. The whole German people remained, according to this Law, under the obligation to 'accomplish the unity and freedom of Germany in free self-determination.'

Secondly, a legacy of the postwar period was the integration of Germany into the Western alliance system. Economic links with the Western powers played an important initial part in binding Germany into Western politics. When in 1947 the Americans launched the European Recovery Programme (or Marshall Plan), they intended to use this to further European integration as a bulwark against Soviet expansion. Then there followed military ties. Germany had been disarmed after 1945. In 1950, Germany pointed out that the West needed more soldiers because of the situation in Korea: if armed confrontation between East and West broke out in divided Korea, conflict might just as easily flare up in divided Germany. The German government used the Cold War as an opportunity to rebuild the army.

The Korean War and rearmament had an important meaning for the new West German political system. Every state believes that an army is an important part of national sovereignty. In classical definitions, sovereignty usually rests precisely in the monopoly of force and coercion. Furthermore, for Germans the army had traditionally played a great part in national self-esteem. As part of the price to be paid for gaining military sovereignty, and for removing the Allied Occupation Statute, Germany agreed to cooperate with proposals for a supra-national European defence force. Then, after France blocked this proposal in 1954, Germany accepted membership in the military organization of NATO. After West Germany joined NATO in 1955, its government declared: 'Now that the Paris treaties have come into operation, the Federal Republic has achieved military control, without which a state is not sovereign.'[1] Being a Great Power once more could no longer, after 1945, be purely and simply a German exercise: it meant in addition accepting a whole pattern of alliances. At the same time, for all the talk about greater supranational integration, these were still alliances between nation-states.

A Divided Country

Though the final Allied declaration of Potsdam spoke of central administrative agencies for Germany, the immediate realization of any centrally unified direction was obstructed by French hostility to anything that might lead to the re-creation of a united country. Already after the First World War, France had tried to establish a separate Rhineland state. The failure to realize this had, in French eyes, led directly to the Second World War. In 1946 and 1947, France was still pressing for a separate Rhineland administration; and the imposition of the Ruhr Statute in 1949 represented a belated half-concession to the French. Some Germans, including Konrad Adenauer, believed the Ruhr statute to be more damaging to Germany than had been the unlucky Versailles Treaty.

After 1947 a new cause of division existed. Soviet policy in its zone hardened, and America's suspicions of the plans of its former ally increased. Anti-communism became a major force behind US foreign policy. In Germany, tension between the USA and the USSR prevented a four-power agreement on economic reform that might have served as a preliminary to the re-establishment of a single democratized state in Germany. Instead, the Western powers – initially only Britain and the USA – went ahead with the creation of their own economically integrated region, the so-called Bizonia. France brought her zone into the Western bloc later in response to American pressure over participation in the Marshall Plan. An exclusively Western economic programme, drawn up and imposed mostly by American planners, then put the seal on the division of Germany.

Both the economic and, later, the political plans for western Germany stemmed initially from Allied proposals. The basis for 1948's economic and currency reform was the realization that the initially very strict limitations on economic activity were unrealistic. The USA had first acted on the basis of the second Quebec conference and the Joint Chiefs of Staff (JCS) directive 1067 of September 1944. The Control Council in March 1946 set out a Level of Industry Plan, in which the target level of output was that of 1932, in other words the depth of the interwar depression. Soon the permitted production ceilings went up, but there were still severe restrictions on the scope of Germany's economic recovery. Only a currency reform could eliminate the monetary chaos that was the legacy of the Third Reich's inflationary financing of rearmament and war. It was an American plan (Colm-Dodge-Goldsmith) that set out the method of cutting the surplus of German money – and the German economic experts only found out at the last moment. They were taken in buses with frosted glass windows to a military base at Rothwesten, where they worked out only the minor and subsidiary details of the reform. Everything, from the name of the new currency (Deutsche Mark) to the proportion by which old accounts should be cut down, had been presented to them without discussion. Currency reform had to be prepared in great secrecy, partly in order to take the population by surprise and to prevent a pre-reform scramble out of the old currency. The Americans also needed to keep the Soviets out of the reform plans.[2]

The liberalization of the press, and the creation of a radio system independent of direct government control, occurred at the insistence of the Allies, and to the dismay even of many German democratic politicians. More generally, at the outset, the constitutional creation of the Federal Republic also came out of Allied demands, plans and pressures. Since 1945, the Western powers had been active in political re-education, denazification of the civil service (including the very important teaching profession), and in encouraging democratic operations at least on a local and regional basis. Even this step towards democratization on a local level presented the new, would-be politicians with problems. The communal parliaments, mayors, *Land* parliaments and Minister-Presidents installed by this exercise stood in an awkward position. They never quite knew whether they functioned as agents of the Allies or as representatives of the interests of their electors against the pressures of the Allies. This uncertainty later became an agonizing dilemma for national politicians in the early years of the Bonn Republic.

The proposal for a government for all the western zones came from the London conference of March 1948, attended by Britain, France and the USA, and the Netherlands, Belgium, and Luxembourg – but not by the USSR. The London conference drew up the basic plans subsequently presented in July at Frankfurt to the Minister-Presidents of the three western zones: these included a Constituent Assembly, and a German legislature, administration and judiciary. Germany was to have a federal system, with its obviously American overtones. But at the same time, the Frankfurt proposals reserved extensive rights for the Allies to intervene in German foreign affairs and trade policy, as well as to impose demilitarization and reparations.

The German politicians hesitated, partly because of the proposed extent of Allied control, partly because of the way the constitutional provisions were supposed to work (they weakened the central state and gave a great deal of influence to the state – *Land* – governments), but also because acceptance of these proposals meant the abandoning of United Germany, as well as of sovereign Germany. As the hardening stance of the SED in the eastern zone, and the Soviet blockade of Berlin, made this point seem less real, and as the responsibility for German disintegration appeared to shift to Soviet intransigence and belligerence, the last objection vanished. The reality of a Soviet threat disposed Germans to go along with the Western powers. So the Minister-Presidents of the German *Länder* accepted the Allied scheme with only a few modifications: the original constituent assembly envisaged by the Allies was now called the Parliamentary Council. It would draw up a Basic Law rather than a Constitution (which implied too great a degree of finality). Most importantly, the politicians would not have to expose their product to a referendum, which could only have led to bad-tempered nationalist denunciations of their sellout.

German national pride had suffered a succession of hard blows. The economic and social situation remained highly precarious. At first the currency reform produced mostly unpleasant effects: prices for clothing and textiles shot up in the latter half of 1948, so that for a substantial part of the population they became unaffordable. The constitutional settlement had been a humiliating external imposition on Germany. As Konrad Adenauer, the Christian Democratic (CDU) leader who was to become the first Chancellor of the Federal Republic, observed: 'the liberation is a cruel and harsh disappointment. If there is not a miracle, the German people will slowly but surely be destroyed.'[3]

That miracle actually lay in the presence of the Allies. The deep gloom of 1948 and 1949 gave a chance to the new political movements to establish their legitimacy. They could identify themselves by their opposition to the occupying powers. Adenauer built up a personal mystique on this basis. He had been dismissed by the British in October 1945 after only a few months as Mayor of Cologne. Everywhere in his zonal authority, he noticed that the socialists were working very closely with the British authorities. This allowed him to attack the SPD as the 'government party', and to blame it (quite unfairly) for the economic problems of the postwar period.[4] In the 1949 elections to West Germany's first parliament, Adenauer still complained that Britain, ruled by a Labour Party government, was imposing an alien socialism on a reluctant Germany. The CDU would provide a defence against this attempt.

The socialist leader Kurt Schumacher played the national card as frequently and with as passionate and genuine a conviction as did

Adenauer. He had suffered for ten years as a prisoner in Dachau and survived only because of a remarkable psychological stamina. He saw himself as the heir to the Lassallian tradition in German socialism which combined social reform and patriotism. In the mid-nineteenth century, Lassalle had seen a weak and disunited Germany subject to the impositions of Vienna, Paris and London. After Hitler's war, Germany lay at the mercy of foreign states just as she had done after Napoleon's war. Already on 6 May 1945, before the official capitulation of Hitler's Reich, in his first public statement Schumacher had explained that 'the victors are now going to make their peace terms, not ours'.[5] The Soviet manipulation of eastern zone politics became clear to him at an early stage. He quickly recognized that the development of the SPD in the eastern zone and its fusion with the communists into the United Workers' Party or SED had turned it into a Soviet puppet, and he was unwilling, as a result, to work with the Soviets. On the other hand, he believed that Adenauer had sacrificed an opportunity for German unity by collaborating with the Western Allies: for him, Adenauer stood to Washington as Ulbricht stood to Moscow. In a famous accusation, on the occasion of Germany's agreeing to set up the International Ruhr Authority, he called Adenauer the 'Chancellor of the Allies', and was expelled from the parliamentary session. In 1952, when Germany concluded a treaty with the Western Allies in Paris in lieu of a final peace treaty, Schumacher described the occasion as a 'naked celebration of the victory of a clerical coalition over the German people . . . Whoever agrees to the General Treaty stops being a good German.'[6]

Progress for Germany could only take place in a national setting, since in the absence of an effective national policy other states – the USA or the USSR – would exploit Germany and sap the strength of her economy. Schumacher tried to distinguish between the true nation and a discredited nationalism. Nationalism in his eyes meant the manipulation of the nation's interests for the advantage of someone else. When the SED in the Soviet zone wanted to play the nationalist card about united Germany, he explained: 'Nation and nationalism are in principle irreconcilable opposites. Whoever wants to be a good German cannot be a nationalist' (1946). Later he defended the integrity of Germany: it was a cultural entity which should not be sacrificed for the sake of foreign notions of grand politics, whether these came from Paris, London, Washington or Moscow. 'Germany is a part of Europe which cannot be thought away. She is not the glacis of other European countries, she is Europe itself' (1950).[7]

For both of the major West German political movements, Christian democracy and socialism, nationalism remained in the later 1940s a vital consideration – despite the experience of National Socialism, and even at a time when it made little sense to speak of the nation. The parties and their leaders performed complex political manoeuvres in order not to appear anti-national.

The strength of reactive nationalism in fact moulded the shape of postwar politics. It made the position of a governing party precarious, in that any unavoidable compromises with the Western Allies, or – though this was less likely – with the Soviet Union, incurred immediate unpopularity. At the same time the national problem, if appropriately handled, gave politicians an opportunity. Any measure that carried political odium, any unavoidable but detested policy, could be carefully presented so as to appear as a policy imposed by the Allies and not the invention of Germans.

The precarious position of governing parties also made the position of the parliamentary opposition much easier. From a nationalist standpoint, the obvious course when faced by a hostile world imposing unacceptable conditions on Germany was to retreat into political opposition. This strategy, characteristic of Weimar politics, dominated SPD thinking until the end of the 1950s. Socialists rejected both the notion of a closer relationship with the SED, or with possibly reformist elements within it (such as the Herrnstadt group); but they also opposed economic integration in Europe and military association with the West. The powerful argument against Adenauer's rearmament proposals, first within the context of the European Defence Community and then in NATO, was that they constituted a revival of German militarism in which old Wehrmacht officers could creep back into political affairs, and also that they did not serve Germany's interests, and indeed exposed Germans to the risk of a new war.

In addition to moral or pacifist objections, many Germans could only see an army limited by the Allied restrictions. They feared that the regulation of their weaponry would be so severe as to leave their country with under-equipped troops destined to be the cannon fodder of the next world war. Even the more generous terms of the European Defence Community accepted by the German government in 1952 still put the twelve German divisions under non-German command (though in 1954 the Community collapsed when the French Assembly voted against it).[8] Here Adenauer's government faced a dilemma. Only by accepting the EDC could Germany ensure the end of the Occupation Statute and the attainment of full sovereignty. But the EDC meant the end of military sovereignty and the surrender of German interests, in theory to those of the Western community of nations, but in practice to the requirements of French power politics.

The division over national issues in the 1950s helped to create the two-bloc system characteristic of West German politics, but not of behaviour in either the Kaiserreich or the Weimar Republic. Government and opposition parties are part of the Anglo-Saxon political tradition, but had not been part of German life. At the outset of the Bonn Republic a national cross-party solution and national politics appeared to many as the time-honoured way of dealing with political crises in Germany – as was, in fact, reflected in the curious relationship between the SED and the other non-communist parties in the National Front of the eastern part of Germany. In the West, many leading figures within the two largest, but not yet dominant, parties – the SPD and the new CDU – argued the need for a Weimar-style 'Great Coalition' to solve all the appallingly complex and emotionally difficult problems facing the new state. In the SPD Carlo Schmid, and in the CDU Jakob Kaiser, Karl Arnold and Werner Hilpert, took this position. But Kaiser's position crumbled in the light of the ferocious intensity of Schumacher's nationalism and also of the extent of the SPD's proposals for nationalization. The other CDU leaders reluctantly accepted Adenauer's rule, with the SPD consigned to opposition.

The ease of opposition for the SPD made it important for the CDU to establish a governmental party, and this division between opposition and government helped both parties to establish clearly defined identities. By 1961 there were only three parties represented in the Bundestag: the CDU/CSU (the CSU or Christian Social Union is the Bavarian equivalent of the CDU); the small liberal Free Democratic party (FDP); and the SPD.

Apart from national issues, economic policy divided opposition and government. Initially, the CDU had taken an ostensibly antagonistic stance towards market capitalism. Big business in Germany had been – so at least it was widely believed – responsible for the rise of Hitler. Then, in the impoverished conditions of the postwar world, the securing of fuel and food supplies took on an urgent priority. A planned economy looked the obvious solution. Jakob Kaiser favoured a wide-ranging nationalization, and the CDU's 'social committees' drew up the Ahlen programme, which contained many socialistic aspects. Already in 1946, however, in the party programme drawn up at Neheim-Hüsten, a compromise solution recorded that 'the socialization of parts of the economy is at the moment not practical, since the economy is not free. In the later settlement, economic and political considerations – but above all the general good – will be decisive.' The responsibility for failure to achieve an ideal economic settlement lay with the foreign powers, 'since the economy is not free'. This was a highly characteristic manoeuvre in the explanation of a failure to implement popular policy choices. The fact was actually that at least the British authorities unambiguously favoured the extension of state ownership in the German economy. Gradually the CDU became bolder in its advocacy of a free market alternative, or of what it styled the social market economy (*soziale Marktwirtschaft*).

It was also the Allied position which made feasible the free market course associated with Ludwig Erhard, the economic director of the Anglo-American Bizonia. Erhard argued that the policies of control and rationing under the Nazis and also under the Allies had not solved Germany's economic problems. In 1948, at its party congress, he persuaded the CDU to 'reject the failed policy of a state-directed planned and command economy'.

The currency reform of June 1948, prepared by the Allies, presented the Germans with a chance to introduce on their own initiative an extensive liberalization, an end to price controls and the removal of rationing. Decontrol reflected the priorities of Erhard and attracted Adenauer politically because it meant a decisive break with the SPD. It also encountered considerable scepticism on the part of the Allies. Liberalization undoubtedly made more goods available, though it meant that price increases (particularly for textiles) put many items out of the reach of ordinary consumers. A free market replaced an administered rationing with rationing through prices, and this appeared at least for a short while as anti-social. It took time before the growth set off by the currency reform and the economic liberalization outweighed the in-equitable effects of the workings of the free market.[9] Erhard worried sufficiently to send out his secretary Ella Muhr on regular missions to check the high-street prices of textile goods. Though prices slipped back in 1949, Germany's economic problems had not vanished. In spring 1950 and in the winter of 1951/2 unemployment rose to almost two million, and Germany had a major balance of payments difficulty. The Americans – whose Marshall Plan had been indispensable for the mixed story of German economic recovery so far – began to demand the reimposition of controls and the end of a crazed experiment in free-market economics. The CDU also suffered badly in electoral terms from its early experiment. In the Bundestag elections of 1949, 31 per cent of voters had chosen the CDU. Subsequently there were further setbacks in the federal state elections. In an opinion poll of spring 1950, only 28 per cent claimed to be 'generally satisfied' with Adenauer's policy.

However, in the early 1950s the tide began to flow in the other direction. The governmental party no longer suffered because of its position. Economic and foreign policy matters became an advantage rather than a handicap for the ruling party, and one that translated directly into increased CDU votes. The turning-point came with a foreign policy success: the creation of the European Coal and Steel Community in April 1951, and the general treaty concluded at Paris with the Western powers in 1952 which promised the end of the Occupation Statute. Schumacher and the SPD attacked the ECSC, the European Defence Community and the Paris treaty (all of which depended politically on each other) as a sellout to the interests of French heavy industry. However, Germany's advantages appeared quickly – certainly by 1955, when the general treaty came into force.

The Western treaty stood as a foreign political achievement only because of the staggering economic recovery of the early 1950s. Revival produced an auspicious environment for the democratization of politics. The Korean War provided a stimulus to the world economy, and Germany's balance of payments problem corrected itself. By 1952 the direction of West German politics for the next decade had been set – towards Adenauer's quarrelsome senescence and towards the less than charismatic Chancellorship of his successor Erhard (1963–6). The CDU and CSU were the major beneficiaries. Throughout the 1950s their support climbed: to 45.2 per cent of the votes in the Bundestag election of 1953, and 50.2 per cent in 1957 (the only time any West German party ever achieved an overall majority in parliament). The SPD in opposition gradually improved its performance as well, though it stayed a long way removed from power and without any obvious coalition partners.

The CDU developed a new national style in the 1950s. It would be a mistake to suppose that Adenauer's Rhineland Catholicism meant the absence of any nationalism. The vigour of the economy helped him to present national issues with far greater authority. West Germany claimed to represent the whole German nation, and refused to have diplomatic relations with any state recognizing the GDR (the so-called Hallstein doctrine). A particularly proud moment came in 1955 when Adenauer went to Moscow to bring back German prisoners of war held in the Soviet Union. Adenauer's West Germany spoke, it seemed, for all of Germany – even in dealings with Russia.

Adenauer became self-conscious about his success. At the beginning of the 1950s Bonn was still a makeshift capital sited in a small and provincial university town. Gradually German self-representation became more elaborate. Adenauer complained that Bonn did not have enough red carpets or luxurious furniture. 'If I', he told some German journalists half jokingly, but with an underlying seriousness, 'want to become a Great Power – and we Germans must become this – I must start to behave like a Great Power.'[10]

Identity and the Wirtschaftswunder

The Federal Republic's claim to be a Great Power depended more and more obviously on the strength of its economic performance. From 1950 to 1961 real GNP *per capita* in West Germany doubled. This became known as the 'economic miracle', or *Wirtschaftswunder* (a phrase originally used to describe Hitler's economic recovery in the 1930s. Erhard himself disliked the term and did not use it.) His *Wirtschaftswunder* did more than guarantee the political success of the CDU in the 1950s: it generated for Germany a new national legitimacy and a new national image. This Germany based itself on social and geographical mobility, newly acquired riches, Americanization, but also on a low level of political participation.

Germany had a new and uprooted population. Refugees from areas that had once been included in Germany (and after 1945 were in Poland, the USSR or Czechoslovakia), and more and more in the 1950s also from the GDR, found new homes in the Federal Republic. By 1960 18.4 per cent of the German population were expellees from the east (*Vertriebene*); in addition another three million had come from East Germany. One-quarter of government employees were *Vertriebene*.[11] Refugees concentrated in particular areas – Bavaria, Schleswig-Holstein, Lower Saxony – and often brought about a transformation of the regional economic and social structure.

After a decade of impoverishment and malnutrition, Germans started to eat with substantial appetites again. Erhard, a plump figure generally photographed with a cigar, became the physical incarnation of German-ness. In the early 1950s he worked with the phrase 'a refrigerator in every household'. The refrigerator conjured up an American image of growing wealth, unequally distributed but producing eventual benefits for everyone:

> When I have been pleading for an expansion of consumption
> beyond what is needed to satisfy basic material requirements, and
> saying that it was our aim to enable every household, and
> particularly every worker's household, to have durable goods such
> as a refrigerator, a washing-machine, a vacuum cleaner and
> whatever else modern industries can provide, I have been told to
> reckon out what a pensioner receives or can earn and to reveal the
> secret of how these goods can be brought within his reach. My
> answer is that of course pensioners cannot be among the first to
> benefit from the growth of consumption. In America it was not the
> poorest people who first had motor-cars. But we have seen over and
> over again how today's luxuries become tomorrow's utilities.[12]

The Americanization of Germany was generally not a conscious process. When the American impact was too direct and too carefully thought out, it usually misfired. The Potsdam conference had provided explicitly for the re-education of Germans, but the programme soon ran out of steam. It turned out that, in the American vision, jazz was to be an important part of Germany's education in democracy. Many Germans reacted sceptically, and the organized tour of Louis Armstrong in 1952 proved to be less than successful.[13]

American culture had at first a rather limited effect on Germany. In general, the 1950s were less a decade of transatlantic-style transform-ation than of the revival of a traditional and ostensibly depoliticized and sanitized kitsch. Sentimental 'home films' (*Heimatfilme*), presenting an idealized version of life in rural Germany, dominated the cinema. Probably this provided an agreeable contrast with the reality of a changing Germany. It also meant an end to the concept of direct political propaganda – whether for Nazism or for democracy – on the screen. Bobby E. Lüthge, the scriptwriter of a film with a title highly typical of the 1950s, *Green is the Heath*, explained: 'The sentence about the "education of the public" is still out of the Goebbels box of tricks. No one wants to pay good entrance money just to be taught something . . . The objection that films [such as *Green is the Heath*] can never reach a high artistic standard may be accurate – but it shows what level is appropriate for the majority of the great German public.'[14]

Lüthge's view accorded closely with the feelings of Germans in the 1950s as recorded by opinion surveys, which noted a general distrust and lack of interest in politics. In 1952 Germany once more had the old national anthem; but only the third verse of Hoffmann von Fallers-leben's 'Deutschland, Deutschland über alles' was to be sung on state occasions:

> Unity and Right and Freedom
> For the German Fatherland
> Let us strive in brotherhood,
> Heart with heart and hand with hand.
> Unity and Right and Freedom
> Are the guarantors of fortune,
> Blossom in the sun of this good fate,
> Blossom, German Fatherland.[15]

The restoration of the 'Deutschland' hymn had so little impact that in 1955, in a radio prize competition – in which presumably candidates had every incentive to remember – three competitors were unable to recite the text.[16]

The biggest cultural transformations were certainly non-political: the motor car and the nylon stocking. Political tones crept in, but only occasionally and by indirect association. The automobile, for instance, was identified with America, as were chewing gum and nylons. Erhard's promise of American life revolved around the automobile as well as the refrigerator.

The car brought mobility to Germany's new population. In the 1930s motorization had been a political motto, designed to bribe Germans into acquiescence under the dictatorship. But it had remained largely a slogan: the number of cars per head of population remained substantially higher in France, for instance. In the 1950s motorization became a reality and the car the symbol of a new Germany. In 1950 Germans had 515,600 private cars, in 1960 4,066,000 (and in 1980 23,191,600). These machines stamped the national perception of the 1950s in just the same way as the railway had made the 'economic nation' of the 1850s.

The story of the German stocking also had some political suspense. Unfortunately for the western zones, Germany's prewar hosiery industry had been sited in Saxony, in what became the GDR. The Soviet zone administrators boasted of their advantages: they could blackmail the West with stockings. As Fritz Selbmann, who later became the GDR Minister for Mining and who was in charge of the reconstruction of the Saxon economy under Soviet occupation, put it in 1947: 'Women in the western zones will have to go in bare feet until their husbands send us steel and coking coal.' The story of the relief of the western zones belongs to Cold War heroics. Pennsylvania miners collected money to buy up old cotton machines, many of which had originally been made in Germany, and then send them back across the Atlantic. A synthetic stocking made in a variety of nylon, called Perlon, dominated the German market: whereas in 1949 only 700,000 pairs of stockings were sold in Germany, by 1953 the figure was 58 millions, of which 55.6 millions were in Perlon. Hans Thierfelder, who built up from nothing a plant making one-eighth of the total German stocking output, explained why the new product was such a success: 'Because of war work at the lathe, because of long standing on tramcar platforms and in queues, because of hoarding expeditions made clinging to the running boards of motor vehicles, German female legs became stronger and calves bigger. With this market analysis it was possible to give the fine mesh stocking such a secure position relative to the prewar period that it no longer slipped.'[17]

These were the unpolitical or apolitical faces of the national revival of the 1950s.

A New German Consensus

The cultivation of economic dynamism and a fundamentally passive foreign policy based on anti-Sovietism and integration into Western Europe came by the end of the decade to underlie all West German political assumptions. The Treaty of Rome (1957) created the European Economic Community, an extension of the principles of the Coal and Steel Community. In it, Germany traded off the loss of parts of her traditional sovereignty for faster growth, in the belief that this could in turn – though only in a rather long run – be translated into political power. However, for Germany this surrender of sovereignty remained incomplete. The legacy of the 1950s was only a one-legged commitment to Europe as a way of expressing German nationality. Originally, there had been two sides to European integration, both originating in French plans. It was the plan of the French Foreign Minister Robert Schuman that had led first to the ECSC and then to the EEC. The second aspect was the defence plan which originally stemmed from René Pleven. But though the French government accepted the European Defence Community as a modified version of the Pleven plan in 1952, two years later the French assembly voted to reject the EDC. The consequence of 1954 was the orientation of the European idea towards economics and growthmanship at the expense of political and military integration. This in turn allowed the state that was best at economic management and expansion greater political room for manoeuvre within the European framework.

After 1955, when Germany became sovereign, she decided to use some of this room. She rebuilt her army at breakneck speed, to the astonishment and mistrust of some German generals who felt that a slower build-up might produce a militarily more effective force. She also turned her attention to the issue of nuclear weapons, withheld from her in 1955 by the West European Union (an organization of NATO's European members).

Political conditions outside Germany helped the Federal Republic. The German role within Europe became easier because of the political change in France in 1958. Adenauer depended on the closer relationship he could establish with de Gaulle; and this depended on the association of German economic strength with French political assertion.

The new self-confidence on the West German political scene had consequences for the parties. Schumacher had died in 1952, and the SPD's nationalism gradually faded into an acceptance of the new style of Bonn politics. The party marked the new direction at the Bad Godesberg congress of 1959. To begin with, it accepted the rapid social change that had taken place during the 1950s. Even in theory it no longer made sense for a socialist party to concentrate on an exclusively working-class constituency. The SPD could never form a majority in elections solely out of working-class votes (and in 1953 the SPD in fact, according to opinion surveys, had only won 48 per cent of working-class votes).[18] So the SPD needed a wider constituency, among the expanding professional middle classes, and proposed to win this by accepting the principle of the social market economy: 'The Social Democratic Party therefore favours a free market wherever free competition exists. Where a market is dominated by individuals or groups, however, all manner of steps must be taken to protect freedom in the economic sphere. As much competition as possible – as much planning as necessary.' Moreover, a new external policy was required. The continuing reality of the Cold War, and especially the harsh lesson of 1958, when Stalin's successor Khrushchev threatened Berlin once more, brought the SPD to acquiesce in the main lines of Adenauer's foreign policy: 'In accordance with the Basic Law [the SPD] strives for German unity in freedom. The division of Germany is a threat to peace. To end this division is a vital interest of the German people.'

The later 1950s so successfully pushed the SPD into the Bonn consensus that new political opportunities arose in the next decade – opportunities which altered the shape of Bonn's politics. As the distinction between the two parties eroded, the idea of the two-party system started to crumble. The two main parties having arrived at a consensus on economic and international issues, a SPD–CDU coalition no longer appeared implausible. This realization shook up the parties themselves. First of all, the existence of a general consensus made the internal politics of the ruling CDU–CSU–FDP coalition and of the CDU itself more fissiparous because the socialist opposition looked less menacing. In fact in the early 1960s a bitter division over foreign policy issues ran, not between the CDU and the other parties, but within the CDU between 'Europeanists' who claimed to stand in the Adenauer tradition and 'Atlanticists' who associated with Erhard.

The story of this split had begun with the Berlin crisis of 1958–9, when the USSR threatened the western link of West Berlin. The USA and Britain for a moment even appeared to some prepared to accept a neutralized Berlin. West Germany's most loyal support came from France. In the following year the French–American strain became highly visible as France launched a programme to develop her own nuclear deterrent. In 1962 the USA responded with a scheme for a 'Multilateral Force' (MLF) which required France to buy Polaris missiles and use them under American supervision. France resisted, and forced the abandonment of MLF. At the same time de Gaulle made a highly successful visit to Germany, and the warmth of relations on that occasion led to Adenauer's conclusion in 1963 of the Elysée treaty of friendship. Erhard saw it as his principal goal to restore harmony in American–German relations.

The divisions over foreign policy raised questions about domestic economic issues. Rearming Germany was expensive. When the small liberal party in 1966 rejected a proposal for tax increases and asked for defence cuts instead, Erhard fell and his place was taken by the SPD–CDU 'Great Coalition' under the Chancellorship of Kurt Kiesinger, with the SPD leader Willy Brandt as Foreign Minister.

The alternative to the CDU–FDP bloc had emerged from the political shadows. Once the Great Coalition was established, it made some cautious policy moves in the direction of the left: towards Keynesian policy with the 'Law on Stability and Growth' (1967), and in foreign terms towards the opening-up of relations with the East European states (with the exception of the GDR).

In domestic politics, the experiment could hardly be reckoned a success. The Great Coalition posed a political problem reminiscent of Weimar: no really effective political opposition existed in parliament (there was only the small FDP, which was excluded from power, but found it difficult as a party of the centre to criticize the right–left coalition). The CDU was divided, while the SPD faced the opposition of many of its younger members, who felt sceptical about the coalition course.

The odd testimony to the success of Adenauer's vision in establishing too much political consensus in West Germany was the collapse of social consensus. Consensus need not always generate stability; and conversely major political conflicts can create legitimacy and political integration. Too much surface harmony may produce breakdowns, as small but intellectually potent groups feel that they have been pushed to the margin. In the 1950s and 1960s, literary figures such as Günther Grass and Heinrich Böll complained about the excessive conformity of life in the Federal Republic. The materialism of the *Wirtschaftswunder* department-store society became a cliché among the intelligentsia. Consumerism, went the theory, had killed the German soul and destroyed moral realities. Garden gnomes, senseless foreign travel, luxury cars – all these were indicted as emblems of the *Wirtschaftswunder*. According to the new stereotype, Germany was becoming a nation of 'lotto players who look for salvation in riches and gains, or of cosmopolitans who annually travel abroad to flee from their own history and their own society'.[19] The rejection of commercial values for the sake of something deeper or higher had a long German tradition. When in the

1960s the materialist economic consensus entered coalition bargaining as the political orthodoxy, that complacent orthodoxy provoked revolt.

The great achievement of 1948–9 had been the creation of bipolar political life: government versus opposition. In the mid-1960s the dangers of an excessive degree of parliamentary consensus soon became apparent: opposition moved out of the political parties and onto the street, and later a small part carried their political journey further, into terrorist associations. On the left, an Extra-Parliamentary Opposition (APO) emerged as the SPD could no longer win the confidence of student radicals. The party had become too big, bureaucratic and bourgeois. A demonstration against the Shah of Iran on 2 June 1967 in Berlin, at which a student was shot by a plainclothes policeman, set off a massive protest movement. Students organized protests and marches and were able to achieve many of their immediate demands concerning reform of the university system, but none of their larger demands – German support for non-Western liberation movements, or the abolition of capitalism in West Germany.

On the right, the Great Coalition helped to stimulate the first re-emergence since the early 1950s of a neo-fascist party (the NPD). By the mid-1950s recalcitrant nationalists and the far right had been integrated electorally into the CDU/CSU, and were tamed by the prospect of opposition from the left. Once the CDU started to work with a left-wing party, however, old resentments reappeared. The NPD drew its support almost exclusively from older voters, and usually from the countryside. It won modest successes in *Land* elections from Hesse (November 1966), where it gained 7.9 per cent of the vote, to Baden-Württemberg, where in April 1968 it reached 9.8 per cent. By 1969, however, when the next federal elections were due, the party's support had dropped and it polled only 4.3 per cent, less than the 5 per cent required to qualify for parliamentary representation.

The development of extremism of the left and right came at the same time as a small economic crisis. In 1967 real GNP fell for the first time in the history of the Federal Republic (though only by 0.2 per cent). The weak economy emphasized the lesson already drawn from the 1950s and from the Weimar Republic: that the legitimacy of the West German political system depended on a strong economic performance. The depression did not, however, last long. In addition, effective parliamentary opposition politics began again after 1969.

The 1970s provided a mirror image of the political scenery of the 1950s. Both decades began with a ferocious war between the parties on external issues. From 1969 a SPD–FDP Great Coalition ruled in place of the Great Coalition. Its major achievements in the early years were in foreign policy: the continuation of the opening-up of Germany towards Eastern Europe. Germany should establish trade links and political contacts with Czechoslovakia, Hungary and Poland. Though this line had already been pursued even in the Erhard years (with Gerhard Schröder as Foreign Minister), *détente* in Europe became the hallmark of Willy Brandt's Chancellorship. In August 1970 a treaty was signed in Moscow with the USSR, and in December 1970 Brandt went to Warsaw to initial a similar agreement with Poland and give virtual recognition of Poland's Oder–Neisse frontier.

These treaties prepared the way for a Four-Power Berlin treaty in which the USSR committed itself to an acceptance of the independent status of West Berlin (September 1971). This in turn provided the political starting-point for a 'Basic Treaty' (December 1972) between the GDR and the Federal Republic, which included the *de facto* mutual recognition of the two German states, and the non-diplomatic representation of each state with the other. Step by step, international treaties had regulated the issue of the two Germanies and had defused 'the German problem'. Brandt's *Ostpolitik* appears in retrospect as an inexorable consequence of the international framework of those years. It bears the same relationship to the *détente* pursued by Nixon, Brezhnev and Kissinger as Adenauer's strategy of Western European integration does to the era of Stalin and Foster Dulles.

Within Germany, Brandt's policy became as controversial as Adenauer's pursuance of integration with the West at the price of German unity had been in the earlier decade. The CDU argued that the text of the Brandt treaties limited German rights to self-determination and for this reason violated the Basic Law; and that the frontier question should be explicitly reserved for the future (general) peace treaty to wind up the Second World War, of which there was still no sign. The bilateral treaties that Brandt concluded had, they argued, merely narrowed the options for the eventual peace treaty.

Ostpolitik also led to problems in the FDP/SPD coalition. In the FDP, a number of parliamentary deputies disliked the change from centre–right to centre–left coalition. The former leader of the FDP, Erich Mende, left the party and joined the CDU. In addition, several politicians close to refugee groups, which felt that their homelands had been betrayed, went over to the CDU, and others suspicious of Soviet motives in the *Ostpolitik* process joined them. By 1972 Brandt's majority had vanished, and the CDU proposed a motion of no confidence, naming as the Chancellor's successor (as required by the Basic Law, which allowed only 'constructive' motions of no confidence) the CDU leader Rainer Barzel.

The no-confidence motion was defeated by two votes because some members of the CDU voted for Brandt's government (on 27 April). On 17 May the Eastern treaties were passed by the Bundestag. The whole crisis put the CDU in as great a predicament as the government, and in a way which was substantially more embarrassing. It would have been an international blow to the Federal Republic if the *Ostpolitik* had collapsed, and if the Moscow and Warsaw treaties had not been ratified. One CDU representative in the upper chamber, Helmut Kohl, speaking as Minister-President of the Rhineland-Palatinate, delicately admitted that 'a failure to ratify the treaties would temporarily involve difficulties'.[20] Barzel originally suggested that his party should vote for the government's slightly watered-down proposal on acceptance of the treaties, but was blocked by the resolute hostility of the Bavarian CSU's stance. Eventually the CDU/CSU agreed to abstain on the motions to ratify the Warsaw and Moscow treaties, though a few deputies voted against ratification, defying Barzel's party line (10 in the case of the Soviet, and 17 against the Polish motion which was thornier because of the direct relevance of the Oder–Neisse issue). The SPD was rewarded by an election in which it achieved its highest ever share of the vote (45.8 per cent).

The legacy of 1972 was the incorporation of *Ostpolitik* into the existing consensus of the Bundesrepublik. The CDU now had to accept as an international reality something that it had begun by viewing as a national betrayal. It was, to take a Weimar parallel, like the DNVP partly voting to accept the Dawes plan. The right had to come to terms with a new foreign policy. After 1982, with a CDU government in office in Bonn once more, affirmation of the Eastern treaties of the early 1970s became a regular ritual of reassuring the world about West Germany's dependability and renunciation of bellicosity.

The consensus created in the early 1970s expressed itself in the new popularity of the Bonn Republic's political symbolism. In the 1976 federal elections, both the major parties set the West German flag (the old republican black-red-gold colours) at the centre of their campaigns.

The Breakdown of Consensus

By the end of the 1970s, however, the situation changed and the whole issue of a Federal German consensus appeared once more highly problematic. The new consensus and stability of the 1970s had depended on three pillars. The first was the Adenauer legacy of a Western orientation that included simultaneously collaboration with Germany's western neighbours (as well as Italy) and with the USA. The second lay in the *Ostpolitik* of the Brandt era. Thirdly, the key to the gradual building-up of Germany's political power lay in the strength of the economy. This became particularly evident as Vietnam weakened the position of the USA, and in 1971 this frailty led to the first of many dollar crises. The strength of the Deutsche Mark and of the German economy gave West Germany a louder voice in world economic diplomacy.

These three pillars eroded softly but steadily through the decade. First of all, the new American uncertainty about global commitments in the post-Vietnam period affected relations with Europe. In 1975 the USSR began a political push in Africa using Cuban troops as a proxy. Could this be mirrored in Europe? Without American guarantees, the Federal Republic's security situation would be untenable. It was with the aim of fixing these guarantees that, in 1977 in London, Brandt's SPD successor Helmut Schmidt sounded the alarm over the Soviet deployment of intermediate-range nuclear missiles in Eastern Europe (SS-20s). His proposal became what was to be called the NATO 'twin track' decision: that the USA should station short- and intermediate-range nuclear missiles in Western Europe and Germany, while negotiating for the removal of Soviet equivalents from the Warsaw Pact countries.

The parliamentary decision on the actual stationing of the US Cruise and Pershing II missiles in Germany provoked massive demonstrations during the 'hot autumn' of 1983. The course taken by the public debate on nuclear weapons reduced rather than augmented the trust between the two sides of the Atlantic. Long before the stationing actually occurred, Schmidt started to sound sceptical when he addressed German audiences. The missiles question generated controversy within the SPD, which affected his government's stance. Many Germans, especially on the political left, presented the Americans as gun-slinging cowboys from the Wild West, and now felt threatened by a tactic that had originally been designed to reassure. They pointed out that the weapons, if used, would be used on Germany. In Washington, on the other hand, the twin-track stationing produced a political frustration with Europe: were not the Europeans, and especially the Germans, miserably ungrateful allies? President Carter found Schmidt by far the most irritating and arrogant of European politicians. In 1980, in an emotional encounter, Schmidt – according to Carter – 'objected to parts of SALT II, complained about our [the USA's] inadequate aid to Pakistan, accused me of not being sincere in negotiating for nuclear arms control, remarked that Germany was not our 51st state, claimed that Vance had failed to carry out a promise to amend UN resolution 242'. In short, the USA could do nothing right.[21]

The Reagan presidency did little to build Atlantic bridges: when the President spoke about strengthening defences and developing the Strategic Defence Initiative he sounded reckless and naive to many Europeans. Even when the regime turned to accepting disarmament, it did this without consulting the European governments. Particularly after the Reykjavik summit of 1986, Europeans were terrified by the apparent radicalism of what Washington was prepared to give up. The German right, in the CDU and CSU, had always been among the most enthusiastic advocates of collaboration with the USA. It now felt that Germany might be left alone, in the political rain, outside any American 'nuclear umbrella'. The CSU, and the right of the CDU, found it hard in 1987 to come to terms with the abandonment of the Cruise and Pershing stationing for the sake of an intermediate arms agreement and the implementation of the 'zero option', eventually agreed at the Washington summit (December 1987).

Each end of the German political spectrum was left with a distrust of American motives or American consistency or both. In the 1960s, though there had existed a crude populist anti-Americanism of the 'Yankees go home' variety, all the major political parties unambiguously supported the American presence. This consensus came under strain in the 1980s.

One small incident illuminated symbolically the shift away from America. After 1945 the reconstruction of West German cities had been carried out in a modernist idiom, which owed something to the *Bauhaus* of republican 1920s Germany but had been transmitted at second hand, through American intermediaries. German architecture had been Americanized. An emblem of this was the Berlin Congress Hall, constructed in 1957–8 as a joint American–German project by Hugh Stubbins with Werner Düttmann and Franz Mocken. The building relied on prestressed concrete and looked, the Berliners said, like an open oyster on a slab. In May 1980 the prestressed concrete unstressed and the Congress Hall fell apart. It was a nice symbol for the disintegration of the first pillar of the German consensus.[22]

A second pillar was being eroded at the same time less than a hundred miles away from Berlin. The strains in the Atlantic relationship appeared particularly obviously at the moment that the presupposition of *Ostpolitik* was also disappearing. Brandt's policy made little sense without the belief that Eastern Europe was fundamentally stable under Soviet control, with only the possibility of a gradual and politically unexciting and untraumatic liberalization. In retrospect perhaps historians can detect signs that this picture underestimated the volatility of Eastern Europe. In December 1970, the month Brandt initialled the

Warsaw treaty, unrest in the shipyards of Gdansk unleashed a movement that soon brought down Brandt's Polish host Wladyslaw Gomulka. In 1976 and 1980 there was renewed instability in Poland. The long war in Afghanistan from Christmas 1979 showed a Soviet Union that could not deal with all the problems on its frontiers; it also showed a country willing to take military risks if it felt that it might achieve local advantages. In 1980 the Solidarity crisis in Poland raised a new range of possibilities, though only for a brief time.

Solidarity took as one of its themes hostility to Yalta (where, in the Poles' eyes, their country had been handed over to Russia by the West). It raised the intriguing possibility of a disintegration of the central European order created at Yalta and Potsdam. If this system were really to collapse, a united Germany might become possible again. Such a Germany might even extend its cultural and economic orbit further east. Central European intellectuals, notably the Czech writer Milan Kundera, began to talk with a new enthusiasm about the old (and formerly exclusively German) concept of Mitteleuropa. It looked as if Kundera was moving into the political territory that in 1848 the Czech professor Palacky had refused to occupy.

Mitteleuropa, if it were ever to be realized, would swallow up and destroy the West German state. West German politicians confronted the difficulty that an ending of the system and suppositions of *Ostpolitik* would carry with it the destruction of the whole political basis of the state within which they operated.

The link between the question of *Ostpolitik* and the stability of Eastern Europe accounted for an often observed German peculiarity: the hostility with which a substantial part of the German press viewed the emergence of an intellectual and working-class reform and opposition movement in Poland. Those publications such as *Der Spiegel* and *Die Zeit* which had been central in the advocacy of *Ostpolitik* particularly disliked the instability engendered by the Eastern bloc reform movement. It was not so much that traditional German Polonophobia had lingered on; rather that any idea that Eastern Europe might change directly affected the political balance within Germany, and brought the whole issue of the Federal Republic's existence into doubt.

Finally, the third pillar tottered. The *Wirtschaftswunder* began to falter. There were two severe shocks as a result of the oil price hikes of the 1970s: in 1973, after the Middle East War, and again in 1979. In 1974 the growth rate of real GNP was cut to 0.5 per cent and in 1975 GNP fell by 1.6 per cent. In 1980 growth slowed down again. In 1981 real GNP fell by 0.2 per cent, and in 1982 by 1 per cent. Germany had grown used to dynamic but steady growth. The SPD election campaign in 1976 had referred to a 'Modell Deutschland', setting the pace for the rest of the world. Now a new mood set in. Analysts dealt with Germany less as an example of economic and social success than as an instance of 'Eurosclerosis'. This had the following characteristics: a very expensive welfare state, a government committed to the subsidization of agriculture and of declining heavy industries, and unions pressing for wage rises. At least in the popular press, there were accusations that the Germans had become lazy.

Whether there was really a widespread collapse of confidence about the social order as a result of the weaker economy is open to debate. In an opinion survey of young people in 1987, 75 per cent reported that they saw the future 'optimistically', and 36 per cent believed that 'economic conditions' would be 'better' in five years' time; by contrast in 1962, during the classic period of the *Wirtschaftswunder*, only 21 per cent had expressed this belief.[23] Greater uncertainty, and difficulties in finding employment, may have made younger Germans more conformist and more prepared to accept their society, rather than more rebellious.

The political consequences of the growth crisis are much easier to describe than its implications for the social psychology of Germans. The economic crisis of the early 1980s played a major part in the disintegration of Helmut Schmidt's coalition government with the FDP. The social–liberal coalition lasted thirteen years in all. In response to the depression, the FDP demanded tax- and spending-cuts to help business through the depression; the SPD on the other hand tried to defend the *status quo* and oppose any social retrenchment. In 1982 the FDP changed sides, and voted in a constructive no-confidence proposal for a conservative–liberal coalition under the Chancellorship of the CDU politician Helmut Kohl.

This change became known as the *Wende*: a fundamental political transformation. There had in fact been a more general crisis of Bonn politics than that of a simple transition from centre–left to centre–right alliance. The parties lost confidence in themselves. After its change of 1982, the FDP feared that it would fall below the 5 per cent electoral barrier. The big parties found it difficult to keep their support: the SPD's share of the vote slid from its 1972 high. By the 1980s alternative parties emerged to the left of the SPD – the Greens – and, though less significantly, to the right of the CSU – the Republicans.

Green support came predominantly from younger voters: in 1987 17.4 per cent of the party list votes of those aged between 25 and 35 went to the Greens (for voters under 25, 15.5 per cent).[24] The movement represented an often strained coalition between ecologists, student revolutionaries from the late 1960s, pacifists, farmers threatened by nuclear power plants, Christians and single issue campaigners. One wing (the 'realos') aimed at participating in political coalitions, and would be willing to work with the SPD in return for concessions on ecological issues and especially on the dismantling of nuclear power plants and the removal of atomic weapons from Germany. The 'fundis', on the other hand, demanded a root and branch approach to political issues and wanted to achieve a far-reaching transformation of society. Modern capitalism was incompatible, they believed, with the interests of man and of nature. Both these groups advocated a loose nationalism: a hostility both to the super-powers and to the economic order they represented; and a desire for a reunited, neutral and pacifist Germany. They believed that cooperating with youth and church groups in 'the other Germany' offered a way out of the present difficulties.

The existence of this substantial group to the left of the SPD posed a problem for that party. Was it possible to work at coalition-building while ignoring the Greens? Holger Börner, the SPD Minister-President of Hesse from 1976 to 1987, was at first one of the bitterest critics in the SPD of the Greens, and drew parallels between their behaviour and that of the Nazis. Then he tried to work in a governing coalition with them, which collapsed over the nuclear power issue. Johannes Rau, the SPD's candidate for the Chancellorship in the federal election of 1987, ignored the issue by saying that he was aiming at an absolute majority and therefore did not need to think of coalitions. That most people in the party knew that this was not a realistic goal contributed to the SPD's demoralization in the campaign and its poor performance in the elections. Rau's strategy failed decisively. In *Länder* government, Greens and the SPD started to work together again.

Part of the parties' problem was connected with the decline in political morality. Traditionally, political corruption played little part in German public life. In Italy or Austria or France scandal and 'affairs' had played a well-recognized part in the political game. Germany traditionally had also had political instability; but she had suffered from ideological politics and not from graft. Germans had expected, and obtained, remarkably high standards of public behaviour. In the spectacularly unstable Weimar Republic, the most wide-ranging corruption scandal had involved nothing more than a fur coat for the wife of Berlin's Lord Mayor. Even the 1970s still appeared relatively free from scandal. Brandt's replacement by Schmidt came after an espionage affair in which Brandt's personal adviser was uncovered as an East German agent. But few people drew major lessons about standards of public life from this affair, and it involved no corruption.

Matters were different in the early 1980s. The biggest and most destructive affair was the Flick scandal, involving all three major parties. The giant steel concern had traded donations to political parties in return for tax exemptions. But the implications of the affair went wider: the two men who had played the most prominent roles in the political crises of 1972 and 1982 respectively, Rainer Barzel (CDU) and Count Otto Lambsdorff (FDP), also stood in the centre of the Flick affair. It only emerged in 1984 that Barzel had been paid 1.7 million Marks by Flick to stand aside as leader of the CDU and allow Helmut Kohl to run as the candidate for the Chancellorship in 1976. Lambsdorff was the man who had designed the FDP's reversal of alliances: as Economics Minister he had put forward a package of spending cuts that he knew would be unacceptable to most of the SPD. The Lambsdorff memorandum tore Helmut Schmidt's Cabinet apart and let the FDP move to coalition with the right. Though there is nothing to connect Flick to this specific move, Flick provided a context of scandal.

Then it appeared that some of the key defections from the SPD and the FDP over *Ostpolitik* during the 1970s had been financed by business interests. The Bundestag deputy Karl Geldner had been tempted to move from the FDP to the CSU with money provided by a small packaging firm in Lippstadt; the SPD deputy Karl Wienand himself organized a small vote-buying ring against the Brandt government.[25] There could be no more striking revelation of the sinister role of German business money in politics. Had an industrial lobby almost succeeded in shifting the Bonn regime to the right in 1972, and then actually succeeded in doing this ten years later, in 1982?

On the sidelines of Flick, smaller-scale affairs emerged. In Berlin the CDU and the SPD were both deeply involved in a building scandal. The SPD had problems with the trade-union-owned building company Neue Heimat. Also in 1982, it emerged that Albert Vietor and his immediate subordinates had made private profits (allegedly around one hundred million Marks) out of Neue Heimat's building operations. Leading trade union officials had also made large personal fortunes out of the firm; among them Heinz Otto Vetter, the head of the General Federation of Trade Unions (DGB), and Eugen Loderer from the largest of the German unions, IG Metall.[26]

Barzel had been elected President (Speaker) of the Bundestag, and had to resign because of the Flick affair. His successor, Philipp Jenninger, tried to defend the Bonn Republic against the larger accusations: 'This Republic is not a bought republic. We have a stable democracy, which is respected all over the world and has won the friendship and confidence of many peoples . . . We are in this house as deputies directly legitimized by the will of the people; and we are here to serve our people. We are not primarily here to make money.'[27] It was a remarkably peculiar defence of the style of Bonn politics, made as if the speaker was standing on the edge of a political and moral sewer. Briefly interrupted by German unification in 1990, disillusionment with the parties and politicians continued to grow in the early 1990s.

The break-up of the old consensus of the 1950s and 1960s raised the problem of the nation again. In the midst of political graft and corruption, it is tempting to think of a large ethical unit, the nation standing above the political fray. When we have our feet in the gutter, we are most inclined to look up at the stars. For a part of the left, a new vision of Germany provided a way out of the foreign policy dilemma: a neutral and united Germany could pull one half out of NATO and one half out of the Warsaw Pact. According to the Berlin Green Party, the new state could be non-aligned and demonstrate to the world the possibility of a new global, and genuine, *détente*.

The SPD itself adopted a defence strategy which preserved the framework of NATO while eliminating much of the substance of an Atlantic alliance. In 1985 a former SPD Parliamentary Secretary of State in the Defence Ministry, Andreas von Bülow, prepared a paper arguing for a central European zone in which only explicitly defensive weapons would be permitted. 'Both sides must dismantle their capacity to attack and invade the opponents' territory.' The title of the Bülow paper, 'Defence without Superpowers', pointed up the dramatic character of his conclusions. In 1986 the leading party theoretician Egon Bahr set out a plan for a nuclear-free zone in central Europe, to be established by means of a West German dialogue with the East German SED. The call for armed forces that were 'unambiguously defensive and not contrary to the goal of a peaceful European order' in the SPD Congress resolution of August 1986 represented a watered-down version of Bülow's theses. Finally, in August 1987, the SPD, together with the SED Central Committee's Academy for Social Sciences, produced a paper on 'Ideological Clashes and German Security'. This suggested the respecting of 'the legitimate security interests of the other side', and argued that 'military doctrines explicitly directed towards defence and security against attack would serve this goal'. In other words, the defensive and European argument of the Bülow paper appeared directly from, and with the approval of, the East German SED.[28]

Bahr explained that the closer relationship of the two Germanies need not conflict with the Warsaw Pact or NATO treaties: the German states should, being presumably eternally feminine, simply behave like modern women: 'The two German states should behave in an emancipated way. If a woman behaves in an emancipated way, that does not mean that she violates existing laws.'[29]

The right had also tried to formulate a new approach to foreign relations. Issues of national policy have since 1982 been bitterly contentious within the CDU/CSU/FDP coalition government. For them, the issue of German unity became once more alive. This represented a major change from the 1960s and 1970s, when, in the aftermath of the Berlin Wall and in the epoch of postwar 'realism', the division of Germany looked, for practical purposes, permanent. The main task of German politicians at that time lay in dealing with international realities without eating too many of their words, and those of the Basic Law, on the subject of German unity. In 1966, for instance, the conservative Bavarian politician and leader of the CSU Franz Josef Strauss said more or less categorically: 'I do not believe in the re-creation of a German national state, even within the boundaries of the four zones of occupation.'[30] German unity could only be re-achieved – if at all – within an overall European context.

By 1986 little doubt existed that the German question had once more been raised. The right of the CDU and the CSU attacked 'a failed policy of *détente*' and revived the notion that only the final peace conference (still of course to take place) could settle Germany's frontiers – thus implicitly claiming a revision of the Oder–Neisse line. Helmut Kohl agreed to attend a meeting of Silesian expellees in June 1985, and although his speech was sober and restrained (and included a statement that Poland and the Federal Republic had no 'territorial demands' against each other), his presence provided a political signal.

The new politics required a reinterpretation of the German past, and the cultivation of a new national style. Kohl and Strauss asked that Germany should 'walk tall' in the light of her great historical and cultural traditions. They talked about the German past in a different tone from that of the Federal President Richard von Weizsäcker, who in his speech on 8 May 1985 described 8 May 1945 as a 'day of liberation' and spoke about the contribution of the USSR to the defeat of Hitler. At a meeting of the CDU federal committee on 8 December 1986, Kohl explained that 'to attain a free united Germany . . . is the historical task for our generation'. He called the political prisoners in the GDR – estimated to number 2,000 – 'our countrymen' and described them as detained in 'concentration camps'.[31] After the conservative–liberal coalition retained power in the January 1987 elections, Kohl's government declaration raised the theme of unity yet again: 'We wish that all Germans may one day be united in common freedom in a European order of peace. German policy also means for us: bringing people together because they belong together. Therefore we must always keep alive our consciousness of the unity of our German nation, and this includes remaining true to Berlin.'[32] In 1987 the CSU party congress passed a resolution calling for the renaming of a square as the 'Place of German Unity' in each Bavarian town.

On 28 October 1987, when he laid the foundation stone for a German Historical Museum in Berlin, Kohl made an even more far-ranging statement about the modern Germanies and their relationship with the past:

> We can do justice neither to past nor to future generations if we do not know where we come from, if we do not know the history of our people and do not remind ourselves of it – in its heights and in its depths . . . Certainly the peoples of the Central European area have common historical and cultural roots – this we will see clearly in the German Historical Museum . . . The museum that is being built not far from, but not in the shadow of, the Wall will deepen the consciousness of the togetherness of people in the divided Germany.[33]

The Bitburg incident also demonstrated Germany's new-found willingness to flex her muscles on the international stage. As a public gesture of acceptance of the new Germany, and as a commemoration of 1945 as the beginning of democratic reconstruction and of the Atlantic alliance, President Reagan scheduled a visit to German soldiers' graves for the fortieth anniversary of the end of the war. The President would deny that the Germans bore any collective guilt for the crimes of the Second World War. However, the cemetery selected, at Bitburg, contained the graves of 1,995 German soldiers, including those of 49 members of the military organization of the SS. A major press campaign in the USA urged Reagan to abandon the visit, but this course would have been a humiliation for Kohl and might have undermined the President's argument about German collective non-guilt. Instead an uneasy compromise involved Reagan in a visit to Bitburg as well as the concentration camp of Bergen-Belsen and the grave of Konrad Adenauer in Rhöndorf. In this way, the Reagan visit could illuminate the dark and the light side of the German past: the price exacted from the world by the German nation as well as the price paid by German nationals. Adenauer represented a symbol that both prices had been historically 'paid off' through the passing of time.

One explanation of the new nationalism interpreted it simply as a response to the domestic (and exclusively West) German situation:

according to this view it followed from arcane political manoeuvrings. Strauss in particular wanted to destroy the FDP by discrediting the policy of *Ostpolitik* and *rapprochement* with the East associated with the FDP Foreign Minister of the Kohl government, Hans-Dietrich Genscher, who had held that office throughout the whole of the Schmidt Chancellorship as well. He also tried to win votes away from the small Republican party on the right, and build up a solid rightist voting bloc. The CDU/CSU should span the whole political range, from the centre to the right, and there should, he argued, be no 'democratically legitimated party' to the right of the Christian parties.[34] On the left, there was a parallel tactic. The SPD could perform a similar trick in attempting to reverse the drift away from the big parties: it might denounce the CDU's over-servile acquiescence in American plans, and warm up the old charge of the 'Chancellor of the Allies' for use against Kohl.

The Reagan visit in 1985 served as a demonstration of how the national references had become associated with party political points and with specifically West German perceptions. The SPD did not appear at Bitburg, and instead held their own 'peace discussions' at Nuremberg (with a symbolism in the choice of location: the former city of the Nazi rallies should be reclaimed for peace and democracy). Reagan refused to receive the leader of the SPD, ex-Chancellor Brandt, as had been customary for the leading German opposition politician on previous American presidential visits. Was this intended to put the SPD outside the pale of a new German national consensus?

The German issue became a sophisticated way of playing out conflicts about the distribution of power, and about social and economic policy, within West Germany. In other words, the shifts of the 1980s were partially explicable in terms of the 'manipulated nationalism' already found in nineteenth-century history. But there also has to be an environment in which this manipulation of political meanings takes place.

That was provided by international politics, and not by German events. There the problem lay in the disintegration of Potsdam and the 1945 order. It might be described as the end of the era of the super-powers. Britain disappeared from this stage relatively early, between 1945 and 1956. The American $3.75 billion loan of 1945 put the UK into financial dependence; the world saw the result in the humiliation of British policy in Suez in 1956. Helmut Schmidt put the point bluntly in an interview with a British journalist when he claimed: 'Britain is no longer a developed nation.'[35] From 1971, the American role in Europe has been weakened because of Washington's budget and economic difficulties. The Soviet Union was strained by Vietnam and Cambodia and by Afghanistan; and communist ideology entered a deep crisis. The three powers of Potsdam lost most or some part of their influence in European affairs.

France was, to de Gaulle's chagrin, excluded from the Potsdam conference. But France remained an obvious presence in European political terms. There was a good personal relationship between Kohl and President Mitterrand, and some of the spirit of the 1963 Elysée treaty returned – along with its foreign policy implications. From 1987, and outside the framework of NATO, France and Germany conducted joint military exercises, formed a joint brigade and instituted a Common Defence Council. A *rapprochement* with Paris offered a more certain relationship than the instability of Bonn–Washington relations. It meant a way of reconstructing a more assertive style of German politics, within a European framework, but without requiring a fundamental restructuring of East–West relations that would be so dangerous for Federal German identity.

In 1815, 1918 and 1945 the international order held Germany in check. As the Vienna, Versailles and Potsdam settlements unravelled, Germany began to develop her own reactions. A long-term perspective on German nationality helps in assessing the scope for formulation of policy responses to changes in international politics.

Historically, economic growth provided the *raison d'être* for Imperial Germany, for Weimar and for the West German state. In the 1950s and 1960s European integration provided an attractive activity for the Federal Republic because of the economic opportunities it presented. An export-oriented economy benefited from the liberalization of trade within Europe. The failure of economic growth in 1979–81 contributed significantly to the weakening of the social-liberal coalition government and in turn to the wider questioning of the Republic's political line. It also raised the question – one which became more tantalizing towards the end of the 1980s – of whether there was not a fundamental flaw in the existing world economic order that only Germany (with Japan) could correct.

Germany's economy lay at the heart of discussions about her international role in the 1980s and 1990s. Since the beginning of the 1980s, many American observers adopted a 'locomotive theory' approach to the world economy. International prosperity would only, they said, return when those states with endemically large current account surpluses reflated. Translated into policy responses, this meant that Germany and Japan should pull the rest of the world behind economies which they would be required to stoke. Since some kind of action was usually held to be necessary to deal with a global problem, the USA believed that Germany should 'do something', and that a German adjustment would be easier and more beneficial than an American one involving a move to balanced US budgets. As West Germany operates with relatively small tax cuts, or with minutely calculated minor reductions in interest rates, the US irritation mounted.

The world economy offered a powerful bargaining weapon for Japan and Germany. The Federal Republic, used its leverage both in the West and in the East to take a more open line in *Deutschlandpolitik* and to press for a closer relationship with the GDR. An initial step was the billion-Mark credit to East Germany (in July 1983). In September 1987 Honecker visited Bonn. The attitude of the German political right was sympathetic to the resolution of the German–German problem in the 1980s. Franz Josef Strauss took the lead in setting up the 1983 credit, and four years later Honecker went on from Bonn to an exceptionally warm reception in Strauss's Bavaria. Though the Honecker leadership was not sympathetic to any more intimate understanding between the two Germanies, there always remained, at least in the foreseeable future, the prospect of change. Gorbachev was apparently more willing than his predecessors to experiment in German–German affairs, and the USSR had a more vital role to play in the global diplomacy of the German question than the ageing Honecker. There was also the helpful precedent of Honecker's own accession to power after the application of Soviet pressure on Ulbricht's German policy.

West Germany calculated that economic leverage would shift an Eastern bloc desperately in need of improved technology and imported capital, and that in a new international order computers would figure more prominently than military might. Or, as Strauss put it on the occasion of his visit to Gorbachev in December 1987: 'Mars should leave the stage of events and Mercury should make his entrance.' The German capital market began to open to the Soviet Union as well as to other Eastern bloc countries.[36]

Traditionally, the Western powers suspected German hankerings after unity, regardless of the affirmation of the goal of reunification in the 1955 treaty establishing German sovereignty. In 1984 the Italian Prime Minister Giulio Andreotti made a much cited public statement about the dangers of a united Germany which touched German sensibilities: 'Pan-Germanism must be overcome. There are two German states and there should be two.' The *bon mot* of François Mauriac, 'I love Germany so much that I am glad there are two of them', continued to circulate. Some statements from the USA and Britain indicated a change of stance: a willingness to see a degree of 'openness' in the

German question. The US Ambassador in Bonn spoke of the West's desire to accomplish German reunification, and called for a 'common strategy' to overcome the political division of Europe which runs through the middle of Germany.[37]

That the balance here moved was largely attributable to the economic muscle of West Germany. An indication of how far the world balance shifted was Germany's assumption of the role of world financial and economic preceptor. With the foundation of a strong economy, Germany could now tell the world how to behave. Over the last hundred years there have been several changes of the guard in global economic leadership. At the end of the nineteenth century Britain and the City of London imposed an orthodoxy on the rest of the world: balanced budgets along with political acquiescence in a City-dominated world system represented the price for importing British funds. During the 1920s American lending took the place vacated by the British – but without an overall vision or a sensitive political touch. After 1945 the American grasp became firmer: first as an extension of US government policy, with American economists advising European governments; then in the 1950s more as a private affair of businessmen employed in multinational corporations teaching better business techniques to the Europeans. After 1971 the US position crumbled.[38] In the 1980s the USA became the world's largest net debtor. It was now Germany which assumed the mantle of fiscal rectitude and preached about spending restraint, realistic tax packages and balanced budgets. The ability to deliver this message in an emphatic and forceful way was itself a symbol of a new sense of national mission.

The 1980s presented many opportunities for a reformulation of German nationalism. The new national identity could certainly be defined in a negative way: as *not* National Socialism. Was there anything more positive? Some of the signs were hopeful. A whiff of political corruption hung in the air of the 1980s; but were not the stories of the 1980s the revelations and unmaskings of earlier problems – which at the time had been concealed? It may be better to accept scandal openly than to adhere to a set of political beliefs which so elevate the state and its service as to demand that politicians see themselves as acolytes committed to a virginal purity as they genuflect before the altar of the Fatherland. The political affair after all plays a perfectly normal role in the ordinary life of most well-run and democratically ordered political systems.

The democratic system in West Germany survived a switch from right to left in the 1960s, and back again in the 1980s: was this not a sign of political maturity and health? Government and opposition currently fight more embittered conflicts than they have done during most of the 1960s and 1970s; but was it necessary to read the breakdown of a possibly stifling consensus as a sign of decay? Getting rid of the notion that nationality has to have an exclusive and narrowly defined social, political and economic ideology meant an important step towards a less vulnerable identity. In the past it had been possible to provide many answers to the question 'What is German?' – a question which seemed to demand only one right answer. In this context, defining nationality meant loading the charges for a political explosion.

The hope lay in a national identity that was not the outcome of a self-conscious process of formulation, leading to a single correct solution, but rather meant the business of reconciling different perceptions and life-styles within the framework of a common social life. Ending a tortured quest for *the* German identity, *the* German national character, and for an overall plan for national development, would provide a calmer and more stable political setting. In other words, a parliamentary system with conflicts, clashes and unharmonious disputes would operate as a focus for a national legitimacy centred on institutions and on the constitution. But then the revolution of 1989 raised the question of German nationhood in an unmistakable and urgent way.

10

The German Revolution of 1989 and its Aftermath

In 1989–90 an apparently stable German world collapsed, and with it a world-view. Before 1989, complicated systems of thought and interpretation had evolved in both German states not only to explain the present, but also to describe why it would be stable and enduring. The majority of the German political élite – politicians, civil servants, journalists, academics – in the West as well as in the East had come to accept the division of Germany as a permanent feature of political life. Some had even welcomed it. For many younger West Germans, the great post-war traumas of the Berlin blockade or the construction of the Berlin Wall belonged to a pre-history that lay too far removed to affect the present. In short, before 1989 East Germany was increasingly unknown and ignored.

Dealing with the GDR as a state had helped to create an impression of permanence. Erich Honecker made a state visit to the Federal Republic in September 1987; and even such conservative politicians as Franz Josef Strauss turned themselves into advocates of billion Mark credits for the GDR. It is true that Strauss continued to demand an end to the Wall, and that, when Honecker came to Bonn, Chancellor Helmut Kohl made explicit his state's commitment to the Basic Law and its preamble's reference to one German people. But in 1987 Honecker and his regime looked secure; no one would have imagined that four years later he would be facing criminal charges for his part in the decision to shoot fugitives crossing the GDR's frontier.

In retrospect, many people have asked why so many Germans mistook the character of the GDR and the possibilities for change[1]. West Germany, the creature of the Cold War and the division of

Europe, was peculiarly slow to realize how the circumstances that had produced it were changing. It is now clear that the events of 1989 were not simply part of a German story, but that the German revolution began with a deep-seated crisis of both communist ideology and Soviet power politics. The German response to these events was peculiar but characteristic – a product of the German mental and political world that has been described in previous pages. At first Germans treated the development as a particular German problem. Then, faced with a complete geopolitical transformation, they clutched at the idea of economic logic and economic necessity. German unity could be treated most harmlessly, they felt, if it were to be presented as a commercial transaction, a matter of rescuing a bankrupt enterprise. Institutional adaptation and the psychological and social strains of adjustment in this manner could be pushed to one side. This approach brought great dangers, which became apparent with an appreciation of the tremendous economic difficulties associated with unification of East and West. The institutional, psychological and social strains started to interfere with the smooth process of economic transition. Quite soon, and quite predictably, commentators were speaking of a moral as well as an economic crisis.

The failure of the communist system had very deep roots, reaching back well before Mikhail Gorbachev was appointed Secretary General of the CPSU. Its most dramatic initial manifestation was the outbreak of massive working class unrest in Poland in the summer of 1980: unrest which at the time deeply troubled many in East and West Germany because of the inherent likelihood of a destabilization of the geopolitical balance.

It was also in Poland that in June 1989 multi-party elections were held which permitted the expression of opposition to communist rule (although the outcome of the election was distorted by a rigged system of representation). The consequence of this election was the appointment in August of Poland's first postwar predominantly non-communist government. Similar developments occurred in Hungary, with the toleration of non-socialist parties, the legalization of strikes, the promise of free elections (and the holding of free by-elections), the rehabilitation of the victims of 1956, the abandonment of the appellation 'People's Republic', and the changing of the name of the communist party. One other highly symbolical act, the dismantling of the barbed wire fence on Hungary's western frontier, had far reaching implications. At first it might have appeared as no more than just a pleasant gesture: President George Bush was presented with a piece of barbed wire as a memento of the lifting of the Iron Curtain. But the consequences for other east European states, and particularly for the GDR, were profound. The Hungarian action underlined the fact that socialism in eastern Europe had depended for its concrete realization on the restriction of the freedom of movement of people.

Relatively large numbers of East Germans fled across the Hungarian–Austrian frontier illegally, since they did not have the correct papers. On some days hundreds moved in this way: in August 1989 five thousand in all crossed in this fashion. Others camped in Hungary waiting for an opportunity to move. The opening of the Hungarian frontier to Austria even to East Germans (11 September) provided a way out of Hungary's embarrassment, at some cost to its relationship with the political leadership of the GDR; but very large numbers now moved over the border in a dramatic vote of no confidence in the ability of the GDR regime to fulfil its own promises. Some 15,000 went in the first three days. When the GDR tried to prevent East Germans moving to Hungary, other Germans went instead to the West German embassies in Prague and Warsaw and demanded a passage to the West. Taken back eventually on trains running through East German territory, these refugees were cheered by crowds in the country they were leaving – another very clear and dramatic display of profound disaffection.

Widespread discontent in the GDR had already begun with protests against the manipulation of the local elections of 7 May 1989. The official results reported a turnout of 98.77 per cent and a vote of 98.95 per cent for the government's candidates (there were no alternatives), but in Berlin opposition groups maintained that the true turnout had been lower by some 12 per cent and the 'yes' vote by 7 per cent. Then later in the summer the events in Hungary transformed a small and heroic resistance to state cheating in elections into a mass movement on the streets.

The celebration of the GDR's fortieth anniversary on 7 October made the extent of the German crisis obvious. The population was clearly impatient with the SED leadership, and Gorbachev seemed to share this feeling when he visited Honecker. He spoke of the dangers facing those who failed to learn the lessons of history: 'if we are late we will be punished'. Here was the signal that the USSR expected rapid change in the GDR, given in an even more explicit manner than the humiliating departure of Ulbricht seventeen years earlier. The GDR lost if not its mandate from heaven at least its mandate from Moscow.

At the same time the commander of the Soviet troops in East Germany stated that he would not participate in a forcible repression of reformist movements. There would be no German Tiananmen square to crush the series of mass demonstrations held in many cities, but most dramatically on Monday evenings in Leipzig. Soviet troops did not move out of their barracks. On 2 October there had been just a brave 15,000; on 9 October 70,000 marched shouting 'Gorby, Gorby', as well as 'We want to stay [in the GDR]'. This was the decisive demonstration, and its peaceful outcome, the product of new Soviet thinking, set off an avalanche of demands. On 16 October 150,000 East Germans demonstrated, on the 23rd 300,000, on the 30th another 300,000, and on 4 November one million marched in East Berlin for democracy and free elections. A substantial part of the East German population was now on the streets, and this new popular power swept away first Honecker, and then later his successor Egon Krenz. On 9 November, the frontiers between the GDR and West Germany and West Berlin were opened, and millions of East Germans surged across amid tumultuous scenes of celebration. Most did not want to stay in the West: but during 1989, 340,000 East Germans went permanently to the Federal Republic. The outflow continued at a rate of over two thousand a day until the GDR elections in March 1990.

By December 1989 the communist party had lost almost all self-confidence, shrunk, and renamed itself as SED-PDS (Party of Democratic Socialism), and later simply as PDS, in an effort to mark a distance from the Stalinist past. It abolished the Central Committee and the Politbureau, the organs of the Leninist party. The old leaders were arrested and charged with corruption and 'abuse of power'; crowds also broke into the offices of the security police in their search for evidence of the criminal behaviour of their former leaders. On 7 December the parties of the previous national bloc met together with representatives of seven oppositional groups at a 'round table' which began to take decisions and assume some of the functions of a government. The round table agreed to hold free elections in May 1990, which were subsequently moved forward to 18 March. The Ministry of State Security and the secret police ('Stasi') were simply disbanded. History text-books needed to be withdrawn from East German schools.

West Germans enthusiastically cheered the developments on the other side of the border as what Helmut Schmidt in *Die Zeit* called the first genuinely mass democratic revolution in Germany, and one that on the whole was surprisingly peaceful. The German revolution in its turn also had international consequences in eastern Europe: the disintegration of the SED's grip on power provided a model for popular demonstrations in Prague which ended communist power there, and an attack on the Bulgarian party leadership and even a public questioning of the monopoly of the CPSU in the Soviet Union.

Only in Rumania, where the removal of the Ceauşescu regime cost the lives of almost 80,000 people, was the revolution violent. Rumania taught the Germans a grim lesson. The fall of Ceauşescu occurred on the same day as the opening of the Brandenburg gate (which had been the symbol of German division), and the massacres conducted by the Rumanian secret police over-shadowed the celebrations and reflections in Berlin. They demonstrated the extent to which all East European regimes had relied on terror and the secret police. Rumania seemed to play the role of nineteenth-century Poland, as the Christ of nations which bore all the sacrifices of a heroic struggle for freedom; and after Ceauşescu's fall, many East Germans realized that they were living their own combats vicariously. After the Rumanian revolution, political debate in the GDR focused on the role of the Stasi, and the failure to act decisively in order to prevent the Stasi regrouping under another name discredited the government of the reform communist Hans Modrow.

The events in East Germany were themselves a product and an extension of the international crisis of communism, as well as of Gorbachev's intervention. Germany was still very obviously a focus of international power politics. Since divided Germany represented the major European legacy of the Second World War, and since Germany was the focus at which the Cold War in Europe had broken out, an end to the East-West tensions of the Cold War epoch spelt the disintegration of those international brackets that had led the two Germanies securely clamped in place in post-war Europe. The German possibilities arose out of these world political developments rather than simply out of the immiseration and discontent of East German people and the petty repressiveness of their regime. Because of the sweeping character of global changes, East Germans simply realized that there was now a realistic chance of a complete political transformation in their country.

Germans were bewildered at being confronted by a new world order that was not of their making. The rapidity of the collapse of the Yalta-Potsdam system left a profound uncertainty. Nobody on either side of the abruptly dismantled fences and walls knew quite how to act.

The GDR faced political and economic disintegration. The two were connected, since one of the most powerful claims of the GDR to legitimacy in the 1960s and 1970s had rested on the promise of effective economic management as a consequence of scientific planning. Until the last moment, Honecker told Gorbachev that the GDR needed no *perestroika* because of the superiority of its economic performance. In October 1989, he was still boasting to the Soviet leader about the

GDR's megabyte chips. It was rather too late and rather too absurd – as Gorbachev very clearly and publicly noticed. His only response to Honecker's claims was a chilly and dismissive 'Tsss'. Slower growth in the 1980s and a widespread awareness that living standards lagged far behind those in the West undermined this sort of justification. Western television showed almost all the population of the GDR nightly how the other half lived.

Growth rates in East Germany had fallen continuously from 5.5 per cent in 1984 to 2.8 per cent in 1988. There were major technical lags; although East Germany was often held to be the centre of East bloc electronics and computer technology, and there were some plants which exported cheap electronic typewriters and printers to world markets, the lag in high technology electronics was as much as fifteen years. The share of GDR engineering products in the total trade of OECD states fell from a respectable 3.9 per cent in 1973 to 0.9 per cent in 1986[2]. By the late 1980s, even the USSR was rejecting GDR exported goods because of their unreliability. The overall picture was highly depressing. In 1989 labour productivity in the GDR was estimated to be less than half that in West Germany[3]. To the popular eye, the difference was graphically presented by the lines of small, slow, noisy and polluting cars – Trabants ('Trabis') and Wartbugs that crossed from East to West in November 1989. To the popular nose and lung, the smog of industrial Saxony carried the consequences of environmental backwardness.

Economics also pointed the bankrupt system in a new direction of increasingly necessary collaboration with and dependence on the West. For years, the GDR had been kept alive by financial assistance from West Germany, by flows which by 1989 amounted to DM4000 million annually (this figure includes both government to government payments for such items as road usage with sums sent by private Germans to their friends and relatives in the East). It was a substantial amount, equivalent to over half the value of German-German trade.

At the end of the 1980s, a potential existed for a much closer economic relationship between the two Germanies. East Germany had a highly trained and qualified work force, and the perception that with new investment and modern technology a new economic power might be created amounted to one of the most pressing arguments for unification. For many West German firms the new markets that might be opened in eastern Europe provided an additional incentive to invest and produce in the GDR. In addition, once the Wall was broken down and a free movement of labour could begin, unification appeared to have an economic inexorability: rather similar to the momentum that existed in the mid-nineteenth century for the creation of nation-states because they provided larger economic areas. This was just another, twentieth-century, case of Ludwig August Rochau's view of nation-building as a commercial transaction.

The economic situation required a political response. Without closer political links which might provide a new stability, an economically collapsing GDR would find itself drained dry by the superior attractions of its western neighbour. The exodus would simply take place at an even faster rate than before the demolition of a Wall which had originally been intended to prevent such losses of population, or become a daily flow of commuters living in cheap housing in the East and working for high hard currency wages in the West.

The future of political parties in the East looked uncertain. In other Central European countries, notably Hungary, the return to a normal political life after the one-party regime appeared much easier. The end of the communist monopoly of power simply produced a restoration of a much older political pattern that had prevailed during the interwar and the immediate postwar years – a party of the left, and a liberal and a conservative party. The dramatic alteration was that all the modern parties accepted the market economy (in the old Hungary both the left and the populist peasants' party had not); at the same time they all agreed on the need for a Hungarian state. The political clashes that remained took the form less of debates about the fundamental nature of policy (which was to be both national and market-oriented) than about style and emphasis.

The disintegration of the GDR by contrast left a vacuum in political life. In the eastern half of Germany, it was not as easy to revive old political traditions as in genuine nation-states such as Poland or Hungary. There existed no convenient history of organized party political life from the interwar years or even earlier upon which to fall back. The 1920s and 1930s were overshadowed by the rise of National Socialism; and after 1945 there was not even the brief democratization that survived briefly in post-war Czechoslovakia or Hungary. When the inhabitants of the GDR thought about political involvement, they did not normally associate this with parties.

In the GDR in 1989 there emerged both broad based coalitions of opposition movements and groups that looked for West German partners. Among the former, the major distinction between New Forum and the Christian movement Democratic Start (*Demokratischer Aufbruch*) lay in their different stance towards unification, with a sceptical New Forum and a rather more sympathetic Democratic Start. For the groups searching for a western model, the party appeared as a necessary device for the rapprochement of political systems. The eastern CDU had formerly been a party in the SED-led national bloc, which then asserted its independence and its desire for integration with the West. The DSU (German Social Union) adopted in East Germany the mantle of the Bavarian CSU. The eastern social democrats (first SDP, then openly SPD, the same name as in the West) represented a new initiative, looking to the western SPD for inspiration and rejecting marxist theory and the label 'socialism' completely. Even the SED, which renamed itself the Party of Democratic Socialism (PDS) under their new leader Gregor Gysi, tried rejuvenation through the adoption of ideas from the West German New Left. The absence of traditions on political life meant a growing use of the West German system as a pattern for how to organize politics. This development represented a remarkable testimony to the success of the Federal Republic over the past forty years in building a political system in which institutions attain that deep legitimacy that can only be a product of time and use and custom.

The full extent of the eastern political catastrophe, however, only became apparent later, after German unification in October 1990. The legacy of totalitarianism in the East proved to be the impossibility of normal politics. The ubiquitous role of the Stasi in the GDR, and the continuing stream of revelations about its activities, discredited the new political élite. Already during the campaign for the elections of March 1990, some candidates were suspected of activities as Stasi agents. Immediately after the elections, the SPD leader Ibrahim Böhme, who for most of the campaign had seemed likely to be the next Minister-President of the GDR, resigned his part suspicion. The CDU leader Lothar de Maiziere who did become Minister President eventually in 1991 resigned as Deputy Chairman of the German CDU because of Stasi allegations. In autumn 1990, when elections to the *Landtage* of the (now former) GDR were held, many of the leading candidates were western politicians. Carpet-baggers seemed preferable to Stasi agents. By 1992 the last eastern Minister-President of an eastern *Land*, Brandenburg's Manfred Stolpe, was under heavy attack for his past contacts with the Stasi. The political and emotional legacy of the Stasi state made impossible the development of a native political élite. In this way it quickened the merging of eastern into western political culture.

The convergence had begun much earlier. Although many foreign observers as well as SED spokesmen and the leaders of New Forum initially denied it, from the beginning of the mass demonstrations in October 1989 demands for German unification played an important part for some protesters. Even early in the Leipzig marches, the West

German national anthem with its opening line '*Einigkeit und Recht und Freiheit*' ('Unity and Law and Freedom') was sung, although by no means all the participants agreed with the implied demand. Some placards bore the slogan '*Deutschland einig Vaterland*' ('Germany One Fatherland'), a quotation from the embarrassing text of the GDR's national hymn. Opinion polls claimed to show that, by the end of 1989, between a quarter and a half of the East German population supported reunification[4]. When Chancellor Kohl visited Dresden in December for talks with the new Prime Minister of the GDR, he was greeted by crowds chanting for unity and waving national flags from which the GDR's symbol had been removed. By the time of the March 1990 election, most East Germans believed that relatively quick unification, even though it might bring traumatic adjustment costs, represented the only way out of the GDR's political and moral, as well as economic, catastrophe.

In the campaign, Chancellor Kohl gave a powerful boost to the three conservative and Christian parties (CDU, DSU, and Democratic Start) that he had personally pushed into an election coalition, the Alliance for Germany. He attracted far larger crowds than any other politician from West or East, in part at least simply because he embodied the authority of the West German state. At Erfurt there was a crowd of 130,000, at Chemnitz 200,000, and in Leipzig over a quarter of a million. He was introduced to his audience as the new Bismarck. His critics argued that he had turned an opportunity for democracy in the East German parliamentary election into simply a part of the West German political scene, a preliminary to the Bundestag campaign. It was without doubt largely due to the presence of the West German parties and the attractions of 'Our Chancellor' that the Alliance raised its vote from predictions of 10 per cent in January to 48.15 per cent on the day of the election. It was, as a hastily revised *Spiegel* title page put it, 'Kohl's Triumph'.

The SED-PDS claim that two different states had created two different nations and two identities looked ludicrously wrong; but with it the deduction that the GDR had a separate entity disappeared also. The GDR's existence was too much associated with the SED's ideology and too little linked with anything else for it to survive the intellectual bankruptcy of communism. One version of this argument had indeed frequently been presented by the SED's ideologists: that a capitalist Democratic Republic alongside a capitalist Federal Republic would be a historical duplication or redundancy. In addition, as communist rule ended all over eastern Europe, the ideological cement that had previously held the Warsaw pact together crumbled; and with this the most obvious power political obstacle to German unity was removed.

Even for those in the SED and in the left opposition movement who preferred a continuation of two Germanies, and campaigned against *Ausverkauf* (sell out, liquidation sale) and *Anschluss* (annexation, with an emotive echo of Nazi Germany's seizure of Austria in 1938), there was a search for appropriate traditions. The profound political uncertainty led to a quest for renewed constitutional forms that replicate older German patterns. The PDS leader Gysi advocated a return to a traditional federal structure in the GDR with a restoration of old-style *Länder*, as well as a decentralization and a devolution of power to local units modelled on the post-Napoleonic Stein-Hardenberg reforms. In practice, these reflections represented an endorsement of the legitimacy and antiquity of those German historical traditions most consciously taken up in the political framework of the Federal Republic. The logic of German political culture began to defeat even its critics.

For West Germany, it was certainly not easy to be chained by national and historic links to an almost moribund political and economic body. There were plenty of reasons to worry that a secure and stable West German order might be infected by the miasmas coming off the eastern cadaver. Economically, western workers feared that the inflow of a vast new labour supply could be calculated to undermine their bargaining position and security. Guaranteed West German citizenship under the provisions of the Basic Law meant that pensioners could come to claim West German payments even though they had made no contributions to the insurance funds, or that students could take western government grants, or that sick people could receive medical attention. A whole galaxy of costly claims now confronted West Germany.

In the tumultuous months of the winter of 1989–90, the initial reaction of all the West German parties to the startling ideological, political and economic collapse of the GDR was highly confused. Questions about how the addition of nearly seventeen million East Germans would change the political balance in Germany produced only uncertain answers. Would the new Germans, repelled by the experience of socialism, vote for the CDU-CSU (as many previous refugees and expelled people from Poland and GDR had done before them)? Would they, brought up in a predominantly non-Catholic culture, feel suspicious of Christian democracy and move towards a moderate SPD? Or perhaps would they, suffering the consequences of environmental disaster, vote for the Greens? Would they support a resurgence of violent and radical ultra-right nationalism? Would they behave in a familiar fashion at all? The major oppositional movement New Forum proclaimed that it was not a political party but a broad movement; it nevertheless prepared to put up candidates for the 1990 elections. In a coalition with other protest movements in the 'Alliance 90', it won eventually merely 2.9 per cent of the vote.

Often it was difficult to avoid the impression that the German question provided such an embarrassment to all parties that they wished it might somehow be avoided. It had been much easier to denounce the Wall and the separation of Germany as barbaric when there existed little prospect of imminent demolition. Initially, the German response to the new situation elevated the future of Germany above politics. Rarely has there been such harmony in the West German Bundestag as in the two great debates of the fall of 1989 on the German issue. On 11 November 1989, immediately after the opening of the Wall, Chancellor Kohl used words almost identical to those of Willy Brandt for the SPD, Theo Waigel for the CSU, Genscher for the FDP and Antje Vollmer for the Greens: 'freedom', he said, 'remains at the centre of the German question'. The inhabitants of the GDR needed to be allowed to decide their own fate. Brandt and Kohl in particular developed a remarkable similarity of outlook on the German question. Kohl's later ten point programme for German unity via confederation (28 November) provoked a second round of West German unanimity, though this time with the exception of the Greens who criticized the Kohl plan from the outset.

These were impressive demonstrations of a West German capacity to create consensus. They were essentially restatements of that system worked out between the late 1950s and the early 1970s. The SPD had to accept western integration, including the military alliance system, and the CDU-CSU later came to terms with *Östpolitik*. But equally characteristic was the rapid breakup of the initially agreed position as it became clear that it provided little basis for dealing with the realities of the current situation. Having established a verbal agreement, the parties then feared that this might be used for electoral advantage, with a new Bundestag election due in December 1990. Thus the SPD rapidly retreated from its early acceptance of the Kohl ten point plan. Even the FDP declared doubts because the programme did not explicitly guarantee the Polish-German frontier as the line of the rivers Oder and Neisse, although this border and the 1970 Warsaw Treaty had been accepted quite specifically with the votes of the CDU in a Bundestag resolution on 8 November 1989 (as well as by Chancellor Kohl emphatically in an address to expellees from the eastern areas on 21 October.

There was an almost formulaic quality to these set-piece debates. First the consensus is arrived at, and then it becomes possible to chip away at the other parties for not observing the consensus. The process betrayed a great vulnerability, the result of uncertainty about the shape of political life in the future and of helplessness in the face of great historical developments. Western uncertainty appeared remarkable in the face of the fact that developments in the East had demonstrated the powerful attractions of both political and economic aspects of the West German example: Bonn's effectively working democracy and the vitality of the compromise economic order characterized as the 'social market'.

The political divisions which followed from the new possibilities lay as much within the established West German parties as between them. In the SPD, Willy Brandt recognized the historic chance for recreating a German unity, and saw the process as natural and inevitable: 'what belongs together will grow together'. He was the party's most obvious, and most successful, asset in the GDR election campaign. On the other hand, Oskar Lafontaine feared the destabilization that unification would bring, through the addition of large numbers to the work-force, to the social harmony of the Federal Republic. In a similar development, those within the CDU most concerned with social policy – such as Labour Minister Norbert Blüm – were most troubled by the new mobility of labour.

Within the CDU and CSU a different kind of division existed between the majority of the parties and a relatively small minority, linked with refugee groups, who insisted that the German-Polish frontier on the line of the rivers Oder and Neisse should not be regarded as definitive. This dispute was complicated not simply by tactical and electoral considerations and a fear of losing voters to the far right, but also by the rather convoluted legal principles underlying the 1970 Warsaw Treaty. West Germany had accepted the Oder-Neisse line; but legally could not conclude any internationally binding treaties on behalf of a future unified German state. Adherence by the West German government to the 1970 Warsaw formula was undoubtedly correct from a strictly legal standpoint, and it may have helped to pacify the far right in Germany, but not surprisingly it terrified the Poles and other Europeans. In the end, after a long and embarrassing period of hesitation, and public conflict between the Chancellery and the Foreign Office, Chancellor Kohl's government accepted the principle of an international guarantee of the Oder-Neisse line. The fissures that appeared within existing parties late in 1989 heralded a new era in which the answers to political questions no longer fitted neatly into the old categories.

Finding answers to the new challenges became harder because the guiding principles of politics in the Cold War era no longer applied;

and also because of a radical uncertainty about Germany's new position. On the one hand Germany had a new and obvious strength. On the other hand, many realized that the origins of a new order lay in three heterogeneous and fortuitous elements: first, the breakdown of East Germany, secondly the new fluidity of the international system, and thirdly the legal provisions of West Germany's Basic Law. Both the preamble and Article 116 had set out explicitly the right of all Germans to self-determination: the German government was to speak not just for those within the boundaries of West Germany, but for all Germans.

The actions of West German political leaders could not affect any of the fundamental impetuses towards unity; and in consequence they realized that their position was to be takers rather than makers of history. It is extremely frustrating for politicians at any time to believe that they are prisoners of events. It was especially so at a time when the new international fluidity presented an opportunity and a challenge to German leaders.

Here a generational shift in Germany had a considerable significance on political attitudes and behaviour. In the immediate postwar period, Allied pressure and interventions gave opportunities for the creation of relatively stable and secure political systems in both Germanies. External limitations were necessary for the new political order. Germans could usefully describe hardships and unpopular policies as the product of Allied demands. One generation later, the same external pressures were no longer interpreted as the intrusion of objective circumstances but rather as an occasion for a legitimate grievance. Bearing a historic responsibility for the crimes of the Nazi era and of the Second World War could not be expected to involve the imposition of a perpetual self-denying ordinance in international politics. Such an ordinance seemed legitimate and appropriate to the postwar generation, which reacted rightly and strongly against the German past. But it is a restriction that a third, post-postwar generation found impossible to comprehend and easy to reject.

The Bavarian Minister-President Franz Josef Strauss formulated the point clearly when he dictated in his (posthumously published) memoirs: his country should not and could not 'remain a wishy-washy state or a kind of semi-colony under international tutelage, controlled from outside'[5]. The General Secretary of the CDU, Volker Rühe, explained similarly that 'we require no approval from abroad for the confederative steps. This is simply an affair of the two German states.' But this new consciousness of Germany's peculiar position was not just an obsession of politicians of the right. At the SPD's Berlin Congress, Willy Brandt carefully explained: 'Forty-five years after the end of the war, the category victor and vanquished is no longer valid. However great the guilt of a nation, it cannot be paid off through a decreed and indefinite division.'[6] Kohl significantly announced his ten point plan without consultations in Washington, London or Paris, or even in Brussels.

Germany (even West Germany on her own) had become a Great Power once again, and had to face the choices and opportunities entailed: but also the problem that there are no longer the excuses for failure and impotence that are available to the small players in the international game.

The result of German developments was a change in the behaviour of the other players. On the Soviet side, there were contradictory statements. Privately, some influential figures in Soviet policy-making had come to believe, even before 1989, that German unity was historically unavoidable. In the summer of 1988, for instance, a prominent Soviet general told the astonished British politician Enoch Powell in a television interview that there was no doubt that German unity would come. Eduard Shevardnadze, the Soviet Foreign Minister at the time of German unification, later wrote that he had begun to believe in the inevitability of a united Germany in 1986: 'I said that in the near future the German question would define Europe.'[7] At first, the most promising strategy from the Soviet point of view appeared to be an attempt to use the German question as a way of destroying the opposing military alliance, NATO. The USSR could bargain German neutrality in return for unity, since it would clearly be impossible for two parts of a single state to belong to rival military alliances.

On Soviet television on 16 November 1989, Mikhail Gorbachev said that 'discussions about reunification would mean an interference in the affairs of West Germany and the Democratic Republic': in other words, the Germans should be left alone to decide their fate. On the next day, these words were removed in the *Pravda* report of Gorbachev's declaration. Instead, Gorbachev then explained that German unification was certainly possible and even perhaps desirable, but that it should be the affair of the next century. On 29 November the Soviet Foreign Ministry spokesman made this point very clearly by stating that 'there is not one country in Europe today which would endorse reunification because of the consequences for the stability of Europe. The question is not on the agenda today'.[8] By February 1990, after a visit of Chancellor Kohl to Moscow, Gorbachev declared his acceptance of German unity, though he still demanded that the new state should not in its entirety be a member of NATO.

In July 1990, Kohl visited President Gorbachev at Stavropol in the Caucasus, and the USSR agreed to NATO membership for Germany, in return for substantial German financial help disguised as payments towards the expense of transporting and resettling the Soviet army in Germany. With the Stavropol agreement, there were no more obstacles in the way of international agreement on the German issue. On 12 September, the Foreign Ministers of the wartime coalition – France, Great Britain, USA and USSR – signed the treaty on 'the final settlement [of the Second World War] in respect of Germany', together with the two German states. They thus endorsed German unity, which they stated would occur within the context of a 'united Europe' in which Germany would be 'an equal and sovereign partner'. The text's confusion – how could Germany be sovereign and at the same time part of united Europe – reflected the embarrassment that the German question posed for the other members of the international order.

But it was not simply for the USSR that these great ambiguities over the German question existed. The same was just as true for the western powers. In America and Britain, domestic discussions over national decline reappeared in the guise of concerns about the influence and power of Germany. France, which had mastered its imperial past rather better than Great Britain, remained much more immune to this debate, but feared that the new enlarged economic and demographic size of Germany would destroy the delicate balance in German-French relations which had been at the centre of France's European policy.

In the USA after a decade of increasing trade deficits opinion polls revealed that Japan was considered to be more of an enemy than the Soviet Union. An economically powerful Germany added a new, European, dimension to the economic challenge to US hegemony. For traditional British conservatives, and at least in this regard Mrs Thatcher was one, the return of a strong Germany set the final seal on Britain's decline as a Great Power whose foreign policy had for centuries rested on the idea of preventing an imbalance of power in Europe. Now the European balance had changed completely. She was quoted as saying: 'We must get used to the idea that in the future there will be one country in Europe that is stronger than all the rest'.[9]

In addition to these concerns, there was also a fear that Germany might be lured away from the West by Soviet offers of support for the unification process at the price of neutrality, that Germany might draw a political lesson from a justified acknowledgement of the role that Gorbachev had played in making unity possible, and that German 'Gorby-mania' might be more than just a passing fad.

NATO's goal since 1967 had publicly and explicitly been a unification of Germany within the framework of the western alliance; but the 1967 Harmel Report was drawn up at just the time when detente and the apparent stability of the GDR made this objective less of a practical reality than it had previously been. When President Reagan called on President Gorbachev to demolish the Berlin Wall in 1987, it still appeared as simply a rhetorical gesture. The US position remained in public unchanged, and was reformulated by President George Bush after the Malta superpower summit in December 1989 as 'German unification should occur in the context of Germany's continued commitment to NATO and to an increasingly integrated European community'. But the practical significance of the insistence on the alliance and the European framework became a rather novel one: it meant an attempt to put a brake on German developments. The same stance was adopted by President Mitterrand (who saw the European Community as providing the major restraint on over-rapid German developments) and Mrs Thatcher (who preferred to use the North Atlantic Alliance as the confining force).

These considerations also led to the Strasbourg European Community summit's guarded endorsement in December 1989 of German unification within the European framework. They arose out of a wish to depoliticize the German question by thinking in as coldly rational terms as possible about the economic logic of integration. Kohl frequently made this point about global integration and unification as a way of reassuring other states. German unity, he explained to a hostile Mrs Thatcher, should be synchronized with a European political union. The nation is no longer the most appropriate framework for economic decision making, and it helps to think of wider and larger units. If German nationality and sovereignty are a possible threat, can the dangers not be removed by thinking of bigger areas? Here there was a reversion to a rather old and familiar German position: economics are easy, but politics requires much more learning. If there are no adequate existing institutions, the Germans have often hoped that they might materialize simply as a result of growth.

The speeding up of unification in 1990 after the March elections occurred not just because of Bonn's belief that it was necessary to seize a moment of opportunity with regard to Soviet policy (because there might be a return to pre-Gorbachev style authoritarian communism). Bonn was primarily worried about the movement of East Germans across the border into West Germany; and at the beginning of February the Chancellor and his advisers came to the conclusion that only the rapid introduction of the Deutschemark in the East could prevent the emptying of the GDR. The decision to exchange the eastern Mark with the DM at the rate of one to one was made in Bonn, against the advice of the economic experts and the Bundesbank. Kohl later said: 'I don't have any alternative. If we don't carry out economic and monetary union, then we face the risk that in the summer we will have 500,000 people coming here from the GDR'.[10]

The monetary union came into effect on 1 July 1990 and from this moment speedy political union became imperative. Otherwise, the argument went, East German destinies would be controlled by the economic decisions made by the Bonn ministries and the central bank in Frankfurt, but East Germans would have no possibility of influencing decisions. By the time of monetary union, many of the normal state functions of the GDR had come to an end; monetary union simply completed the GDR's political vacuum. A complicated legal process, involving German constitutional law (the application of newly constituted Länder in the East to join the Federal Republic under Article 23 of the Basic Law) and international law (the rights of the Four Powers, ended by the Two plus Four Treaty), was rushed through to allow political unification of the two Germanies by the beginning of October.

The German unity established on 3 October 1990 was in purely practical terms the accomplishment of the Deutschemark – as an instrument in dealing with the USSR, and as an irresistible attraction for the population of the GDR. In the immediate aftermath of unification, economics continued to dominate the political scene. The debate between parties in the elections in December 1990 to the first Bundestag of united Germany concentrated on a cost-benefit calculus about the German revolution. Helmut Kohl won the election convincingly, in large part because he appeared as the historic figure who had created German unity; but at the same time, he also thought it necessary to boost the performance of his party by a promise that unification would not be financed through tax rises. His opponent, the SPD leader Oskar Lafontaine, responded with a negative strategy of insisting on the exorbitantly high costs of unity. These warnings may have been justified by the experience of the deep depression in East German industrial production in 1991 and 1992, and by the enormous costs of restructuring East German industry. But in the circumstances of December 1990 they were quite useless: they proposed no realistic alternative to Kohl's strategy, and they alienated eastern voters.

Concentrating on the business aspects of unity generated a great vulnerability in German politics. What possibility is there for creating new and satisfactory political institutions on such a basis? The makers of the new Germany could either point to the economic logic of the process or to its cultural appeal. The former may provide only unsatisfactory grounds for a creation of new bonds of loyalty. Since the SED tried to justify its control of power more and more in terms of what I have called the theory of an 'economic nation', or what its former leaders saw as the opposition of a Germany of the proletarians to a Germany of the bourgeois, the argument about the economic determination of state forms and the necessity for economic reasons of a greater Germany looked dubious as well to many East German citizens. But it was this case which initially appeared to be the most immediately compelling and pressing reason for unification: that the alternative was complete collapse in the East. Sometimes the idea of economic necessity transformed itself into utopian hopes. One of the slogans of the March 1990 elections had been: 'Helmut, take us by the hand, Lead us to the economic miracle land'. Can a vision of a way out of bankruptcy be a foundation substantial enough on which to build a new German state?

It is hardly surprising that many prominent East German critics and dissidents rejected such an economistic argument, and offered instead ideas of a cultural community. Inhabitants of western Germany such as Günther Grass or of eastern Germany such as Christa Wolf or Stefan Heym or former GDR citizens such as Uwe Johnson had long in their writings discussed the effects of division. They hoped that their reflections and creations might play the same role in transcending the divisions created by frontiers that Goethe and Schiller did in the small state Germany of the late eighteenth century. There might, in short, be a cultural answer to the political problem.

In the West, Günter Grass set out this solution quite explicitly: 'of all areas, it is the most sensitive, the most fragile – culture – that has survived the division of Germany best ... With a new cultural understanding, a confederation of both German states would have the chance to define a national understanding – two confederated states, one cultural nation'.[11] The dissident marxist thinker Rudolf Bahro warned about abandoning a 'Trabi-Deutschland' simply to move into a 'Mercedes-Deutschland'. The West German philosopher Jürgen Habermas complained after the GDR elections of a 'DM-Nationalismus', and the 'barren emotional territory, where nationalist blossoms shoot out of the arrogance of economic domination'.[12]

The PDS leader Gregor Gysi tried to use this theme when he warned against an 'impending domination by capitalist magnates'. The election propaganda of his party warned against an *Anschluss* by the Federal Republic. The most striking rejection of the wish to be integrated into a colossal new economic super-state came from the novelist Stefan Heym in circumstances that in retrospect appear tragic. He stated at a press conference in Berlin that there existed a danger that the GDR would be 'sold out' or 'taken over' by a Federal Republic which would turn united Germany into a bleak landscape dominated by powerful corporations: it would be the 'Germany of Messerschmidt, Mercedes and Herr Herrhausen of the Deutsche Bank.' Though there was no direct connection between the events, two days after Heym's declaration, the only person he mentioned by name as the most obvious and prominent representative of the economic idea of unity was assassinated by West German terrorists.

Alfred Herrhausen, the chief executive of the Deutsche Bank, had indeed been a powerful and articulate proponent of unification, of Germany as a powerful economy existing in a Europe driven by the logic of economics. For Herrhausen, Germany could not live for ever without a national identity, and he explained to British journalists only days before his death that German unification was both 'desirable and inevitable'. Or, as he wrote in a speech for an American audience, 'I feel it to be a mistake if Germans do not recover their identity within a European context'.[13] It is not too fanciful to follow the British journalist David Marsh who saw Herrhausen like Walther Rathenau as a martyr to a vision they had of Germany: they were symbols of a development against which many wanted to fight ferociously. Though Heym could not have foreseen Herrhausen's murder, neither did Karl Helfferich intend to cause Rathenau's death when he made his fanatical attack in the Reichstag on 21 June 1922, the day before Rathenau was killed as he drove to his work down the *Königsallee*.

The East German intellectuals and the West German terrorists made clear how deep the resentments run against a Germany produced less by Germans than by economic logic and international movements, and how explosive the German mixture can be. A very different threat to emerge was that from a West German far right, which offered a new version of militant German nationalism: in the European Parliament elections of 1989, a party calling itself 'Republican', led by Franz Schönhuber, won seven per cent of the overall vote, and in parts of Bavaria fared even better with scores over twenty per cent. After the breakdown of the SED's control, Schönhuber claimed to have established branches of his part in the East. The high vote of the Republicans was due to anti-immigrant feeling, to discontent over the government's handling of population movements from Eastern Europe, to disillusionment with corruption in the big Bonn parties, and to the death of Franz Josef Strauss who had been capable of integrating traditional right wing attitudes within a modern and fundamentally moderate mass party. The new party rejected internationalism in all forms – whether superpower pre-eminence, concessions to the East, or international flows of populations. In the course of 1991–2 it derived further support all over Germany from worries about the pace of European integration, a popular backlash against the Maastricht proposals for European monetary and political union, and the threatened abolition of the Deutschemark; but above all from the increased flow of people, mostly from eastern Europe, claiming political asylum under German law.

The asylum issue also provided one of the triggers for violent explosions of racial and national hatred among neo-fascist youth groups in both western and eastern parts of Germany. Most terrifyingly, in the eastern riots in Rostock in August 1992, large numbers of bystanders cheered and encouraged the youths. The motivation of the rioters and their supporters ranged from frustration at the lack of opportunities in the East, complaints that the Bonn politicians had neglected the former GDR, a wish to demonstrate power and aggression, and a desire to appear in the substantial television and press coverage of the riots.

The concerns of the intellectuals and the violence of the extreme right are only symptoms of a general malaise of a Federal Republic engaged in a search for a new political style. Since 1989, there has been a foreign policy debate that reflects the crisis of identity of a state that has suddenly become a major power and that is surprised about its own role; and a loss of nerve and confidence in the major political parties, the institutions that had been the pillars of post-1949 West German democracy.

The January 1991 Gulf War demonstrated the problems Germany would face in a world in which the defining international problem no longer lay in East-West relations. At the outbreak of the war, the SPD's chairman Hans Jochen Vogel had said that he was disturbed by the actions of the US-led anti-Iraq coalition. Initially Chancellor Kohl and Foreign Minister Genscher were non-committal, and appeared slow to accept that the military defence of Kuwait was justifiable and necessary. As a result of the late support, and the nervous feeling in Washington that Germany had been unsupportive, Germany – together with Japan, which behaved in a similar way – were pressed and then agreed to make very substantial payments towards the costs of Operation Desert Storm. The politics of evasion turned out to be expensive for Germany.

The Iraq debate raised constitutional questions about whether German troops could properly be used for any purpose apart from the defence of Germany and commitments within the NATO treaty area. At the same time, the debate became a highly moralistic one, concerned with the circumstances under which states should use force, and the peculiar responsibilities of German policy. As the past perpetrator of military aggression, did Germany have a peculiar historic duty to avoid military conflict, and work towards peaceful resolution even if this meant accepting injustices; or did the past rather impose on Germany the special mission of resisting aggression?

Later in 1991, the disintegration of Yugoslavia and the war between parts of the former federation brought a new version of this dilemma. With support from all the major political parties, the government coalition led the way in the international diplomatic recognition of Slovenia and Croatia, and put the European Community under pressure to follow the German example. The combination of enthusiastic action on the diplomatic front and an inability (because of the German Basic Law) and an unwillingness to engage in military action meant that Germany in practice could do little to affect the outcome of the exceptionally brutal and destructive war between Serbia and Croatia, and between Serbia and Bosnia. The European Community found it almost impossible to devise a common policy towards the former constituents of Yugoslavia, and impossible to halt genocide. Both the Gulf and Yugoslavia demonstrated not the power, but the impotence of the new Germany.

The wars of 1991–2, and the debate over the pace of European integration raised questions about the character of the new German state that the political élite wished to avoid. How far had Germany become a normal state with normal interests? Those who insisted on German peculiarity developed a peculiar nostalgia for the confined state of the Cold War period. Some features of this nostalgia seemed very peculiar. Intellectuals who had previously criticized Adenauer's restorationism now saw him as the man who created stability by accepting the partial state of the western zones. Adenauer became the subject of a retrospective idealization[14]. The yearning for the past was driven by the rejection of the present.

The party debate about the new German problems followed more directly from the economic problems that had been at the heart of German reflection about nationality and statehood. The old political system found it difficult to come to terms with the slower than anticipated economic recovery of eastern Germany. In the past, both the major movements – CDU and SPD – had depended on economic growth to produce resources that would be available for redistribution and for the building of political legitimacy. When it became evident that the costs of restructuring the East would place a real burden on the West, the scope available for redistribution contracted, and the political parties found that their relation with their traditional supporters became strained. They needed to appeal to new groups of voters, and as they modified their message they appeared to be more and more cynical.

It was characteristically President Richard von Weizsäcker who, as on previous occasions in his Presidency, presented himself as the voice of morality correcting the vices of the political system. He both called on Germans to make greater sacrifices as part of the unification process, and argued that the parties had lost their function and sense of purpose and now stood in the way of genuine and effective democracy. Instead of parties debating issues and solving problems, they had 'instrumentalized' policy issues for the sake of electoral advantage. 'We live in a demoscopic democracy. It seduces parties to listen to society, identify issues, make a programme out of them, and then beam them back at society in order to get a mandate for the next legislative period.' The former SPD leader Oskar Lafontaine complained that German politics appeared to be conducted 'under the influence of valium'[15].

The criticism may have been appropriate, but appeals to sacrifice have to be accompanied by a vigorous defence of the purpose of the sacrifice. The absence of such a purpose appeared most strikingly when German politicians tried to define away the German problem by placing it in a broader context. For most of post-war history, German choices had been limited by the international system. After 1989, the instinctive German reaction meant searching for equivalent ways of constraining German choices and opportunities.

The double crisis – of Germany's external position and her political structures – produced an attempt to escape the problem by Europeanizing it. It was a German flight away from Germany. Kohl argued that Germany was already the most European country because she possessed the longest frontier and the most neighbours[16]. Such a strategy contained the obvious danger that Germany's neighbours would see the European rhetoric as a way of dressing up German power political interests – interests that Germany was not willing openly to acknowledge. As a result, disenchantment with the European ideal outside Germany increased; and the German purpose of seeking a secure international framework for domestic politics was frustrated.

Europeanization at the same time challenged the most powerful emblem of German success since 1945, the Deutschemark. With the Maastricht conference, a populist revolt began against the major political parties. The most striking headlines came in *Bild-Zeitung*: 'Our beautiful money. The Mark will be abolished'.[17] International constraints clashed with the German symbol.

Germany in 1989 had been politically and intellectually unprepared – or rather prepared in the wrong way, armed with the simple assumption that economic growth held the answer to political problems. As a result, the euphoria briefly associated with unification turned to bitterness, frustration and a new German malaise. The festival of 1989 was followed by a terrible hangover.

11

Conclusion: Cycles in German History

In 1870 and 1939 and 1914, the German question destroyed the existing international order. In 1806 and 1989–90 German changes profoundly altered the international balance. Then, as now, German politics were part of a much broader international system, and changes in Germany carried implications that reached far beyond German borders. After 1989, Helmut Schmidt wrote that, simply because Germany has 'more neighbours than any other people', it is more difficult for Germans to live in tranquillity. François Mitterrand reminded Germans of history: 'Remember the words of Napoleon: every state follows the politics of its geography.[1]

Was there something peculiar about German development apart from the chance of geographical position at the fulcrum of the international balance? Was there, to use the German expression, a *Sonderweg*? A path in internal development of such historical peculiarity that it led inexorably to 1933 and 1945, but then also to the peaceful democratic revolution of the GDR in 1989? And a path that caused Germany so frequently to disturb the European balance?

We should treat any claim of this sort – that the origins of the peculiar development lie within German society rather than stemming from circumstances in the international system – with some initial scepticism. After all, most nations consider themselves to be in some way unique, and often with rather little objective justification. There are British, American, French, Japanese, Russian, Italian, Swiss 'peculiar paths' with their own substantial literature, both academic and non-academic, devoted to chronicling their peculiarity. Even Luxembourg and Liechtenstein have their own roads to modernity.

Since at least the end of the nineteenth century, a social historical interpretation of the German experience has enjoyed considerable popularity. It was originally the political instrument of left liberal critics of the Kaiserreich, who argued that what was wrong with Germany was simply that there were not enough of them, and besides that, that they did not have any political power. There was in Imperial Germany, they explained, a modern economic and industrial system – and it would have been hard to argue with that – but there had not been a bourgeois revolution of the type that had been found in Britain or France. The First World War and the collapse of Imperial Germany did not solve the problem. 1918–19 was a political, and not a social, revolution. The old élites – in business, the civil service, the army, the judiciary – remained important in the Weimar Republic, and undermined democracy from within. Their influence and their intrigues put Hitler into power.

Looking back on the past century, one modern writer says: 'The German society of the time did not become bourgeois, but remained quasi-feudal. Industrialization in Germany failed to produce a self-confident bourgeoisie with its own political aspirations.' Or, from another author, 'Germany had never experienced a successful bourgeois revolution. This resulted in a lack of questioning and opening up, or at least loosening up, of traditional structures.'[2] A pre-modern élite stayed on; and felt increasingly uneasy with the social revolution created by industrial society. Thus it adopted more and more risky measures – particularly in foreign policy – in order to generate a bogus national consensus. This vulnerable social constellation led to war in 1914 and 1939. The theory could explain both repressive and authoritarian domestic policies and external adventurism with a single concept: a deficit of modernity among Germany's ruling élites.

It was a view put forward by Max Weber in 1895, by Thorstein Veblen in 1915, and in the interwar period by Eckart Kehr and Hans Rosenberg. After 1945, its tenets are expressed most clearly by Alexander Gerschenkron, Ralf Dahrendorf, Volker Berghahn, and by Hans-Ulrich Wehler. Arno Mayer has extended the concept into an analysis of the whole ruling order in prewar Europe. Though it is in general a feature of left liberal critiques of German society (it is with all the above writers), it has crept into and influenced a great deal of other work. It appears with respect to an earlier period – rather bizarrely but quite powerfully – in the work of Friedrich Meinecke, who derived the political incapacity of Prussia at the beginning of the nineteenth century from the excessively privileged position of the Prussian aristocracy, and pointed out that the great Prussian reformers were either non-Prussian or non-aristocratic or both.

After 1945, critics continued to analyse the problem of German élites. According to a widespread interpretation, the Federal Republic represented the restoration of an older Germany, in which a continuity of élites perpetuated the German past. These élites, it was claimed, continued to attempt the imposition of authoritarian solutions to political problems: banning left wing activists from civil service employment in the 1970s, creating a police state in response to the threat of terrorism, or siting nuclear power plants and stationing missiles without consulting the people.

Such an interpretative tradition of looking for social continuities distinguished itself sharply from the old concerns of the Prussian school of historians, who had their own thesis on German peculiarity. Her uniqueness came – if not from inherent superiority – from her peculiar geographical position in the centre of Europe (the *Mittellage*). Place and space determined race. This was argued by Leopold von Ranke, by Arnold Heeren, and by Otto Hintze. In the twentieth century, explicit versions have been put forward by Ludwig Dehio, David Calleo, and Michael Stürmer. It is a stance usually, but not always, associated with political conservatism. When taken to explain the weakness of German liberalism it may well take the form of a critical argument – as with the case famously argued by Sir John Seeley that the internal freedom of a people decreases in proportion to the pressure exerted on its boundaries by other nations. Heeren used the *Mittellage* as an argument against national unity: the transformation of Germany into one state 'would have been the grave of German improvement and European freedom' he wrote in 1830[3]. Sir Lewis Namier derived a devastating criticism of German liberalism from an analysis of how the 1848 revolutions took place in the geographic middle of other nationalist revolutions.

Not all modern historians feel that the Germans are really so peculiar or that they are imprisoned by geography or a unique social constellation. Instead, some recent writers attempt to show Germany as a normal nation with a quite normal past until the exceptional events of the third and fourth decades of the twentieth century. Thomas Nipperdey, David Blackbourn and Geoff Eley have spent considerable energy, imagination, and perspicacity in demonstrating the modernity of the Wilhelmine Empire and its culture. This was materialist, commercial and entrepreneurial, open to advances in the sciences and to modernist culture, and self-critical in the fashion of modern satire. The critiques offered from the 1890s by the Munich magazine *Simplicissimus* or by Heinrich Mann (most famously in his novel written before the First World War, but only published in 1918, *Der Untertan*) of the Wilhelmine order are turned round: instead of proving that fin de siècle Germany was feudal and reactionary, they prove that she was sufficiently modern to be able to sneer at herself. Nipperdey points out the diversity of German traditions, and that 1933 is not the ultimate realization of the whole German past. Eley's concerns are slightly different – and above all less concerned with the tone of political culture – than those of Blackbourn and Nipperdey: he is chiefly interested in showing the emergence in nineteenth-century Germany of 'a mature capitalist society'[4]. But it is an argument which certainly confirms the view of Blackbourn and Nipperdey.

The interpretation advanced here is closest to the third of the sketched out models.

First, it should be clear from the analysis given in the main part of this essay that the author believes Germany from the 1870s to have been indeed highly modern. From the middle of the nineteenth century Germany had successfully caught up with her western rivals. This view was also held by most contemporary observers of the Kaiserreich.

One of the curiosities of the critical 'social history approach' of Weber and Veblen as an analysis is that historically it appeared so late in time. It took surprisingly long for middle-class Germans to discover that there had been no bourgeois revolution. This interpretation is in fact a product of the bitter political turmoil during the Chancellorship of Leo von Caprivi in the early 1890s. In a sense it is nothing more than party propaganda directed against the Prussian aristocrats and the Agrarian League. Until the 1890s, it was much more usual for analysts to reflect, when they pondered the differences between Germany and England, that Germany was so very much less aristocratic than the island state. Germany was more middle class because the civil service mattered rather more. Hegel had viewed Germany as the land of the bureaucracy, which constituted what he called the 'universal class'. This was also, for instance, the line advanced very powerfully by the Swiss lawyer Bluntschli. At the beginning of the 1890s this interpretation was still the obvious one. At the time when the landless Caprivi became Chancellor of Germany, the English Prime Minister was the highly aristocratic Lord Salisbury – the heir to a title, and estate and fortune, and an instinct for politics that went back to the sixteenth century.

Secondly, it would be unwise for any analyst to ignore the importance of Germany's position within the international order. The external European and then world setting moulded the ideas developed by the nationalists. Early nineteenth-century German nationalism can only be understood as a rebellion against the circumstances of international politics, a rejection of Napoleon and Metternich. Bismarckian Prussia could grow into united Germany because of a vacuum in European politics after the Crimean War. At the same time, in 1871 a new European order was created. The new Germany had pushed up as far as she could against the limits tolerated by Britain and Russia, and Bismarck had to declare her to be now a 'satiated power'. In the last third of the nineteenth century, the existence of a powerful and united Germany presented a new force for the destabilization of international politics. One of the reasons why German policy was so erratic and incalculable – always consistently anti-French, but then anti-Russian as well, and finally anti-British – was the novelty of the German state as a political unit. It tried to secure stability by building a system of alliances, which looked like threats to those powers outside the German alliance system. It wanted to win equal rank by acquiring an overseas empire, as Britain or France had already done; but this only led it into frenetic competition. Once the nation had been made, it existed in a context of great power clashes. The rapid growth of Prussian-German power made many of its followers and worshippers believe that for Germany nothing was impossible. Some Germans became infinitely confident about the possibilities open to the new Germany. Since the German Empire could never accomplish all the goals posed by national-ist thinkers, Germans found this international system almost as limiting and restricting as that of Napoleonic or Congress Europe, and developed a similarly nationalist and hostile response.

Smaller and less powerful states could easily view themselves as victims of oppression from their neighbours, and of an international power game played out at their expense. Germans, whose state had become an Empire which viewed itself as a major player in that international game, could not offer the same excuse for national failures. They could not see themselves as a small country, victimized by bullies next door. When national ideologues looked for constraints on Germany's room for manoeuvre, when they realized that the nation could not do all that it set out to do, they concluded that the fault lay in internal weakness. The national strength had been sapped by some domestic difficulty, perhaps by an enemy from within.

However, there is a sociological explanation for the odd course of Germany's development. The German peculiarity lay in the fact that it had a substantial bourgeoisie with a powerful and independent culture, and which thought in a 'modern' direction, before there were really any of the substantial economic and political changes that accompanied industrialization. This middle class imagined a vision of the nation and proposed schemes on how to realize their ideal: through education, the construction of uplifting public monuments, and through economic advance. This group looked at the French, English, and American models of modernity as a way to shape the new organization of the nation.

There have been two misleading assumptions about the 'bourgeoisie' which have obstructed useful analysis of the development of nineteenth-century German politics. One is that this should be a class necessarily identified with political liberalism. The German middle classes looked instead rather to cultural politics and unpolitical culture. The other error is that the bourgeoisie are a product of the industrial revolution and that they specialize in industry and commerce. It is conceivable that a prosperous urban class should indeed have these attributes, but the world is full of bourgeoisies that have little to do with modern industry. The German example is only one. The development in the first half of the nineteenth century in Berlin or in southern Germany of employment by the state, of university life, and of a very extensive and unusually literate culture are phenomena that are quite independent of the stirrings of manufacture in the distant Rhineland or Saxony.

As a class the bourgeoisie was intellectually rather than nationally defined. What distinguished it was its vision of identity and society. This bourgeoisie was the principle bearer of national thought and of nationalist doctrine. It looked continually at other cultures and other bourgeoisies. It had an obsession with the geographic position of Germany – with the *Mittellage*. It combined the intellectual assertion of national identity with two other realizations. First, that national unity required a stable social order which economic prosperity alone could supply. Secondly, that national units needed an economic backbone if they were to possess a military capacity. In this regard, Prussia had moved ahead in the 1850s while Austria had stood still (and been crippled by the impact of the economic crisis of 1857). The military victory of Prussia over Austria in 1866 at Sadowa made this a finally conclusive lesson. These two doctrines were the legacy of national inferiority and humiliation in the first third of the century.

In the last third of the nineteenth century, however, the situation that had prevailed in the first third had been turned around. Germany possessed a major economic force: this gave German decision-makers a greater arsenal with which they could manoeuvre on the battlefields of international politics. It made the nationalists more conscious of the strength of their country, and more eager to use that strength assertively.

On the other hand, the governments of Imperial Germany could not provide results that lived up to these expectations and demands. A new generation of nationalists insisted that the state should follow policies that were more aggressive and radical. Others rejected the whole set of assumptions that underpinned state nationalism based on economic prosperity. They revolted against materialism and the cult of mammon. After the First World War, as the economic climate became highly changeable, the search for radical prescriptions for a new nationalism became more frenzied, and provided the climate in which National Socialism could grow as a successful political movement. Only total defeat in 1945 ended this quest.

The story is one of generational revolts against previous generations' assumptions about nationality. We might generalize about the development of views about Germany in the following way. National identity is built around perceptions of what it had been some time in the past, say in our parents' generation. Partly this is simply because ideas always require some time to be disseminated. But more important than this is the reactive quality of visions of nationality: the mental pictures of identity we elaborate represent a response to a past phenomenon which creates a different and new one. (If we view it as a mathematical function, we might say it was autolagged.) The new represents some form of reaction against the old. This reactive quality is likely to be least prominent in cases where institutions, with their solid dependability, provide a bedrock of continuity from which change and adaptation may emerge.

Where this is absent, there is room for greater swings of opinion and attitude. Where national identity is artificially constructed out of a series of intellectual endeavours, rather than growing slowly out of the day-to-day humdrum life of institutions, identity can be recast and reformulated much more easily. In such a radically unstable set-up, the scope for clashes between generations becomes greater. Of course even in the best families, and in the most stable societies, there are generational conflicts. Think of Absalom's defiance of David. But when we cannot agree about any framework within which arguments and discussions and combats take place, such conflicts become incapable of resolution. German history has had many such youth revolts, from the reaction of Young Germany against the German confederation, through the Nietzschean upsurge before the First World War, the Nazi youth's rejection of stuffy Weimar values, to the student revolt of the 1960s and the Greens' attack on an older generation, and, after 1990, the revolt of the neglected youth of the former GDR.

There have also been profound generational contrasts in political style: the hard-headed realists of the 1860s who pushed to replace the dreamers of 1848; the new imperialists of the 1890s who rejected the complacent Bismarckian view of Germany as a satiated state; the advocates of mass politics after the First World War in which the Front Generation discarded Wilhelmine smugness; the restorers of bourgeois politics after 1945 reacting against the anti-bourgeois revolt of National Socialism; the Europeanists of the 1950s casting off the politics of nationalism. Helmut Kohl's generation, which grew up politically and intellectually in the 1950s and in the aftermath of Hitler's war, built its identity around the European promise, and it is quite conceivable that a new generation will reject the premises of the older generation. There are many indications that Kohl is aware of this threat and that he believes it necessary to proceed with European integration at such a fast pace in order to create an external framework that will constrain the freedom of manoeuvre of a successor generation of politicians. The curse of generational conflict seems likely to reappear. A discontinuity of élites offers a rather better way of explaining German politics in the past but also in the future than an insistence on the perpetual survival of old élites.

The explanation for the dramatic swings lies in the institutional flux that characterized German history. In the nineteenth and for most of the twentieth century, Germany was a political territory in which institutions failed to give any true stability and continuity. Germans looked to foreign models for inspiration, and attempted to assimilate these in a theory of Germanness. Each process of adoption proved to be problematic, and gave rise to a generational reaction and rejection. In the first half of the nineteenth century, the examples would be the protest of gothicizers against neo-classicals, of nationalist populists against humanistic educators. This cycle of rejection also applied to other measures of the effectiveness of national integration, and in particular to the one that from mid-century became crucial to Germans' view of themselves: the performance of the economy.

German nationalism had appeared first without any political content, as an expression of a sense of cultural community. As a reaction to the French Revolution, and to invasion and occupation by the revolutionary and Napoleonic armies, it acquired a political edge. Nationality defined itself in opposition to the contemporary order of international politics, rather than as a more positive doctrine. It remained opposed to the world order of Metternich's system. In the middle of the nineteenth century, economics became the central consideration for nationalists. Prosperity alone could sustain the social community essential to national integration.

Only in the middle years of the nineteenth century did the nation-state represent in size the appropriate unit for economic development. Before that, economic life had centred on regions; by the beginning of the twentieth century, the cheapening of transport made larger multi- and cross-national units more attractive. Economic logic seemed to produce a *Mitteleuropa* (as later it could create an EEC).

For some time, the nineteenth-century vision of prosperity sustained the national community. It depended on a perception in which a whole society operated to the advantage of at least most of its politically expressive members. A strong economy, which Germany had in the later nineteenth century, was an essential condition for this way of thinking about nationality. Strains came once either too many expectations about what economies could do were generated, or when the economy encountered crisis. By the end of the nineteenth century, there was a powerful political and cultural reaction: even prosperity encountered the generational revolt.

This was even more evident after the First World War. As the economy collapsed in the Weimar Republic, so this nineteenth-century, 'economistic' view of nationality vanished. Political and cultural ideals of national existence re-emerged, in very radical guises. National Socialism in particular drew its appeal from a claim to transcend those economic interests which had divided rather than united Germans. It constitutes the most alarming example of generational revolt against the past and especially against the 'economic idea of the nation'.

We may then speak of a cycle of answers to the problem which Germans so insistently posed themselves: what constituted national identity? It moved from cultural to political to economic and then back to a series of cultural claims. This is the peculiar cycle that justifies a German claim to uniqueness.

After the Second World War, the old concept of the nation lost almost all its meaning. In the later 1940s, Germany and German identity appeared severely discredited, even to many Germans. This is easily the most striking case of a reaction to the immediate past. For a while, it seemed that there had really been a 'zero hour' (*Stunde Null*), in which Germanness was obliterated from the language of political conduct.

However, a new cycle of identities appeared by the 1950s as once more a different sort of nationalist response emerged. The German Federal Republic and the German Democratic Republic both began their life uncertain about any reason for existence. Politicians felt acutely aware that they operated in the artificial environment generated by international conflicts and pressures. There was little doubt that they were the prisoners of the Potsdam settlement. By the 1950s, in both states, economic growth proved to be a powerful machine for generating political legitimacy (as well as more material goods). This creation of legitimacy occurred within an international framework which favoured the growth view of politics, and which through promoting international economic integration and cooperation speeded the process along. In addition, in the eastern bloc the Council for Mutual Economic Assistance (Comecon), and in western Europe the ECSC and then the EEC and European Community helped create an international as well as a domestic legitimacy for the German states.

Given the cyclical interpretation suggested here, we should not be surprised by the revival of political and cultural nationalism in the 1970s, when the German states on both sides of the Iron Curtain experienced economic problems. The rejection of the orthodoxies and the received wisdom of elder generations indeed took place. It is true that the reaction was not as severe as that of the early and mid twentieth century, but then, it might be said, neither was the economic crisis. The shift in the way the nation is conceived is only a partial and limited one: towards a vision of national existence still primarily focused on the economy, but treating this in a much more national setting, instead of the internationalist one of the 1950s. The strong West German economy offered a lever for the assertion of national interest. In the 1980s, political leadership in the international sphere meant for both German states the flexing of economic muscle.

Then at the end of the 1980s, an economic crisis was the trigger for the collapse of legitimacy of the communist East German state. As the GDR disintegrated, German unification frequently appeared to have been driven by economic logic, so that the extension of the Deutschemark to the East in July 1990 required the political follow-up of unification on the third of October.

The German problem for over a century has been the heavy economicization of political life, and a concentration on the values generated by material culture. In the past this has produced a dynamic stability, but also periodic instability and breakdown. Since the Second World War, debates about the stability of Bonn politics have come and gone: in the late 1960s and early 1980s, the instability of Bonn was a fashionable topic, and less so in the 1950s, or in the later 1980s. In the early 1990s, the theme of a crisis of political institutions and parties became acute once more. Germans, and others, will ask whether the revolution of 1989–90 ended the period of growing political and institutional stability that had marked the forty years' existence of the Federal Republic.

The process of unification shook German political institutions. The successful federalism of the old Federal Republic was strained by the necessity in the new Federal Republic of making large redistributive transfers between *Länder*. In 1991, it was calculated that almost half of income in the eastern parts of Germany was derived from transfer payments. As its institutions came under challenge, Germany responded by trying to share the burden of decisions to a wider set of institutions so that the *Länder*, and the Bonn government, and the European Community would all play a part. Chancellor Helmut Kohl's insistence on making German and European integration parallel processes derived not only from concern with foreign reactions to German power, and a French wish to harness Germany, but also from a German fear of German power. The political historian Hans Peter Schwarz had spoken about Germany's *Machtvergessenheit*, Germany's forgetting of power politics. After 1989 Germany was afraid of power politics, and afraid of herself.

The idea of dividing politics up into tiers and ensuring that there was not anywhere a locus of political decision-making too concentrated began with Kohl's ten point programme of 28 November 1989. The key to the plan was the recognition that 'state organization in Germany has always meant confederation and federation ... We could use these historical experiences again today.' The seventh point gave the European framework, 'the radiance and attraction of the European community is and remains a constant in all-European development. We wish to strengthen it further ... We understand the process of rewinning German unity to be a European concern. It must therefore be undertaken in conjunction with European integration.' The *rapprochement* of the two Germanies was to be part of a wider process in which the reforming central and south-east European economies would be brought into an association with the European Community in order to reduce the differences of wealth and incomes within Europe. The Strasbourg summit in December 1989 adopted many of these suggestions in a spirit of Franco–German cooperation, making the idea of German 'unity through free self-determination' less threatening by anchoring it within the principles of the Helsinki Final Act (a euphemism for the declaration on Basket One of 'the inviolability of frontiers and the territorial integrity of states'[5] and 'the context of European integration'.

On 10 December 1991 at the Maastricht summit, the member governments of the European Community agreed to amend the 1957 founding treaty, the Treaty of Rome, so as to establish monetary and political union. Almost immediately a popular discussion about the integration process began in most European countries, with a referendum in Denmark narrowly voting to reject the Maastricht treaty, and a narrow margin in France approving the treaty. German opinion polls

243

showed overwhelming popular hostility to the idea of surrendering the Deutschemark.

Federalism and the 'German problem' had become the cause of an acute crisis – not only in a Germany wrestling with the costs left by the communist system in the East, but also in the whole of the European state system. Germany moved within months from offering a model of federalism for imitation by the rest of the European Community to providing the nightmare of how federalism can undermine stability and legitimacy.

Germany's federal tradition is indubitably venerable and antique. Within the Holy Roman Empire, it was impossible to say precisely where sovereignty lay. Though the territorial princes often behaved as if they acknowledged no superior, there was a system of imperial courts and thus a judicial process that extended beyond the confines of the territorial state. Inside the territorial states, many decisions were made on very parochial levels, by feudal magnates able to be substantially independent from the interventions of the territorial prince. The resulting impossibility of describing the structure of the Empire in any neat juridical fashion led the jurist Samuel Pufendorf to make his famous reference to the Empire as a 'monster', something that cannot be intelligible or natural, though it may still operate as a political institution (since many institutions are not understandable to those who work within them).

After the destruction of the Holy Roman Empire, there was a German Confederation which contained at the same time a Prussia and an Austria which both had claims to be major and sovereign European powers as well as a Bavaria, a Saxony and a Hanover which resented Prussian and Austrian claims to hegemony. The Empire of 1871 was a federal structure in which the southern kingdoms still retained their own separate armies, and even though the Weimar Republic which followed it in 1919 was more centralized, the *Länder* still had a substantial degree of autonomy. The Federal Republic was a constitutional provisorium, which was intended to be capable of absorbing more *Länder* should circumstances change. Only the Germany of the National Socialist dictatorship was politically a centralized state, centralized in the name of a powerful and destructive ideology. Nazism represented at least in this way a profound break with German traditions, a historical discontinuity.

Federations have an inherent advantage in countries such as Germany where the institutional sense of loyalty is weak, for they disperse centres both of loyalty and of decision-making. Inhabitants could be both Bavarians or Saxons and Germans, and see some political measures taken in Munich or Dresden and others in Berlin. The smaller units are more cohesive than the larger ones, but the wider framework can give a counterweight which for some citizens makes the power of the more immediate unit more bearable.

In addition, if there exists some consensus about the ground rules, different rings of a federal structure become possible. There can be closer unions within loose constellations. It is possible in this fashion to think of the *Länder* of the Federal Republic, which in turn is a member of the European Community, which is itself surrounded by a wide free trade area that includes East European and Russian states.

Originally the most contentious questions for a federation arose in foreign relations. Is the federation to have its own external policy, or does it merely impose certain conditions and restrictions such as the Holy Roman Empire's ban on its members forming coalitions with outside states directed against other members? There could be a division of competence, in which some kinds of foreign policy are left to lower level national states, while overall security issues are dealt with at a federal level or in supra-national institutions, and the broader area simply commits itself to a progressive relaxation of trade controls.

In the twentieth century, the rise of the state as a major economic agent has changed the perspective for federal systems. Making economic policy for areas with very disparate levels of development has a tremendous potential to cause mischief among the members of a federal system. If too many claims and demands are made of a central institution that lacks the capacity to create legitimacy, the expectations prove to be too large and there is collapse. In this regard the future of a European Community extended to take in collapsed socialist command economies is worrying. The EC has its own budget, at present a modest one per cent of the total Community GNP, for making transfer payments (in addition, its price regulation policies mean a far higher supplementary level of transfer); and at the same time it has created a body of law which severely restricts subsidization outside the framework of the community budget. When there are central redistributive institutions that need to decide on the relative merits of claims for structural support from Catalan light industry, Scottish highland farmers, obsolete East German heavy industrial zones (and perhaps in the future also decaying Polish shipyards) there can only be rising political tension. No neutral or scientific solutions can be presented. The only grounds on which the competing demands can be arbitrated depend on prejudice, on local, regional and national affinities and identities. In this way federations can increase, rather than resolve, national feelings and hostilities.

If the central institutions of an economic federation are to avoid this trap and stand any chance of success, they need to be as unpolitical as possible. As long as the consensus of the federal system is fundamentally *laissez-faire* and non-interventionist, conflicts about regional distribution policy are less likely to occur than if the institutions are glued to an ideology of intervention, management and subsidization. Federations and confederations can only survive if they do not claim to be able to do too much as economic managers. The German federations of the eighteenth and nineteenth centuries are a poor model in this process of adjustment to new international realities since they were established before the age of the state as a massive economic redistributor.

The issue of Germany has already given a powerful fillip to the process of European integration because many Germans, and also other Europeans, see a strengthened Europe as a way of balancing and restraining a newly powerful Germany. European integration, with its substantial economic attractions, offers a path out of the German political maze. But some of the German problems begin to reappear on the European level, in particular the combination of economic promise and institutional instability. In addition, there can be no guarantee of the economic promise. Although it is true that growth may come in time to legitimize political institutions, there is a converse side to this argument; and widening Europe by including formerly socialist economies struggling to adjust to a market order is likely to produce economic shocks that will further undermine political legitimacy.

The course of German history has already shown again and again how vulnerable political institutions are when they are guided not by long lasting loyalties but by short term expediency and economic rationale. The German peculiarity, the *Sonderweg*, has been the excessive trust in economics to solve political problems. It resulted in a cycle of state-building followed by outbreaks of violent rejection of new, uncertain, and dubiously legitimate institutions. The German obsession with economics is not a peculiarity that should be inflicted on the rest of Europe simply for the sake of at last finding a solution to the German problem.

Notes

1 Prelude

1 E. Kedourie, *Nationalism* (London 1960), and E. Gellner, *Nations and Nationalism* (Oxford 1983), are the most revealing recent accounts of the process of inventing nationality.

2 For an entertaining as well as profound analysis of Germans and national character, see G. A. Craig, *The Germans* (New York 1982).

3 See on this S. R. Letwin, *The Gentleman in Trollope: Individuality and Moral Conduct* (London 1982).

4 Madame de Staël, *De l'Allemagne*, ed. J. de Pange (Paris 1958), I, p. 61 (first published London, 1813).

5 B. Anderson, *Imagined Communities: Reflections on the Origin and Spread of Nationalism* (London 1983), p. 78. The contrast between 'eastern' and 'western' types of European nationalism – i.e. between Germany and central and eastern Europe on the one hand and Britain, France, Switzerland, etc., on the other – has been most clearly and systematically developed by H. Kohn, *The Idea of Nationalism* (New York 1961). See also H. Seton-Watson, *Nations and States: An Enquiry into the Origins of Nations and the Politics of Nationalism* (London 1977); Also M. Hroch, *Social Preconditions for National Revival in Europe* (Cambridge 1985).

6 F. Meinecke, *Cosmopolitanism and the National State*, trans. R. B. Kimber (Princeton 1970), p. 94.

7 T. M. Knox (trans.), *Hegel's Philosophy of Right* (Oxford 1942), pp. 217–18.

8 B. Goltz, *Die Deutschen. Ethnographische Studie* (Berlin 1860), pp. 1–2.

9 Madame de Staël, *De l'Allegmagne*, I, p. 39.

10 H. von Treitschke, *Politik (Vorlesungen gehalten an der Universität zu Berlin)* (Leipzig 1899), I, pp. 269 and 273.

11 Ibid., p. 29.

12 Goltz, *Die Deutschen*, pp. 4, 7.

13 Ibid., p. 12.

247

14 H. -P. Schwarz, *Adenauer: Der Aufstieg 1876–1952* (Stuttgart 1986), p. 638.

15 Quoted in *Frankfurter Allgemeine Zeitung*, no. 176, 2 August 1986.

16 C. Gluck, *Japan's Modern Myths: Ideology in the Late Meiji Period* (Princeton 1985), p. 20.

17 C. Thomasius, *Deutsche Schriften* (Stuttgart 1970), p. 8.

18 Ibid., pp. 11–12.

19 Ibid., p. 17.

20 Ibid., p. 34.

21 F. Theodor Vischer, *Altes und Neues* (Stuttgart 1889), pp. 139–40.

22 'Die Märker und die Berliner und wie sich das Berlinertum entwickelte', reprinted in T. Fontane, *Politik und Geschichte* (Munich 1969), pp. 739–55. See also P. Gay, 'Probleme der kulturellen Integration der Deutschen 1849 bis 1945', in O. Büsch and J. J. Sheehan (eds), *Die Rolle der Nation in der deutschen Geschichte und Gegenwart* (Berlin 1985), p. 184.

23 L. Gall, *Benjamin Constant: Seine politische Ideenwelt und der deutsche Vormärz* (Wiesbaden 1963).

24 Quoted in T. C. W. Blanning, *The French Revolution in Germany* (Oxford 1983), p. 277.

25 T. Nipperdey, *Deutsche Geschichte 1800–1866* (Munich 1983), p. 311.

26 Published in Leipzig by Franz Peter.

27 J. J. Winckelmann, *Gedanken über die Nachahmung der griechischen Werke in der Malerei und Bilderkunst*, 2nd ed. (Dresden 1756), pp. 2–3.

28 Quoted in E. Butler, *The Tyranny of Greece over Germany* (Cambridge 1935), p. 215.

29 See J. N. Shklar, *Freedom and Independence: A Study of the Political Ideas of Hegel's Phenomenology of Mind* (Cambridge 1976), pp. 57–95.

30 R. Wagner, *Gesammelte Schriften*, ed. J. Kapp (Leipzig 1914), x, p. 14 ('Die Kunst und die Revolution', 1849).

31 B. Hildebrand, *Die Nationalökonomie der Gegenwart und andere gesammelte Schriften*, ed. H. Gehrig (originally 1848; Jena 1922), p. 103.

32 Treitschke, *Politik*, ii, pp. 225 and 227, translated as *Politics* (New York 1916), pp. 246 and 248.

33 Quoted in P. Kennedy, *The Rise of the Anglo-German Antagonism 1860–1914* (London 1980), p. 131. This is the authoritative account of Germany and the 'English model'.

34 See W. J. Mommsen, *Max Weber and German Politics 1890–1920*, trans. M. S. Steinberg (Chicago 1984).

35 O. Pflanze, *Bismarck and the Development of Germany* (Princeton 1963), p. 80.

36 J. Warrack (ed.), *Carl Maria von Weber: Writings on Music* (Cambridge 1981), p. 206.

37 J. Warrack, *Carl Maria von Weber* (London and New York 1968), p. 333.

38 C. E. McClelland, *The German Historians and England: A Study in Nineteenth Century Views* (Cambridge 1971), p. 168.

39 M. Cornicelius (ed.), *Heinrich von Treitschkes Briefe* (Leipzig 1920), p. 327.

40 T. Kohut, 'Kaiser Wilhelm ii and his parents', in J. C. G. Röhl and N. Sombart (eds), *Kaiser Wilhelm ii: New Interpretations* (Cambridge 1982), pp. 81 and 78.

41 Quoted in H. Dippel, *Germany and the American Revolution 1770–1800*, trans. B. A. Uhlendorf (Chapel Hill 1977), p. 311.

42 F. Schiller, *Sämtliche Schriften: Historische Schriften* (Munich 1958), p. 33.

43 M. Howitt, *Friedrich Overbeck: Sein Leben und Schaffen* (Freiburg 1886), I, p. 479.

44 See G. Kozielek (ed.), *Polenlieder. Eine Anthologie* (Stuttgart 1982), pp. 23–4.

45 This book is concerned with the links between state building and national identity. In consequence, it deals only very tangentially with the problems and feelings of those German-speakers who lived in multilingual or multinational states: the Habsburg or Romanov empires, or Switzerland.

46 There are analogies in late nineteenth-century France, where the nationalist right (Barrès and Maurras) attacked as alien and German those political forces they objected to in France.

47 H. Seton-Watson, *Nationalism Old and New* (London 1965), p. 121. Also A. Smith, *Theories of Nationalism* (London 1983), p. 201.

48 J. G. Fichte, *Reden an die deutsche Nation*, Goldmann edition (Munich n.d.), p. 169.

49 An interesting account of the connections between German national development and international politics is given in W. D. Gruner, *Die deutsche Frage: Ein Problem der europäischen Geschichte seit 1800* (Munich 1985).

2 The Origins of German Nationalism

1 J. G. Fichte, *Schriften zur Revolution*, ed. B. Willms (Frankfurt 1973), p. 131 ('Beitrag zur Berichtigung der Urteile über die französische Revolution', 1793).

2 See F. Meinecke, *The Age of German Liberation 1795–1815*, trans. P. Paret and H. Fischer (Berkeley 1977).

3 R. Ibbeken, *Preussen 1807–1813: Staat und Volk als Idee und in Wirklichkeit* (Cologne 1970), p. 371.

4 Ibbeken, *Preussen*, p. 362.

5 P. Paret, *Clausewitz and the State* (Oxford 1976), pp. 160–1.

6 Hesse-Homburg was restored in 1817, making 39.

7 B. Suphan (ed.), *Herders Sämtliche Schriften* (Berlin 1877–1913), V, pp. 135–6.

8 Ibid., p. 141.

9 Ibid.

10 Ibid., p. 538.

11 Ibid., p. 539.

12 Ibid., p. 544.

13 Ibid., XIII, p. 336.

14 Ibid., V, pp. 142–3.

15 Ibid., IX, p. 375.

16 Ibid., V, p. 565.

17 Ibid., IX, p. 377.

18 Ibid., IV, p. 437.

19 Ibid., V, p. 510.

20 Ibid., p. 142.

21 J. W. Goethe, *Aus meinem Leben: Dichtung und Wahrheit* (Berlin 1970 edition), I, p. 320. Also W. D. Robson-Scott, *The Literary Background of the Gothic Revival in Germany* (Oxford 1965), p. 81.

22 On the *Bildungsbürgertum*, see K. H. Jarausch, *Students, Society and Politics in Imperial Germany: The Rise of Academic Illiberalism* (Princeton 1983), p. 157; W. Conze and J. Kocka (eds), *Bildungsbürgertum im 19. Jahrhundert* (Stuttgart 1983).

23 J. G. Fichte, *Schriften zur Revolution*, p. 122 ('Beitrag zur Berichtigung').

24 J. G. Fichte, *Reden an die deutsche Nation* (Munich n.d.) (Goldmanns Taschenbücher), pp. 120 and 171.

25 Fichte, *Reden*, pp. 153, 129, 131.

26 F. Schnabel, *Deutsche Geschichte im Neunzehnten Jahrhundert*, I (Freiburg 1929), p. 443.

27 See D. Watkin and T. Mellinghoff, *German Architecture and the Classical Ideal 1740–1840* (London 1987), p. 90.

28 Ibid., p. 156.

29 Ibid., pp. 159–60.

30 H. Schulze, *Der Weg zum Nationalstaat* (Munich 1985), p. 74.

31 Robson-Scott, *Literary Background*, p. 288.

32 Ibid., pp. 300 and 296. Also T. Nipperdey, 'Der Kölner Dom als National-denkmal', in Nipperdey, *Nachdenken über die deutsche Geschichte* (Munich 1986), pp. 156–71.

33 Nipperdey, *Deutsche Geschichte*, p. 370.

34 H. Heine, *Reisebilder*, ed. W. Vontin (Hamburg 1966) (originally 1828), p. 228.

35 P. A. Pfizer, *Briefwechsel zweier Deutschen*, 2nd ed. (Stuttgart and Tübingen 1832), pp. 349, 5–6, 11.

36 Ibid., p. 321.

37 Ibid., pp. 281–2, 11.

38 Ibid., pp. 145, 335–45.

39 Ibid., p. 343.

40 F. T. Vischer, *Aesthetik oder Wissenschaft des Schönen* (Munich 1922) (originally 1847/8), II, pp. 615–18.

41 L. Namier, *1848: The Revolution of the Intellectuals. The Raleigh Lecture* (London 1946), pp. 121–2.

42 See H. -U. Wehler, *Sozialdemokratie und Nationalstaat* (Würzburg 1962), p. 13.

43 K. Marx and F. Engels, *Collected Works*, VIII (London 1977), 13 January 1849, 'The Magyar Struggle' (Engels), pp. 233, 236, 238.

44 Marx and Engels, *Collected Works*, VIII, 15 February 1849, 'Democratic Pan-Slavism' (Engels), p. 367.

45 Marx and Engels, *Collected Works*, VII (London 1977), 9 September 1848, 'The Danish–Prussian Armistice' (Engels), p. 423.

46 Pfizer, *Briefwechsel*, pp. 174–5.

47 Namier, *1848*, p. 88.

Notes

3 National Economics

1 F. Engels, *Die Lage der arbeitenden Klasse in England. Nach eigener Anschauung und authentischen Quellen* (Leipzig 1845). L. von Stein, *Der Socialismus und Communismus des heutigen Frankreichs* (Leipzig 1842; 2nd ed. Leipzig 1848).

2 L. Untermeyer (trans.), *Poems of Heinrich Heine* (New York 1917), p. 263.

3 Calculated from A. Maddison, *Phases of Capitalist Development* (Oxford 1982), p. 8.

4 K. Borchardt, 'Germany 1700–1914', in C. M. Cipolla (ed.), *Fontana Economic History of Europe* vol. 44I (London 1973), p. 123.

5 See M. Walker, *German Home Towns: Community, State and General Estate 1648–1871* (Ithaca 1971).

6 F. List, *Das Nationale System der politischen Ökonomie*, ed. A. Sommer (Tübingen 1959), p. 175.

7 Ibid., p. 184.

8 See W. O. Henderson, *Friedrich List: Economist and Visionary 1789–1846* (London 1983).

9 F. List, *Schriften, Reden, Briefe*, III (Berlin 1929), pp. 331 and 347–8 (originally essays of 1841: 'Das deutsche Eisenbahnsystem').

10 J. G. Droysen, *Politische Schriften*, ed. F. Gilbert (Berlin 1933), p. 353.

11 W. von Eisenhart-Rothe and A. Ritthaler, *Vorgeschichte und Begründung des deutschen Zollvereins 1815–1834*, III (Berlin 1934), pp. 525–41. See in general W. O. Henderson, *The Zollverein* (London 1939).

12 See H. W. Hahn, *Wirtschaftliche Integration im 19. Jahrhundert: Die hessischen Staaten und der Deutsche Zollverein* (Göttingen 1982), p. 246.

13 H. von Treitschke, *Die Anfänge des deutschen Zollvereins* (Berlin 1872), p. 5.

14 Trietschke, *Politik*, I, p. 367.

15 An interesting account of economic development and nationalism in Germany is provided by R. M. Berdahl, 'New Thoughts on German Nationalism', *American Historical Review*, 77 (1972), pp. 65–80. On the links between economics and liberalism, see J. J. Sheehan, *German Liberalism in the Nineteenth Century* (Chicago 1978), pp. 84–6, 111–12; T. Hamerow, *The Social Foundations of German Unification*, 2 vols (Princeton 1969–72).

16 G. Droysen, *Gustav Adolf* (Leipzig 1869), p. 8.

17 H. Sybel, *Die deutsche Nation und das Kaiserreich: Eine historisch-politische Abhandlung* (Düsseldorf 1862), p. 109.

18 Anon. (L. A. von Rochau), *Grundsätze der Realpolitik angewendet auf die staatlichen Zustände Deutschlands*, I (Stuttgart 1853), pp. 13 and 21.

19 Ibid., pp. 125, 47, and 137–41.

20 Rochau, *Grundsätze der Realpolitik*, II (Heidelberg 1869), pp. 18–19.

21 Ibid., pp. 26–7 and 184–95.

22 K. Marx, 'Preface to the First German edition', in *Capital*, I (London 1970), pp. 19–20. See also pp. 714–15.

23 See T. S. Hamerow, *The Social Foundations of German Unification 1858–1871, Ideas and Institutions* (Princeton 1969), pp. 340–5.

251

24 Published by J. J. Palm and E. Enke, Erlangen.
25 *Fliegende Blätter* (1855), p. 533.
26 H. Rothfels (ed.), *Bismarck Briefe* (Göttingen 1955), p. 345.
27 Ibid., p. 347.
28 Quoted by H. Böhme, 'Probleme der wirtschaftlichen Integration der Deutschen vom frühen 19. Jahrhundert bis 1945' in O. Büsch and J. J. Sheehan (eds), *Die Rolle der Nation in der deutschen Geschichte und Gegenwart* (Berlin 1985), p. 169.
29 D. Stegmann, *Die Erben Bismarcks. Parteien und Verbände in der Spätphase des Wilhelminischen Deutschlands* (Cologne 1970), p. 114.
30 F. Naumann, *Central Europe*, trans. C. M. Meredith (London 1916), p. 137. German edition: *Mitteleuropa* (1915), p. 126.
31 T. Nipperdey, *Nachdenken über die deutsche Geschichte* (Munich 1986), pp. 493–4.
32 S. von Weiher and H. Goetzeler, *The Siemens Company: Its Historical role in the Process of Electrical Engineering* (Berlin 1977), p. 44. P. W. Musgrave, *Technical Change, the Labour Force and Education* (Oxford 1967), p. 50.
33 W. Roscher, *Grundriss zu Vorlesungen über die Staatswirthschaft. Nach geschichtlicher Methode* (Göttingen 1843).
34 W. Roscher, 'Über das Verhältnis der Nationalökonomie zum klassischen Alterthume' (1849) in *Ansichten der Volkswirthschaft aus dem geschichtlichen Standpunkte* (Leipzig and Heidelberg 1861), p. 4.
35 W. Roscher, *Grundlagen der Nationalökonomie* (Stuttgart 1854), p. 41.
36 Roscher, 'Zum Lehre von den Absatzkrisen', in *Ansichten*, p. 308.
37 Ibid., pp. 372–4.
38 Roscher, *Grundlagen*, p. 39.
39 K. Knies, *Die politische Ökonomie vom Standpunkte der geschichtlichen Methode* (Braunschweig 1853), p. 1.
40 Ibid., p. 345.
41 B. Hildebrand, *Die Nationalökonomie der Gegenwart und Zukunft*, ed. H. Gehrig (originally 1848) (Jena 1922), p. 187.
42 Roscher, *Grundlagen* (1854), p. 31; 1906 edition, pp. 54–5.
43 J. C. Bluntschli, *Politik als Wissenschaft* (Stuttgart 1876), p. 165.
44 See H. Reuther, *Die Grosse Zerstörung Berlins* (Frankfurt 1985), pp. 69–74.
45 Ibid., p. 86.
46 H. Fürstenberg (ed.), *Carl Fürstenberg: Die Lebensgeschichte eines deutschen Bankiers 1870–1914* (Berlin 1931), p. 70.
47 See R. Cameron, 'Founding the Bank of Darmstadt', *Explorations in Entrepreneurial History*, 8 (1956), pp. 113–31.
48 Fürstenberg, *Lebensgeschichte*, p. 208.
49 T. Fontane, *L'Adultera* (*Sämtliche Werke: Romane, Erzählungen, Gedichte*, II (Munich 1962), p. 29).
50 H. Kohl (ed.), *Briefe des Generals Leopold von Gerlach an Otto von Bismarck* (Stuttgart and Berlin 1912), p. 209 (6 May 1857).
51 J. H. Clapham, *The Economic Development of France and Germany 1815–1914* (Cambridge 1936), pp. 91, 281, 285.

52 The title of a book by E. E. Williams (London 1896). See also C. Buchheim, 'Deutschland auf dem Weltmarkt am Ende des 19. Jahrhunderts', *Vierteljahrschrift für Sozial- und Wirtschaftsgeschichte*, 71 (1984), pp. 199–216.

53 Roscher, *Grundlagen* (1906), p. 644.

54 R. Martin, *Jahrbuch der Millionäre aus der Rheinprovinz* (Berlin 1915), p. v.

55 A. Wagner, *Rede über die sociale Frage. Gehalten am 12 October 1871* (Berlin 1872).

56 G. Schmoller, *Grundriss der allgemeinen Volkswirtschaftslehre*, II (Leipzig 1900), p. 675.

57 John Kenneth Galbraith (Schmoller's phrase is on p. 323, *Grundriss*, II).

58 H. Böhme, *Deutschlands Weg zur Grossmacht* (Berlin 1966).

59 J. Burckhardt *Reflections on History* (*Weltgeschichtliche Betrachtungen*), trans. M. D. H. (London 1943), p. 57.

60 M. M. Freiherr von Weber, *Nationalität und Eisenbahnpolitik* (Vienna 1876), p. 5.

61 Max Weber, *Gesammelte Politische Schriften*, ed. J. Winckelmann (Tübingen 1971), p. 4.

62 F. von Hügel, *The German Soul in its Attitude towards Ethics and Christianity, The State and War: Two Studies* (London 1916), p. 186.

63 E. Haeckel, *The Riddle of the Universe at the Close of the Nineteenth Century*, trans. J. McCabe (London 1901), pp. 335–6.

64 F. Stern, *The Politics of Cultural Despair* (Berkeley 1961), pp. 155–6.

65 Quoted in H. Delbrück, *Vor und nach dem Weltkrieg* (Berlin 1926), p. 18.

66 E. von Oldenburg-Januschau, *Erinnerungen* (Leipzig 1936), pp. 38, 63. On *Agrarstaat* and *Industriestaat*, see K. Barkin, *The Controversy over German Industrialization 1890–1902* (Chicago 1970).

67 Karl von Einem, *Erinnerungen eines Soldaten 1853–1933* (Leipzig 1933), p. 79. Oldenburg-Januschau, *Erinnerungen*, p. 81.

68 von Einem, *Erinnerungen*, p. 123.

69 J. Steinberg, 'The Copenhagen Complex', *Journal of Contemporary History*, vol. 1, no. 3 (July 1966), p. 25; also P. Kennedy in J. C. G. Röhl and N. Sombart, *Kaiser Wilhelm II: New Interpretations* (Cambridge 1982), p. 149.

70 H. Hauser, *Germany's Commercial Grip on the World* (London 1917), pp. 210, 25; W. H. Dawson, *The Evolution of Modern Germany* (New York 1919), p. 89.

71 Weber, *Gesammelte Politische Schriften*, pp. 14, 19–20.

72 H. -U Wehler, *Sozialdemokratie und Nationalstaat* (Wurzburg 1962), p. 103.

73 R. Fletcher, *Revisionism and Empire: Socialist Imperialism in Germany 1897–1914* (London 1984), pp. 91–2, 148–9.

74 E. Mathias and S. Miller (eds), *Das Kriegstagebuch des Reichstagsabgeordneten Eduard David 1914 bis 1918* (Düsseldorf 1966), p. 38 (note of 10 September 1914).

75 Fletcher, *Revisionism*, pp. 135–6.

76 Mathias and Miller, *David*, p. 49.

77 K. Helfferich, *Deutschlands Volkswohlstand, 1888–1913*, (Berlin 1914), pp. 8 and 5.

78 For one of the most compelling accounts of the mid-nineteenth-century creation

of the 'economic state' (*Wirtschaftsstaat*) see W. Eucken, 'Staatliche Struktur-wandlungen und die Krisis des Kapitalismus', *Weltwirtschaftliches Archiv* 36 (1932), pp. 297–321.

4 The Incomplete Nation-State

1 1880 figures from *Statesman's Yearbook 1888* (London), p. 115; 1900 from *Statesman's Yearbook 1905*, p. 685.

2 See on this H. -U. Wehler, *Sozialdemokratie und Nationalstaat* (Würzburg 1962).

3 M. Gregor-Dellin, *Richard Wagner: Sein Leben. Sein Werk. Sein Jahrhundert* (Munich 1980), p. 209.

4 See R. Wagner, *My Life*, trans. A. Gray (Cambridge 1983), p. 505.

5 Wagner, *Gesammelte Schriften* x, p. 23 ('Die Kunst und die Revolution').

6 Ibid., p. 58 ('Das Kunstwerk der Zukunft').

7 E. Newman, *The Life of Richard Wagner*, IX (New York 1946), p. 481.

8 Translated by William Mann.

9 G. Skelton (trans.), *Cosima Wagner's Diaries*, I (London 1978), p. 753.

10 Wagner, *My Life*, pp. 386–7.

11 *Cosima Diaries*, I, pp. 377–8; II (London 1980), p. 172.

12 Wagner, *Gesammelte Schriften*, XIV, p. 56 ('Deutsche Kunst und deutsche Politik'). *Cosima Diaries*, I, p. 758.

13 Gregor-Dellin, *Wagner*, p. 667.

14 H. Mayer, *Richard Wagner in Bayreuth 1876–1976* (Frankfurt 1976), p. 40.

15 Gregor-Dellin, *Wagner*, p. 665. Translation H. J.

16 *Cosima Diaries*, II, pp. 229, 452, 210–11.

17 Ibid., p. 440 (the entry is for 1880).

18 Wagner, *Gesammelte Werke*, XIII, p. 12 ('Das Judentum in der Musik').

19 *Cosima Diaries*, II, pp. 505–6, 191.

20 Ibid., p. 773.

21 R. W. Gutman, *Richard Wagner, the Man, His Mind and His Music* (Harmonds-worth 1971). D. C. Large, 'Wagner's Bayreuth Disciples', in D. C. Large and W. Weber (eds), *Wagnerism in European Culture and Politics* (Ithaca 1984).

22 W. Schüler, *Der Bayreuther Kreis von seiner Entstehung bis zum Ausgang der wilhelminischen Aera* (Münster 1971), pp. 54, 59–60.

23 F. Nietzsche, *Untimely Meditations*, trans. R. J. Hollingdale (Cambridge 1983), pp. 3, 80.

24 Ibid., pp. 18, 109, 25.

25 F. Nietzsche, 'The Case of Wagner' (1888), and 'Nietzsche contra Wagner' (1888), in A. M. Ludovici (trans.) *Nietzsche Collected Works*, VIII (New York 1964), pp. xxxi and 69–70. On Nietzsche's break with Wagner, see C. P. Janz, 'Die "tödtliche Beleidigung": Ein Beitrag zur Wagner-Entfremdung Nietzsches', *Nietzsche Studien*, 4 (1975), pp. 263–78.

26 T. C. W. Blanning, *The French Revolution in Germany* (Oxford 1983), pp. 289–300. H. -U. Wehler, *Deutsche Gesellschaftsgeschichte*, II (Munich 1987), pp. 355–6. C. R. Friedrich, 'Politics or Pogrom? The Fettmilch Uprising in German

and Jewish History', *Central European History*, 19 (1986), pp. 186–228.

27 S. Volkov, *The Rise of Popular Antimodernism in Germany; The Urban Master Artisans 1873–1896* (Princeton 1978), p. 223.

28 P. Pulzer, *The Rise of Political Anti-Semitism in Germany and Austria* (New York 1964), p. 119.

29 See ibid., p. 249.

30 See especially I. Geiss, *German Foreign Policy 1871–1914* (London 1976), pp. 65–6.

31 H. Delbrück, *Vor und nach dem Weltkrieg: Politische und historische Aufsätze 1902–1925* (Berlin 1926), p. 369.

32 F. Fischer, *War of Illusions: German Policies from 1911 to 1914*, trans. M. Jackson (London 1975), p. 35.

33 H. Pogge von Strandmann, 'Rathenau, die Gebrüder Mannesmann und die Vorgeschichte der Zweiten Marokkokrise', in I. Geiss and B. J. Wendt (eds), *Deutschland in der Weltpolitik des 19. und 20. Jahrhunderts* (Düsseldorf 1973), pp. 251–70. J. G. Williamson, *Karl Helfferich 1872–1924: Economist, Financier, Politician* (Princeton 1971), p. 90. F. Fischer, 'World Policy, Power and German War Aims', in H. W. Koch (ed.), *The Origins of the First World War* (London 1972), p. 93.

34 F. Fischer, *Griff nach der Weltmacht* (Düsseldorf 1961), pp. 116–18, 124.

35 F. Naumann, *Central Europe* (London 1916), p. 63. (German: *Mitteleuropa* (1915), pp. 58–9.)

36 Ibid., p. 118. (German: p. 109.)

37 Ibid., pp. 270, 118, 121. (German: pp. 247, 109, 112.)

38 Ibid., pp. 123, 129, 258, 277. (German: pp. 114, 119, 236, 253.)

39 See G. D. Feldman, *Army, Industry and Labor in Germany 1914–1918* (Princeton 1966).

40 H. Pogge von Strandmann (ed.), *Walther Rathenau: Industrialist, Banker, Intellectual, and Politician, Notes and Diaries 1907–1922* (Oxford 1985), p. 6.

41 Ibid., p. 119.

42 Ibid., p. 224.

43 W. Rathenau, *Von kommenden Dingen* (Berlin 1925) (reprint), pp. 236, 284, 340–1, 99.

44 Ibid., pp. 299–300. Strandmann, *Rathenau*, pp. 183–7.

5 The Weimar Republic

1 Real growth of Net National Product 1871 to 1913; figures from W. G. Hoffmann (with F. Grumbach and H. Hesse), *Das Wachstum der deutschen Wirtschaft seit der Mitte des 19. Jahrhunderts* (Berlin 1965).

2 The title of a book by T. Eschenburg (Munich 1963).

3 F. Fischer, *Griff nach der Weltmacht* (Düsseldorf 1961), p. 565.

4 J. Wheeler-Bennett, *The Nemesis of Power: The German Army in Politics, 1918–1945* (London 1953), pp. 31, 67.

5 A. Hitler, *Mein Kampf*, trans. R. Manheim (London 1969), p. 186.

6 Thomas Mann, *Diaries 1918–1939*, trans. R. and C. Winston (New York 1982), p. 41.

7 See on the Auxiliary Service Law, G. D. Feldman, *Army, Industry and Labour in Germany 1914–1918* (Princeton 1966).

8 See R. G. Moeller, 'Winners as Losers in the German Inflation: Peasant Protest over the Controlled Economy, 1920–1923', in G. D. Feldman (ed.), *Die deutsche Inflation: Eine Zwischenbilanz* (Berlin 1982), pp. 263–75.

9 H. A. Winkler, *Von der Revolution zur Stabilisierung. Arbeiter und Arbeiterbewegung in der Weimarer Republik 1918 bis 1924* (Berlin and Bonn 1984), p. 192.

10 Ibid., pp. 191–3, 198.

11 Ibid., p. 219.

12 J. C. Hess, *Das ganze Deutschland soll es sein* (Stuttgart 1978), pp. 86–9.

13 *Frankfurter Zeitung*, 634, 27 August 1921; 642, 30 August 1921.

14 Ibid., 468, 26 June 1922; 474, 28 June 1922.

15 *Vossische Zeitung*, 240, 8 October 1929.

16 Ibid., 55, 5 March 1925; 53, 3 March 1925.

17 See particularly G. D. Feldman and I. Steinisch, 'Die Weimarer Republik zwischen Sozial- und Wirtschaftsstaat: Die Entscheidung gegen den Achtstundentag', *Archiv für Sozialgeschichte*, 18 (1978), pp. 353–75.

18 See H. James, 'Die Währungsstabilisierung 1923/24 in internationaler Perspektive', in W. Abelshauser (ed.), *Die Weimarer Republik als Wohlfahrtsstaat* (Stuttgart 1987), pp. 63–79. In general on international stabilizations in the 1920s, R. H. Meyer, *Bankers' Diplomacy: Monetary Stabilization in the Twenties* (New York 1970).

19 S. Andic and J. Veverka, 'The Growth of Government Expenditure in Germany since the Unification', *Finanzarchiv*, Vol. 23 (1964), p. 243. See on the political problems of German spending W. D. McNeil, *American Money and the Weimar Republic* (New York 1986).

20 On this see K. Borchardt, 'Zwangslagen und Handlungsspielräume in der grossen Weltwirtschaftskrise der frühen dreissiger Jahre: Zur Revision des überlieferten Geschichtsbildes', most recently in Borchardt, *Wachstum, Krisen, Handlungsspielräume der Wirtschaftspolitik* (Göttingen 1982), pp. 165–82.

21 Lamont papers, Baker Library Harvard, 181–1, 30 August 1929, Morgan to Lamont.

22 E. W. Bennett, *Germany and the Diplomacy of the Financial Crisis, 1931* (Cambridge, Mass 1962), p. 128.

23 H. Brüning, *Memoiren 1918–1934* (Stuttgart 1970). H. Luther, *Vor dem Abgrund 1930–1933: Reichsbankpräsident in Krisenzeiten* (Berlin 1964).

24 C. -L. Holtfrerich, *The German Inflation 1914–1923*, trans. T. Balderston (Berlin 1986), p. 143.

25 R. Neebe, *Grossindustrie, Staat und NSDAP 1930–1933* (Göttingen 1981), pp. 56–7.

26 F. Reinhardt, *Youngplan Menschenexport* (Munich 1929) (September).

27 W. J. Helbich, *Die Reparationen in der Aera Brüning* (Berlin 1962), pp. 15, 28.

6 The Brown Nation

1 See on this especially T. Childers, *The Nazi Voter: The Social Foundations of Fascism in Germany, 1919–1933* (Chapel Hill 1983); R. Hamilton, *Who voted for Hitler?* (Princeton 1982).

2 S. Attanasio (trans.), *Hitler's Secret Book* (New York 1961), p. 19.

3 Ibid., p. 23.

4 N. Henderson, *Failure of a Mission: Berlin 1937–1939* (London 1941), p. 18.

5 See R. A. Blasius, *Für Grossdeutschland – gegen den grossen Krieg. Ernst von Weizsäcker in den Krisen um die Tschechoslowakei und Polen* (Cologne 1981).

6 See R. Overy, 'Hitler's War and the German Economy: A Reinterpretation', *Economic History Review*, 35 (1982), pp. 272–91.

7 W. Jochmann (ed.), *Adolf Hitler Monologe im Führerhauptquartier 1941–1944: Die Aufzeichnungen Heinrich Heims* (Hamburg 1980), pp. 137, 336. J. Dülffer, J. Thies, and J. Henke, *Hitlers Städte: Baupolitik im Dritten Reich. Eine Dokumentation* (Cologne 1978), p. 291.

8 A. Hitler, *Mein Kampf*, trans. R. Manheim (London 1969), p. 239.

9 A. Speer, *Inside the Third Reich*, trans. R. and C. Winston (London 1971), pp. 114–15.

10 B. Miller Lane, *Architecture and Politics in Germany, 1918–1945* (Cambridge 1968), p. 188. Dülffer, *Hitlers Städte*, p. 297.

11 Quoted in D. Welch, *Propaganda and the German Cinema 1933–1945* (Oxford 1983), p. 42.

12 Ibid., p. 45.

13 Goebbels diaries, Institut für Zeitgeschichte Munich, 8 August 1936.

14 *Hitler's Secret Book*, p. 13.

15 Hitler, *Mein Kampf*, p. 288.

16 H. Rauschning, *Gespräche mit Hitler* (New York 1940), p. 29.

17 Jochmann, *Monologe*, p. 256.

18 Goebbels diaries, 22 December 1937.

19 Rauschning, *Gespräche*, pp. 26, 44. Jochmann, *Monologe*, p. 122.

20 Jochmann, *Monologe*, p. 122.

21 Thomas Mann, *Diaries 1918–1939*, trans. R. and C. Winston (New York 1982), p. 150.

22 L. Dawidowicz, *The War against the Jews 1933–1945* (New York 1975), pp. 123–4.

23 For a recent survey of the literature on the national-conservative opposition, see G. Schulz, 'Nationalpatriotismus im Widerstand', in *Vierteljahrshefte für Zeitgeschichte*, 32 (1984), pp. 331–72.

24 Quoted in I. Kershaw, *The Hitler Myth: Image and Reality in the Third Reich* (Oxford 1987), p. 129.

25 See D. Beck, *Julius Leber: Sozialdemokrat zwischen Reform und Widerstand* (Berlin 1983); K. Tenfelde, 'Proletarische Provinz: Radikalisierung und Widerstand in Penzberg/Oberbayern 1900 bis 1945', in M. Broszat *et al.* (eds), *Bayern in der NS-Zeit*, IV (Munich 1981). Also vol. V of *Bayern (Die Parteien KPD, SPD, BVP in Verfolgung und Widerstand)* (1983). For an account in

English of the rapidly increasing literature on popular resistance, see D. Peukert, *Inside Nazi Germany: Conformity, Opposition and Racism in Everyday Life* (New Haven 1987), pp. 101–74.

26 H. Mommsen, 'Social Views and Constitutional Plans of the Resistance', in H. Graml *et al.*, *The German Resistance to Hitler* (London and Berkeley 1970), p. 69. G. van Roon, *German Resistance to Hitler: Count von Moltke and the Kreisau Circle* (London 1971), pp. 359–60.

27 H. Graml, 'Resistance Thinking on Foreign Policy', in Graml, *Resistance*, pp. 40, 54. van Roon, *Resistance*, pp. 257, 349, 260.

28 Quoted in Mommsen, 'Social Views', p. 65.

29 H. Grimm, *Der Schriftsteller und seine Zeit* (Lippoldsberg 1980), p. 82. C. Kessler (trans.), *The Diaries of a Cosmopolitan: Harry Kessler 1918–1937* (London 1971), p. 461.

30 H. Trevor-Roper, *The Last Days of Hitler* (New York 1971), p. 54. F. Gilbert (ed.), *Hitler Directs His War* (New York 1950), p. 159. F. Genoud (ed.) *The Testament of Adolf Hitler*, trans. R. H. Stevens (London 1959), p. 104.

7 Potsdam

1 *Keesings Contemporary Archives* (1945), p. 7179.

2 A. Weber, *Abschied von der bisherigen Geschichte: Überwindung des Nihilismus* (Bern 1946), p. 238.

3 J. Wheeler-Bennett and A. Nicholls, *The Semblance of Peace: The Political Settlement after the Second World War* (London 1972), pp. 147–8. H. Feis, *Churchill, Roosevelt, Stalin: The War They Waged and the Peace They Sought* (Princeton 1957), pp. 273–4.

4 Wheeler-Bennett and Nicholls, *Semblance*, p. 176.

5 There are two Neisse rivers. The difference in location between the Eastern and the Western Neisse (both flow into the Oder) does not seem to have been clear at least to all the Western participants at Potsdam.

6 J. L. Gaddis, *The United States and the Origins of the Cold War 1941–1947* (New York 1972), p. 331.

8 The GDR

1 See W. Leonhard, *Child of the Revolution*, trans. C. M. Woodhouse (London 1975) (originally 1957), pp. 346–50.

2 J. Hacker, *Der Ostblock: Enstehung, Entwicklung und Struktur 1939–1980* (Baden-Baden 1983), pp. 543–4.

3 Ibid., p. 545.

4 *Neue Zürcher Zeitung*, no. 34, 12 February 1987.

5 Ibid., no. 274, 26 November 1985; no. 293, 18 December 1985.

6 H. Nicolson, *Diaries and Letters* vol. III: *1945–1962*, ed. N. Nicolson (London 1968), p. 116. See also H. Feis, *From Trust to Terror* (London 1970), pp. 283–4.

Also G. D. Neef, 'The Failure of Quadripartite Negotiations for Economic Reform and the Blockade of Berlin: American Policy, Currency Reform and the Division of Germany 1945–1948', Cambridge University PhD, 1986.

7 The document is reproduced in R. Steininger, *Eine Chance zur Wiedervereinigung? Die Stalin-Note vom 10. März 1952* (Bonn 1985), p. 282.

8 'Auferstanden aus Ruinen / Und der Zukunft zugewandt, / Lass uns dir zum Guten dienen, / Deutschland, einig Vaterland. / Alte Not gilt es zu zwingen, / Und wir zwingen sie vereint, / Denn es muss uns doch gelingen, / Dass die Sonne schön wie nie / Über Deutschland scheint.' (Johannes R. Becher: 'Nationallied der DDR'.)

9 A. J. McAdams, *East Germany and Détente* (Cambridge 1985), pp. 50 and 60.

10 A. Kosing and W. Schmidt, 'Zur Herausbildung der sozialistischen Nation in der DDR', *Einheit*, 1974/2, pp. 179–88.

11 H. Axen, 'Die DDR und der Grundwiderspruch unserer Epoche', *Einheit* 1984/9–10, p. 826.

12 A. Abusch, 'Kunst, Kultur und Lebensweise in unserem sozialistischen deutschen Nationalstaat', *Einheit* 1971/6, pp. 728, 730.

13 McAdams, *East Germany*, p. 143.

14 H. Weber, *DDR: Grundriss der Geschichte 1945–1981* (Hanover 1982), p. 125.

15 Quoted in *Frankfurter Allgemeine Zeitung*, no 9, 12 January 1987.

16 W. Brus in M. Kaser (ed.), *The Economic History of Eastern Europe 1919–1975*, III: *Institutional Change Within a Planned Economy* (Oxford 1986), pp. 19, 95.

17 McAdams, *East Germany*, pp. 45, 58.

18 E. Honecker, 'Unsere Republik – Staat des Friedens und des Sozialismus', *Einheit* 1984/9–10, p. 774.

19 *Neues Deutschland*, 21/22 January 1984, 'Aufruf zum 35. Jahrestag der Gründung der Deutschen Demokratischen Republik'.

20 'Über Heimatsgeschichtsschreibung', *Einheit* 1984/12, p. 1119. The major GDR biographies are: K. -H. Börner, *Wilhelm I: Deutscher Kaiser und König von Preussen: Eine Biographie* (Berlin 1984); E. Engelberg, *Bismarck: Urpreusse und Reichsgründer* (Berlin 1985); I. Mittenzwei, *Friedrich II von Preussen: Eine Biographie* (Berlin 1979).

9 West Germany

1 Quoted by C. Greiner in L. Herbst (ed.), *Westdeutschland 1945–1955: Unterwerfung, Kontrolle, Integration* (Munich 1986), p. 270.

2 See E. Wandel, *Die Entstehung der Bank deutscher Länder* (Frankfurt 1980), p. 118.

3 H. -P. Schwarz, *Adenauer: Der Aufstieg 1876–1952* (Stuttgart 1986), p. 552.

4 Schwarz, *Adenauer*, pp. 534–6.

5 L. J. Edinger, *Kurt Schumacher: A Study in Personality and Political Behaviour* (Stanford 1965), p. 148.

6 Edinger, *Schumacher*, p. 163. Schwarz, *Adenauer*, p. 947.

7 A. Renger (ed.), *Kurt Schumacher, Bundestagsreden* (Bonn 1972), pp. 126, 77.

8 See N. Wiggershaus, 'Effizienz und Kontrolle', in Herbst (ed.), *Westdeutschland*, pp. 253–65.

9 See K. Borchardt and C. Buchheim, 'Die Wirkung der Marshallplan-Hilfe in Schlüsselbranchen der deutschen Wirtschaft', *Vierteljahrshefte für Zeitgeschichte*, 35 (1987), esp. pp. 321–30; I. Turner, 'Great Britain and the Post-War German Currency Reform', *Historical Journal*, 30 (1987), p. 707.

10 Schwarz, *Adenauer*, p. 863.

11 *Statistiches Jahrbuch* (1961), pp. 54–5.

12 L. Erhard, *The Economics of Success* (Princeton 1963), p. 142.

13 *Der Spiegel*, no. 43, 22 October 1952, p. 27.

14 Ibid., no. 9, 25 February 1953, p. 29.

15 'Einigkeit und Recht und Freiheit / Für das deutsche Vaterland! / Danach lasst uns alle streben / Brüderlich mit Herz und Hand! / Einigkeit und Recht und Freiheit / Sind des Glückes Unterpfand – / Blüh' im Glanze dieses Glückes / Blühe deutsches Vaterland!'

16 *Der Spiegel*, no. 30, 20 July 1955, p. 42.

17 Ibid., no. 10, 3 March 1954, pp. 29–33.

18 P. Schindler (ed.), *Datenhandbuch zur Geschichte des Deutschen Bundestages 1949 bis 1982* (Bonn 1983), p. 63.

19 See the speech by President Richard von Weizsäcker, 'Weltoffener Patriotismus', in *Frankfurter Allgemeine Zeitung*, no. 259, 7 November 1987.

20 *Keesings Contemporary Archives*, 1972, p. 25349.

21 J. Carter, *Keeping Faith: Memoirs of a President* (New York 1982), p. 537.

22 It should be added that the Congress Hall was subsequently rebuilt, and reopened in 1987.

23 *Der Spiegel*, 1985, no. 10, p. 91.

24 *Statistisches Jahrbuch* (1987), p. 90.

25 W. Hoffmann, 'Pfrünzen, Freunde und Mandate', *Die Zeit*, no. 44, 26 October 1984.

26 H. Blüthmann and R. Kahlen, 'Hypothek der früheren Jahre', *Die Zeit*, no. 40, 26 September 1986.

27 *Frankfurter Allgemeine Zeitung*, no 251, 6 November 1984.

28 Bülow paper 'Perspektiven für das Jahr 2000. Verteidigung ohne Supermächte', *Frankfurter Rundschau*, no. 212, 13 September 1985. Egon Bahr, 'Ein Plan im Sinne Olof Palmes', *Vorwärts*, no. 43, 25 October 1986. 'Der Streit der Ideologien und die gemeinsame Sicherheit', *Politik*, no. 3, August 1987.

29 Quoted in *Frankfurter Allgemeine Zeitung*, no. 137, 18 June 1985.

30 Quoted in T. Sommer, *Denken an Deutschland* (Hamburg 1966), p. 33. See also F. J. Strauss, *The Grand Design* (London 1965).

31 *Frankfurter Allgemeine Zeitung*, no. 4, 6 January 1987; no. 9, 12 January 1987.

32 *Frankfurter Allgemeine Zeitung*, no. 66, 19 March 1987.

33 Pressemitteilung der Bundesregierung (Federal Government Press release), 28 October 1987.

34 *Neue Zürcher Zeitung*, no. 2, 6 January 1987.

35 P. Jenkins, *Mrs Thatcher's Revolution: The Ending of the Socialist Era* (London 1987), p. 46.

36 *Der Spiegel*, no. 1, 4 January 1988, p. 23.
37 *Die Zeit*, no. 39, 21 September 1984. *Frankfurter Allgemeine Zeitung*, no 8, 11 January 1988.
38 See recently R. Gilpin, *The Political Economy of International Relations* (Princeton 1987), pp. 65–117, 364–408. P. Kennedy, *The Rise and Fall of the Great Powers: Economic Change and Military Conflict from 1500 to 2000* (New York 1987), pp. 514–35.

10 The German Revolution of 1989 and its Aftermath

1 Some convincing answers are given in J. Hacker, *Deutsche Irrtümer: Schönfärber und Helfershelfer der SED-Diktatur im Westen* (Berlin 1992).
2 *Der Spiegel*, no. 41, 9 October 1989, p. 27.
3 *FAZ*, 6 December 1989, p. 19.
4 The former figure comes from the *Spiegel*, working with the GDR's Academy of Sciences and the Bielefeld Emnid Institute; the latter from Marplan. *Der Spiegel*, 18 December 1989, pp. 86–9, and *FAZ*, 27 December 1989, p. 4.
5 F. J. Strauss, *Die Erinnerungen* (Berlin 1989), p. 439.
6 *Die Zeit*, 15 December 1989, p. 2; FAZ, 19 December 1989, p. 3.
7 E. Shevardnadze, *The Future belongs to Freedom* transl. C. A. Fitzpatrick (New York 1991), p. 131.
8 *Die Zeit*, 24 November 1989, p. 6; *Financial Times*, 30 November 1989.
9 *Der Spiegel*, 26 March 1990, p. 182.
10 See D. Marsh, *The Bundesbank: The Bank that Rules Europe* (London 1992), pp. 206–13.
11 *Financial Times*, 4 December 1989, p. 40.
12 In *Die Zeit*, 30 March 1990, p. 62.
13 *Financial Times*, 29 November 1989 and 1 December 1989; *Die Zeit*, 8 December 1989, p. 16.
14 See A. Baring, 'Magnetfeld Europe. Konrad Adenauer war der Wegbereiter', *FAZ*, 29 September 1990. D. Koerfer, *Kampf ums Kanzleramt: Erhard und Adenauer* (Stuttgart 1987). There is a criticism of the Adenauer myth in R. Zitelmann, *Adenauers Gegner: Streiter für die Einheit* (Erlangen 1991), especially pp. 9–27.
15 'Wo bleibt der politische Wille des Volkes', *Die Zeit* no. 26, 19 June 1992; G. Hofmann, W. A. Perger (eds.) *Die Kontroverse: Weizsäcker's Parteipolitik in der Diskussion* (Frankfurt 1992), p. 103.
16 *Financial Times*, 26 November 1991.
17 *Bild*, 5 December 1991.

Conclusion

1 *Die Zeit*, 15 December 1989, p. 1. *Die Zeit*, 30 March 1990, p. 7.
2 R. Dahrendorf, *Society and Democracy in Germany*, New York 1967,

p. 52. (transl.) K. Traynor, H. U. Wehler, *The German Empire 1871–1918*, Leamington Spa 1985, p. 242.

3 A. H. L. Heeren, *Handbuch der Geschichte des Europäischen Staatensystems und seiner Colonien*, 5th edn (Göttingen 1830), p. 416 (English translation (London 1846), p. 480).

4 D. Blackbourn and G. Eley, *The Peculiarities of German History* (Oxford 1984), p. 81. T. Nipperdey, '1933 und die Kontinuität der deutschen Geschichte', in *Nachdenken über die deutsche Geschichte* (Munich 1986), pp. 186–205.

5 August 1 1975 Final Act of the Conference on Security and Cooperation in Europe: 'The participating states regard as inviolable all one another's frontiers as well as the frontiers of all states in Europe and therefore they will refrain now and in the future from assaulting these frontiers. Accordingly, they will also refrain from any demand for, or act of, seizure and usurpation of part or all of the territory of any participating state ... The participating states will respect the territorial integrity of each of the participating states.' These statements do not, in fact, rule out peaceful adjustments, involving no threats to use force, of frontiers.

Index

Index